Donated in memory of
Jean S. Kimball
to the University of Northern Iowa
Rod Library

by her dear friend
Vicki Edelnant

Joyce and the Early Freudians

The Florida James Joyce Series

Florida A&M University, Tallahassee
Florida Atlantic University, Boca Raton
Florida Gulf Coast University, Ft. Myers
Florida International University, Miami
Florida State University, Tallahassee
University of Central Florida, Orlando
University of Florida, Gainesville
University of North Florida, Jacksonville
University of South Florida, Tampa
University of West Florida, Pensacola

Joyce and the Early Freudians

A Synchronic Dialogue of Texts

Jean Kimball

University Press of Florida

Gainesville · Tallahassee · Tampa · Boca Raton

Pensacola · Orlando · Miami · Jacksonville · Ft. Myers

Copyright 2003 by Jean Kimball
Printed in the United States of America on acid-free,
TCF (totally chlorine-free) paper
All rights reserved

08 07 06 05 04 03   6 5 4 3 2 1

Library of Congress Cataloging-in-Publication Data
Kimball, Jean, 1923–
Joyce and the early Freudians: a synchronic dialogue of texts /
Jean Kimball.
p. cm.—(The Florida James Joyce series)
Includes bibliographical references (p.) and index.
ISBN 0-8130-2619-9 (cloth: alk. paper)
1. Joyce, James, 1882–1941—Knowledge—Psychology. 2. Psychoanalysis
and literature—Ireland—History—20th century. 3. Psychological fiction,
English—History and criticism. 4. Freud, Sigmund, 1856–1939—
Influence. 5. Psychology in literature. I. Title. II. Series.
PR6019.O9Z675 2003
823'.912—dc21   2002043034

The University Press of Florida is the scholarly publishing agency
for the State University System of Florida, comprising Florida A&M
University, Florida Atlantic University, Florida Gulf Coast University,
Florida International University, Florida State University, University
of Central Florida, University of Florida, University of North Florida,
University of South Florida, and University of West Florida.

University Press of Florida
15 Northwest 15th Street
Gainesville, FL 32611–2079
http://www.upf.com

For my sister, Dorothy

Contents

Figures

Foreword

Jean Kimball's book is one of the best, if not the best, study of its kind I have read in the last ten years. Wise, balanced, clearly written, extensively researched, thoroughly convincing, without hubris, meaningful, and simply brilliant in its ideas, explications, and insights. One would think that the psychoanalytic ground in Joyce—especially with regard to Freud, Jung, and company—had already been thoroughly covered, but the wealth of new information and connections demonstrably present in this manuscript has uncovered far more than former critics had ever seen.

Some of Kimball's new readings and old and new source connections, and the history behind their inclusion by Joyce, fall like soft rain on parched earth, producing new sensible and ingenious explications of *A Portrait of the Artist as a Young Man* and *Ulysses* and bringing to light not only what we might have suspected about meaning in Joyce but also how much Freud and Jung and their followers have shaped the conscience of modernism itself.

Kimball's careful approach to the minefield of psychoanalytic hubristic claims to providing the final speculative answers to *Ulysses* is augmented by her painstaking research on what Joyce had in his library and what was available in the libraries he is known to have consulted during the time he wrote *Ulysses,* as well as by the justice of her interpretations. Further, when there is either doubt about Joyce's intention or lack of a documented link between the earlier similar texts and ideas he assimilated into his works, it is Kimball herself who informs her readers of what is speculation and what is history—a refreshing and reassuring departure from the state of much Joyce interpretation over the last twenty years.

Zack Bowen, Series Editor

Preface

I was introduced to Joyce's *Ulysses* back in the 1950s in a class, as most actual readers of this monumental novel have been. This was before the various Joyce guidebooks had been published, so we didn't have all the auxiliary information we now have. I was reading Ernest Jones's *Hamlet and Oedipus* at the same time, and when we came to "Scylla and Charybdis," the Hamlet episode in *Ulysses,* I was startled by what seemed to me clear echoes of Jones's book in this ninth episode. Obviously Joyce could not have been influenced by a 1948 book, but the echoes were there. I was not then as attached to James Joyce as I have come to be, but I *was* interested in psychoanalysis and its history and fascinated by Sigmund Freud. When I discovered that Jones's book had its origins in a 1910 essay in the *American Journal of Psychology,* I started seriously on an investigation that has, with intermediate stops along the way, produced *Joyce and the Early Freudians,* a title that links two of the great innovators of the twentieth century. For Joyce and Freud were truly giants, each in his separate field. They shared a certain space in history, and it has been my assumption in writing this book that others besides me would have interest in examining connections between them.

This has been a long journey, and I am indebted in more ways than I can remember to more people than I can remember, let alone name. These debts are institutional as well as personal, and I should like to recognize once again a debt, which all Joyceans share, to the James Joyce Foundation and to the spirit of its founders: Fritz Senn, Thomas Staley, and the late Bernard Benstock. The openness, good humor, and flair, which all these men have combined with their unquestioned literary taste and knowledge, have come to characterize the operations of the foundation. I am grateful for the opportunities provided by this institution to test out insights of my own as well as to become familiar with the insights of others at meetings the James Joyce Foundation arranges and through publications it sponsors.

I should like also to express my gratitude to the National Endowment for the Humanities for a Summer Stipend in 1985, which enabled me to translate several early works by Otto Rank, translations that have contributed to this study.

I have depended greatly on the services of librarians, and wherever they were, they have been uniformly helpful, courteous, and apparently really interested in what I was doing. I wish here to express my special thanks to Mr. L. Köhler at the Zentralbibliothek Zürich, who was extraordinarily generous with both time and interest when I searched for materials at the time of my first Joyce Symposium in 1979 and again in 1984 and 1996 when I returned to Zurich. And here at home, I have been grateful to my department head, Jeffrey Copeland, for his continuing interest and practical assistance.

Because this study has developed over a period of many years, I have been perhaps more aware than some of the way one generation of critics builds on the work of previous generations. My own indebtedness to these earlier critics is acknowledged in the notes, which in some instances go back quite a long way. Joyce has been fortunate in his critics, I think, and, early and late, they hold up well.

A certain amount of the material that makes up this study has appeared, though in different contexts, in articles I have published over the years in various outlets. Although in no case is this material simply a reprint, I have used substantial parts of the following published articles without attribution. For permission to use this material in my book, I am indebted to the following:

To the *James Joyce Quarterly* for material from "James Joyce and Otto Rank: The Incest Motif in *Ulysses,* 13 (Spring 1976): 366–82; "Freud, Leonardo, and Joyce: The Dimensions of a Childhood Memory," 17 (Winter 1980): 165–82; "Family Romance and Hero Myth: A Psychoanalytic Context for the Paternity Theme in *Ulysses*," 20 (Winter 1983): 161–73; and "An Ambiguous Faithlessness: Molly Bloom and the Widow of Ephesus," 31 (Summer 1994): 455–72.

To the *Journal of Modern Literature* for material from "Jung's 'Dual Mother' in Joyce's *Ulysses:* An Illustrated Psychoanalytic Intertext," 17 (Spring 1991): 477–90.

To the University Press of Florida for material from "Growing Up Together: Joyce and Psychoanalysis, 1900–1922," in *Joyce through the
Ages: A Nonlinear View,* ed. Michael Patrick Gillespie, 25–45 (Gainesville: University Press of Florida, 1999).

And to the University of Texas Press for the use of substantial parts of
"Autobiography as Epic: Freud's Three-Time Scheme in Joyce's *Ulysses,*"
Texas Studies in Literature and Language, 31 (Winter 1989): 475–96.

My debt to my sister, Dorothy Allan, is acknowledged in the dedication. Without her quite remarkable encouragement and her equally remarkable assistance to me in other important aspects of my life, I could
not have written this book.

Abbreviations

BK   Joyce, Stanislaus. *My Brother's Keeper: James Joyce's Early Years.* Ed. Richard Ellmann. New York: Viking, 1958.

CDD   Joyce, Stanislaus. *The Complete Dublin Diary of Stanislaus Joyce.* Ed. George Healy. Ithaca: Cornell University Press, 1971.

CW   Jung, C. G. *The Collected Works of C. G. Jung.* Ed. H. Read and others. Trans. R. F. C. Hull. 18 vols. New York/Princeton: Bollingen Foundation and Princeton University Press, 1953–1978.

D   Joyce, James. *Dubliners.* New York: Viking, Compass, 1968.

E   Joyce, James. *Exiles: A Play in Three Acts.* New York: Viking, Compass, 1961.

FP   Joyce, James. "A Portrait of the Artist" (1904). In *The Workshop of Daedalus: James Joyce and the Raw Materials for "A Portrait of the Artist as a Young Man,"* ed. Robert E. Scholes and Richard M. Kain, 56–74. Evanston: Northwestern University Press, 1965.

FW   Joyce, James. *Finnegans Wake.* New York: Viking, 1958.

H   Jones, Ernest. "The Oedipus-Complex as an Explanation of Hamlet's Mystery: A Study in Motive." *American Journal of Psychology* 21 (January 1910): 72–113.

JJII   Ellmann, Richard. *James Joyce.* Rev. ed. New York: Oxford University Press, 1982.

Letters   Joyce, James. *The Letters of James Joyce.* 3 vols. Vol. 1, ed. Stuart Gilbert. Vols. 2 and 3, ed. Richard Ellmann. New York: Viking, 1966.

P   Joyce, James. *A Portrait of the Artist as a Young Man.* New York: Viking, Compass, 1964.

PU   Jung, C. G. *Psychology of the Unconscious: A Study of the Transformations and Symbolism of the Libido.* Trans. Beatrice M. Hinkle. New York: Moffat, Yard, 1916.

SE   Freud, Sigmund. *The Standard Edition of the Complete Psychological Works of Sigmund Freud.* Trans. and ed. James Strachey with Anna Freud et al. 23 vols. London: Hogarth Press and the Institute of Psycho-Analysis, 1953–1974.

SH   Joyce, James. *Stephen Hero.* Ed. John J. Slocum and Herbert Cahoon. New York: New Directions, 1944, 1963.

SL   Joyce, James. *Selected Letters of James Joyce.* Ed. Richard Ellmann. New York: Viking, 1975.

U   (Plus episode and line number.) Joyce, James. *Ulysses: The Corrected Text.* Ed. Hans Walter Gabler with Wolfhard Steppe and Claus Melchior. New York and London: Garland Publishing, 1984, 1986.

U-G   (Plus page number.) Joyce, James. *Ulysses.* Ed. Hans Walter Gabler et al. New York and London: Garland, 1984. (References to critical apparatus or textual notes.)

1

Introduction

Growing Up Together

One of the secrets of the seemingly inexhaustible invitation that Joyce's *Ulysses* offers to interpretation is the character of the connections that Joyce has built into his autobiographical fiction. With his stunning sense for analogy, he has tapped into some of the main arteries of Western thought, which have themselves become intricately interconnected through their shared history. To mention only the most central of these, when he named his novel *Ulysses* and insisted—publicly and often—on the connection between Homer's epic and his novel, he set up resonances not only with Homer's Odysseus but also with the Ulysses of Dante and Shakespeare, as well as with a wealth of commentary on all these poets, not to mention the associations that the church fathers had developed between Odysseus and the figure of Christ.[1]

The intertextual mix was further enriched and diversified by the influence of Charles Lamb's *Adventures of Ulysses*, which was Joyce's introduction to Ulysses as a boy (*JJII*, 46). Lamb's *Adventures* in turn, as the author reminded readers in his introduction, was "designed as a supplement" to Francois Fénelon's immensely popular *Adventures of Telemachus*, listed by Stanislaus Joyce as one of the books his brother had consulted in preparation for writing *Ulysses* (Stanford, *Ulysses Theme*, 276 n. 6). And in Fénelon's *Télémaque* the son's adventures—and his fame as well—parallel the father's, a situation suggestively similar to that in *Ulysses* (Stanford, "First Meeting," 99). Joyce's projection of the hero takes on the weight and some of the complexities of this traditional content. In varying degrees, the same may be said of other texts from the past with which the text *Ulysses* is in dialogue.

Psychoanalysis as Intertext

Psychoanalytic literature, however, was an intertext that was roughly contemporaneous with *Ulysses,* and the relationship between Joyce's texts and the texts of psychoanalysis is somewhat different from the relationship with texts of the past. Often the contemporaneous psychoanalytic texts of the early twentieth century were themselves products of a dialogue with a range of other traditional texts—especially myth, poetry, and drama—many of which were familiar to Joyce. In pamphlet form, Sigmund Freud's 1910 psychobiography of the great Leonardo da Vinci—*Eine Kindheitserinnerung des Leonardo da Vinci* [A childhood memory of Leonardo da Vinci]—was one of three psychoanalytic works that Joyce purchased in Trieste. By 1920, in addition to the pamphlet by Freud, Joyce owned C. G. Jung's aggressively Freudian essay, *Die Bedeutung des Vaters für das Schicksal des Einzelnen* (1909) [The significance of the father for the fate of the individual] and the German translation of Ernest Jones's 1910 essay on Hamlet and Oedipus, *Das Problem des Hamlet und des Ödipus-Komplex* [The problem of Hamlet and the Oedipus Complex] (1911). He later purchased Freud's *Zur Psychopathologie des Alltaglebens* [The psychopathology of everyday life] (1905) in Zurich.[2] It is certainly reasonable to assume that, having bought these early works, Joyce read them and gleaned from them details he could use in his autobiographical portrait of the twentieth-century artist.

In his 1977 *Consciousness of Joyce,* Richard Ellmann included a listing of Joyce's personal library in 1920, the "Trieste Library," which included the four psychoanalytic pamphlets. And, considering his regular stress on Joyce's negative attitude toward the early psychoanalysts, he was surprisingly exuberant about the effect of this psychoanalytic literature on Joyce. The effect, he wrote, "can hardly be overstressed," surmising that Joyce must have recognized "at once that he had here a new continent" (54).

"A new continent" is surely something of an overstatement, since Joyce, like many artists, was aware of unconscious motivations before he knew anything about Sigmund Freud. And Freud has over and over credited the artist with knowing intuitively what he himself was laboring to explain scientifically. "How hard it is," Freud writes, "for a psychoanalyst to discover anything new that has not been known before by some creative writer" (*SE*, 6:205). And he explains elsewhere that "the description of the human mind is indeed the domain which is most [the artist's] own; he has from time immemorial been the precursor of science, and so too of scientific psychology" (*SE*, 9:43–44).

Stanislaus Joyce remembers his brother's experimentation, while both were still in Dublin, with epiphanies—"ironical observations of slips, and little errors and gestures . . . by which people betrayed the very things they were most careful to conceal" (*BK*, 124). This is an endeavor that has an obvious relationship with Freud's observations in *The Psychopathology of Everyday Life* about "slips of the tongue." Stanislaus further observes that once "the revelation and importance of the subconscious had caught [his brother's] interest," these experimental pieces became progressively more subjective and "included dreams, which he considered in some way revelatory" (*BK*, 124–25). Joyce had thus been toying with ideas very close to psychoanalysis by the time he purchased the pamphlets in Trieste and Zurich.

Many of the psychoanalytic texts, however, were significantly based on that special category of autobiographical fiction, the case study, a resource that, especially with the case study's empirical, "scientific" underpinnings, *was* new to Joyce. Furthermore, these case studies reflected actual experiences of actual persons whose lives were roughly contemporaneous with Joyce's, thus harmonizing with the historical/autobiographical impulse that moves so much of Joyce's fiction. Even more, as the case studies and the literature based upon them focused on sexual experiences, they reinforced Joyce's often-quoted conviction that if he "put down a bucket into my own soul's well, sexual department, I draw up Griffith's and Ibsen's and Skeffington's and Bernard Vaughan's and St. Aloysius' and Shelley's and Renan's water with my own." He then followed this pronouncement with the promise that "I am going to do that in my novel (inter alia) and plank the bucket down before the shades and substances above mentioned to see how they like it: and if they don't like it I can't help them" (letter of 11 November 1906 to Stanislaus, *Letters* 2:191).

The psychoanalytic texts available to Joyce during the writing of *Ulysses*—and they were many—offered a range of specific examples that provided support for Joyce's apparent conviction of the universality and power of "the sexual department" of the human soul as well as a revelation of its variety. And although psychoanalysis in the first quarter of the twentieth century obviously lacked the tradition it now has as a literary corpus, it had a developing future that could not have been predicted. Psychoanalytic materials were thus much less stable than the known quantities represented by Aquinas, Aristotle, Dante, or Shakespeare. Indeed, when Joyce tapped into psychoanalytic speculation, even selectively, as he certainly did, he was in touch with a body of work that would itself be enriched, or at least expanded, through developments in psychoanalytic thinking that Joyce could not have anticipated. Certainly he could not have foreseen that the language of psychoanalysis might become so interwoven with the common language of readers as to affect their understanding of his novel. These developments add to the complexity of any consideration of psychoanalytic literature as an intertext.

The scope of this study of psychoanalytic contexts in *Ulysses*, however, is limited to Joyce's appropriations from specific texts produced by Freud and his followers between 1900 and 1922. These are often fragmentary, often striking details lifted from these texts. The study is thus to be distinguished from a psychoanalytic reading of *Ulysses* or a "Freudian" investigation of Joyce's own psyche as it is revealed in the novel. Neither of these is my aim. Nor am I attempting to analyze the characters of *Ulysses* in a psychoanalytic frame, as Paul Schwaber has done so authoritatively in his recent *Cast of Characters*, concluding that Joyce's approach to characterization "dovetails with Freudian psychoanalysis" (13).

It should also be noted that I have excluded *Finnegans Wake* from this study. By the time Joyce wrote and published this later novel, the outlines of psychoanalytic theory were much more firmly fixed than in the earlier time and much more nearly common knowledge. Even by the 1930s we all knew, at least vaguely, what the Oedipus complex was or what a Freudian slip might be. The references to psychoanalysis in the *Wake* are thus of a different kind from those in *Ulysses*. Joyce after all came to psychoanalysis not only early in his career but also early in the history of the psychoanalytic movement, before analytic observations had become established concepts, before Freud's hypotheses had hardened into dogma. In his *History of the Psycho-Analytic Movement* (1914), Freud himself refers to psychoanalysis as "a theory still in the making" (*SE*, 14:26). In the early years of the century that are the focus of this study he was still testing his hypotheses and refining his definitions, as were the writers of varying talents who surrounded him—some of them brilliant and others possibly closer to Jung's unkind description: "a medley of artists, decadents, and mediocrities" (quoted by Jones, *Life and Work*, 2:33). They were excited by the avenues of exploration Freud had opened up, and many of them were publishing articles of varying significance in the four journals that had been founded by the movement between 1909 and 1913.[3]

One of the circumstances that adds to the likelihood of Joyce's appropriating bits and pieces of these texts is that though Joyce (1882–1941) was separated in age by a generation from Freud (1856–1939), his development as an artist between 1900 and 1922 coincided with the origins and early development of the psychoanalytic movement. In addition, he had opportunities, in part simply because of where he lived—that is, in Trieste and Zurich—to interact with the literature of psychoanalysis in a fairly continuous way during important formative years of his growth into a mature productive artist, and there is evidence in his texts that he took advantage of these opportunities. To be sure, the assumption of a consciously crafted relationship between texts, whether we call it "influence" or "allusion," "intertextuality" or "dialogue," is generally a matter of probability rather than proof, and the evidence I offer is admittedly circumstantial and to a degree speculative. But it is my claim that the probability of the existence of a relationship between *Ulysses* and the early psychoanalytic texts is high.[4]

We have known for over twenty years now that Joyce's personal library in 1920 included the four psychoanalytic texts I have listed earlier. Three of them—Freud's Leonardo study and the essays by Jung and Jones—were purchased while he was still in Trieste. These four have been the only works from the considerable output of the early psychoanalysts with which Joyce was provably in contact before the publication of *Ulysses*. It is also true, of course, that two months after his departure from Zurich in 1919, he wrote to Frank Budgen of his irritation at not receiving a promised copy of Jung's 1912 *Wandlungen und Symbole der Libido* [*Transformations and symbols of the libido*] from his friend Otto Weiss.[5] To be sure, Joyce's reference to "Doktor JUNG'S (prolonged general universal applause) Wandlungen der LIBIDO (shouts Hear! Hear! from a raughty tinker and an Irishman in the gallery)" (*SL*, 244) is mocking, but his vehemence, mocking or not, adds to the probability that he knew something more than the title.

These provable or near-provable sources were, I am here presuming, only the beginning of Joyce's acquaintance with the literature of psycho-analysis in the period before 1922. And I propose in this study to examine selectively Joyce's interaction—in most cases not provable, but highly probable and certainly not impossible—with this early psychoanalytic literature and evidence of its incorporation into the text of *Ulysses*. Such a consideration of evidences of a textual relationship between *Ulysses* and psychoanalytic texts, though fragmentary and by no means exhaustive, may lead to a subtly altered understanding of thematic strands in the novel. But what is of equal interest and significance, I think, is that in tracing the development of such patterns of verbal and situational corre-spondences, we may participate in a creative process that is uniquely Joyce's and that reaches its finest, most balanced expression in *Ulysses*.

Freud and Joyce

Most Joyceans are familiar with the remark, reported by Ellmann as one Joyce generally "left to his friends," that the name Joyce meant the same thing in English as Freud in German (*JJII*, 490). But it is an interesting fact that Freud, whose life seems never to have intersected with Joyce's, anticipated the novelist in this name play. In his *Psychopathology of Everyday Life*, which Joyce acquired in Zurich, Freud offers an example of "paramnesia" from his own experience (*SE*, 6:148–50). While he was on vacation, away from all his references, Freud writes, he was working on a passage on daydreams in the manuscript for *The Interpretation of Dreams* and thought of an example he wanted to use from Alphonse Daudet's *Le Nabob* (*SE*, 5:491, 535). This example involved a daydream "hatched out" by a character in the novel, whom Freud remembered as "Monsieur Jocelyn." In this daydream, Monsieur Jocelyn, through gran-diose actions, saves a "great personage," who becomes his munificent benefactor. When Freud finally checked Daudet's novel, however, he could find no such fantasy recorded, and in addition Daudet's character was not named "Monsieur Jocelyn" at all, but "Monsieur Joyeuse."

The name gave Freud the key to a solution to his mistaken memory of the incident: "'Joyeux,' of which 'Joyeuse' is the feminine form, is the only possible way in which I could translate my own name, Freud, into French," Freud writes. He concludes, then, that the fantasy he misre-membered from *Le Nabob* must have been his own, even though he had no conscious memory of it, a repression that Freud attributes to his extreme distaste for the notion of being someone's protégé. "Perhaps," Freud writes, "I invented it myself in Paris where I frequently walked about the streets, lonely and full of longings, greatly in need of a helper and protector, until the great Charcot took me into his circle" (*SE*, 6:149).

Had Joyce come across this passage in Freud's *Psychopathology of Everyday Life*, as he very probably did since he owned the volume, the translation of his own name into French and German must surely have stayed with him, especially as it combines with Freud's description of himself as a lonely young man in Paris. For Freud's situation, as he describes it, is strikingly similar to Joyce's miserable circumstances during his 1903 stay in that same glamorous city (*JJII*, 121–29).[6] It thus seems entirely possible that Joyce himself originated the comment on the interchangeability of "Joyce" and "Freud," drawing on Freud's account (see also Kidd, 81–82).

Nor is the identity of names the only link that has been recognized between the two men. Jung, in his essay on *Ulysses*, identified both as "prophets of negation" (*CW*, 15:121), naming Joyce as Freud's "literary counterpart," who, like Freud, was "the answer to the sickness of the nineteenth century" (*CW*, 15:37). For Lionel Trilling, Freud and Joyce, each of whom had a significant effect on the culture of the twentieth century, were both deeply committed to the ideals of the previous century: Freud "the very type of what David Riesman has called the 'inner-directed' personality which dominated the nineteenth century and constituted its genius," and Joyce "entirely . . . a man of the century in which he was born," a "continuator of the titanism of the nineteenth-century artistic personality."[7]

And if the personalities of Freud and Joyce were fundamentally shaped by nineteenth-century ideals, so, too, distinctive features of their work have their roots in the thinking of the final decade of that century. Gunnar Brandell, discussing the "interrelation between Freud's thinking and certain currents of the literature of his time," maintains that Freud "was at one with the psychology of the modern novel," focusing especially on "that current commonly called 'psychological naturalism' . . . [that] towards the end of the century, . . . merged almost imperceptibly into symbolism" (x).[8] And this amalgam of naturalism and symbolism was identified by Edmund Wilson in his early, remarkably perceptive study of *Ulysses* as preeminently exemplified by Joyce, "a master of Naturalism," who in *Ulysses* "exploited together, as no writer had thought to do before, the resources both of Symbolism and Naturalism" (24, 204).

Henri Ellenberger, too, in his monumental *Discovery of the Unconscious*, has pointed to the "deep-reaching affinity" between dynamic psychology as it was developing toward the end of the century and the spirit of the times, as revealed by "the similarity between patients described by psychiatrists and [characters described] by novelists and playwrights" (283). Ellenberger traces back to the "magnetizers" of the eighteenth century the nineteenth-century preoccupation with the problem of the coexistence of two minds in one person and of their relationship to each other.

In turn, this "concept of the 'double-ego,' or 'dipsychism'" exerted a strong influence on "the systems of the new dynamic psychiatry" (145–47). Such a dipsychism is represented theoretically in the twentieth century by Freud's ego and id and by Jung's ego and shadow. A similar concept is also reflected in the literary world of the late nineteenth century. Ellmann, for example, in his study of Yeats, points to the general acceptance among Joyce and his contemporaries in Dublin of the notion of the self as "binary or double-decked," as well as the tendency of writers "to anthropomorphize each part," and he notes the familiar examples of R. L. Stevenson's *Dr. Jekyll and Mr. Hyde* (1885) and Oscar Wilde's *Picture of Dorian Gray* (1890) (*Yeats*, 72–73). In the twentieth century this double-decked self is dramatized by Joyce in *Ulysses* through Stephen and Bloom.

In addition, Ellenberger maintains that a "major characteristic of the *fin de siècle* spirit was eroticism," especially as it is exhibited in sexual perversions. He points out that some of these perversions—sadism, masochism, fetishism, all of which find a place in Joyce's fiction—were given the names under which they are referred to today through allusion to nineteenth-century authors, and "the scientific description often followed the literary one" (282). Robert S. Steele, too, dismissing the notion that "Freud singlehandedly rediscovered sex just before the turn of the century" as "just not true," points to the "numerous researchers involved in the scientific exploration of sexuality," as well as artists who were choosing the themes of sexual conflict and perversions for their novels and plays. "Freud's power," writes Steele, "lay in synthesizing diverse trends of thought and giving them the trademark: Made by Freud. In the 1890s Freud not only founded psychoanalysis—he gave birth to a legend" (65). And in the 1920s Joyce published *Ulysses*, "the greatest masterpiece of the twentieth century" in Vladimir Nabokov's eyes (57), and gave birth to another kind of legend.

Joyce and the Psychoanalytic Movement

The first edition of *Ulysses* appeared in 1922 at the height of the postwar popularization of psychoanalysis among the intellectuals of England and America.[9] The psychoanalytic movement, heralded by the publication of the first edition of Freud's *Interpretation of Dreams* in 1900, had evolved from very small beginnings in 1902 when the Psychological Wednesday Society, composed of Freud and four of his disciples, met weekly in Freud's waiting room. By the time *Ulysses* was published, the movement was represented by a flourishing International Psychoanalytic Association with members on both sides of the Atlantic.[10] Joyce's publication career also began in 1900, when he was still an undergraduate at University College Dublin, with the appearance of his essay on "Ibsen's New Drama" [*When We Dead Awaken*] in the London *Fortnightly Review* for 1 April (*JJII*, 71–74). His development from the author of this relatively slight essay into the artist who produced *Ulysses*, which Joyce identified for Arthur Power as "the book of my maturity" (36), thus occurred in the same time period during which the psychoanalytic movement grew into a significant influence in the English-speaking world and the world of literary criticism in particular. Freud himself, in fact, laid the groundwork for psychoanalytic literary criticism with his famous footnote in the first edition of *The Interpretation of Dreams* about Shakespeare's *Hamlet* as having "its roots in the same soil as *Oedipus Rex*" (*SE*, 4:264).

Indeed, more than one of Joyce's contemporaries linked the method and content of *Ulysses* with the new psychology. Wyndham Lewis claimed that "it was in the company of that old magician, Sigmund Freud, that Joyce learnt the way into the Aladdin's cave where he manufactured his *Ulysses*" (102), and T. S. Eliot in his widely influential critique of *Ulysses* credited "psychology (such as it is, and whether our reaction to it be comic or serious)" with having helped "to make possible what was impossible even a few years ago" (202). But resistance to the connection also arose early and persisted. In a 1929 article in *transition*, William Carlos Williams, in response to Rebecca West's 1928 essay on *Ulysses*, roundly denounced her "descent to Freudian expedients of classification," which he labeled "a mark of defeat" in a literary discussion (161–62).[11] Twenty-five years later, Joyce's Triestine friend, Italo Svevo, whose *Confessions of Zeno* has been labeled "the first psychoanalytic novel" (Esman, 103), assured the world and himself that by 1915 when Joyce left Trieste for Zurich, he "knew nothing of psycho-analysis . . . [which] thus cannot boast of having fathered Joyce's work" (quoted in Bollettieri, 181).

Ellmann, in both editions of his biography, has diligently reported Joyce's consistently negative comments about Freud and his psycho-analysis, comments that, like so much in Ellmann's biography, have been widely quoted, reinforcing the tendency to deny any direct connection between Joyce and psychoanalysis.[12] And as late as the 1973 Joyce Symposium in Dublin, when Maria Jolas was asked about Joyce's attitude toward Freud and Jung, she could respond that "it was a remarkable sign of his intelligence that he didn't fall for psychoanalysis when it was so current. He started beyond it" (Kain, 128).

This resistance to the investigation of Joyce's possible use of psychoanalytic insights in *Ulysses* was coupled with a lack of information about Joyce's reading after he left Dublin, as if there were, David Daiches suggests, an "unmentioned conspiracy to conceal Joyce's sources on the continent" (Hoffman, 122 n. 19). But in 1977, the darkness lifted somewhat with the publication of Ellmann's listing of Joyce's "Trieste Library," the "only detailed source for information on Joyce's reading over the period during which he was writing the majority of the works which make up his canon," according to Michael Patrick Gillespie (*Inverted Volumes*, 64). And this list, of course, included the pamphlets by Freud, Jung, and Jones. Joyce's purchase of these psychoanalytic texts during his residence in Trieste, a time when his catch-as-catch-can household was habitually and dramatically short on cash, may be seen as solid evidence of his interest in psychoanalytic insights, an interest that obviously must have predated his actual purchase of these pamphlets.[13]

In figure 1.1 I offer an overview of the parallel development of Joyce and the psychoanalytic movement, a chart that is representative rather than comprehensive. In the first column I list published writings of Joyce plus facts of his life that are relevant to his connections with psycho-analysis. I have devoted the next columns of the chart to three of the early psychoanalysts: Freud, the great originator, plus Jung and Rank in the next generation. Although Jung had left the movement well before

1922 and Rank would move toward a final separation from Freud with the publication of his *Trauma of Birth* in 1923, both these men were exceptionally close to Freud and made extraordinary contributions to the movement in its early years.[14] In addition, both had special interests close to Joyce's own. I have listed representative examples of their significant writings and also, as with Joyce, facts of their lives that are relevant to the parallel development I am discussing. In the far right-hand column, then, I list significant events in the development of the psychoanalytic movement.

Of course, there has always been some question about whether Joyce knew German well enough to access these early psychoanalytic writings. Indeed, Svevo's denial of Joyce's knowledge of psychoanalysis was based on his opinion that Joyce's "grasp of German" was too poor to approach these scientific writings (Bollettieri, 179). But Joyce's easy mastery of languages is a fact of his biography, and even as a university student he had learned French and Italian well and had studied Dano-Norwegian in order to read Ibsen in the original. Similarly, in order to translate Gerhart Hauptmann, he attempted, while still an undergraduate, to teach himself German, a language that he had earlier avoided because he disliked it (*JJII*, 76).[15]

By the time Joyce left Ireland in 1904, although he was fluent in French and Italian, his grasp of German was still rudimentary (*JJII*, 87–88). At the Berlitz school in Pola, Italy, however, where he secured his first job teaching English to Italians, he intensified his study of the language, exchanging lessons with the German professor at the school (*JJII*, 188). His further progress in German may be followed in his letters to Stanislaus. On 15 December 1904, he reports that he has "made good progress"; in February 1905 he has "progressed a great deal in German" and declares that by the time his novel is finished, he expects to be "a good German and Danish scholar" (*Letters*, 2:74, 83). And by July 1905, shortly before his son Giorgio was born, he could write that in his nine months on the Continent, he had not only begotten a child and progressed with his writing, but had also learned German "fairly well" (*Letters*, 2:93).

Now, by 1905, Freud—writing in German, of course—had published key texts of psychoanalysis: not only *The Interpretation of Dreams* (1900), *The Psychopathology of Everyday Life* (1901), and *Jokes and Their Relation to the Unconscious* (1905) but also his unsettling specula-

JOYCE (1882-1941)	FREUD (1856-1939)	JUNG (1875-1961)	RANK (1884-1939)	PSYCHOANALYTIC MOVEMENT
1900 "Ibsen"	1900 *Interpretation of Dreams* 1901 *Psychopathology of Everyday Life* 1901/1905 "Dora"	1900 RESIDENT, BURGHÖLZLI 1902 *Dissertation* 1904-7 *Word Association*		1902 PSYCHOLOGICAL WEDNESDAY SOCIETY FOUNDED
1904 "The Sisters" 1904 JOYCE TO CONTINENT			1905 *The Artist* to Freud	
1905 JOYCE LEARNED GERMAN	1905 *Jokes* 1906 FREUD-JUNG CORRESPONDENCE/ RELATIONSHIP BEGUN	1906 "Significance of the Father"	1906 SECRETARY TO SOCIETY	1906 MINUTES FOR SOCIETY BEGUN
1907 *Chamber Music*	1908 "Creative Writers and Daydreaming" 1909 FREUD AND JUNG AWARDED HONORARY DEGREES BY CLARK UNIVERSITY, WORCESTER, MASSACHUSETTS	1907 *Dementia Praecox*	1907 *The Artist*	1907 FREUD SOCIETY IN ZURICH 1908 FIRST INTERNATIONAL PSYCHOANALYTIC CONGRESS
	1909 "Family Romance" in Rank's *Myth* 1910 *Leonardo*	1909 "Significance of the Father" 1909 EDITOR, JAHRBUCH 1910 PRESIDENT OF THE INTERNATIONAL ASSOCIATION	1909 *Myth of the Birth of the Hero*	1909 *JAHRBUCH*
1910-13 JOYCE PURCHASED PSYCHOANALYTIC TEXTS	1911 *Hamlet* footnote expanded by Jones, German Translation 1913 FREUD-JUNG CORRESPONDENCE/ RELATIONSHIP ENDED	1911-12 *Transformations* 1912 *Transformations* 1913 RESIGNATION, JAHRBUCH EDITOR	1911 *Lohengrin* 1912 DOCTORATE, UNIVERSITY OF VIENNA 1912 "Griselda Legend" 1913 "Woman of Ephesus"	1910 INTERNATIONAL PSYCHOANALYTIC ASSOCIATION FOUNDED 1911 AMERICAN PSYCHOANALYTIC ASSOCIATION FOUNDED 1911 *ZENTRALBLATT* 1912 *IMAGO* 1913 *ZEITSCHRIFT*
1914 *Portrait (Egoist)* 1914 *Dubliners* 1915 JOYCE TO ZURICH	1914 *History of Psychoanalytic Movement* 1914 "On Narcissism"	1914 RESIGNATION, PSYCHOANALYTIC ASSOCIATION PRESIDENT	1914 "The Double" 1915 "The Play In *Hamlet*" 1915 RANK TO AUSTRIAN ARMY	
1916 *Portrait*	1916-17 *Introductory Lectures*			
1917 *Ulysses (Little Review)* 1918 *Exiles* 1919 *Ulysses (Egoist)* 1919 JOYCE FROM ZURICH TO TRIESTE 1920 JOYCE TO PARIS		1917 *Psychology of Unconscious Processes* 1921 *Psychological Types*	1917 "Homer" "Folk Epic"	
1922 *Ulysses*				

Fig. 1.1. Joyce and Psychoanalysis

tions about infantile sexuality in *Three Essays on the Theory of Sexuality* (1905). In addition, the first of his brilliant psychoanalytic case studies, the near-novelistic "Fragment of a Case of Hysteria" ("The Case of Dora"), written in 1901, was also published in 1905.[16]

These were the beginnings of a unique body of literature, a peculiar blend of science, autobiography, and myth, which, by its nature, and especially because of its focus on sexuality, was of considerably more than passing interest to the author of *Ulysses*. For Joyce's declaration to Stanislaus, quoted earlier, that his autobiographical fiction, "sexual department," would have universal application and significance was very close to Freud's working hypothesis in his autobiographical *Interpretation of Dreams*.[17] And the psychoanalytic writings that built on Freud's work offered Joyce a kind of scientific confirmation—however dubious the scientific nature of psychoanalysis might be—of the universal significance of sexuality in human life, an area, after all, which he proposed to exploit in his fiction as he found it in himself.

The Textual Interaction: Joyce's Way

A defining characteristic of Joyce's style in *Ulysses* is the number, the variety, and the historical range of other texts he has incorporated into his own, and it is the interaction between the text of *Ulysses* and psychoanalytic texts available to Joyce when he was writing *Ulysses* that is the focus of this study. I should emphasize that in no instance do I intend to claim that the psychoanalytic context is the only context present. Indeed, the multiple interaction of congruent texts is characteristic of Joyce's way, and in this interaction the congruent intertexts confirm one another. Thus when a psychoanalytic intertext appears as well as an Aristotelian text, as it does in Stephen's discussion of the impossibility of proving fatherhood (*U*, 9.827–60), it is my assumption that both sources are implicated and that Joyce's text is thereby deepened and enriched. With any of Joyce's texts it is seldom a question of "either/or" but most often of "both/and." *Ulysses* is surely one of the most redundant of texts, and this is one of its glories.

As pointed out earlier, it is no part of my intention to identify Joyce's psychic needs or to contribute to what Mark Shechner has called "a composite psychoanalytic picture of Joyce's mind" ("Joyce and Psychoanalysis," 418), an aim that he appears to share with Sheldon Brivic, who identifies as his purpose in *Joyce Between Freud and Jung* "to understand the development of [Joyce's] mind as it went into and came out of the works," using as a "main tool, . . . Freudian psychology" (4). My overriding interest has been in the relationship between the text of *Ulysses* and specific texts of the psychoanalytic movement, in the way these texts talk to one another. This is a textual study, not a psychological one. Although my primary focus is psychoanalytic texts that are woven into *Ulysses*, I also consider in some detail a series of traces in the little overture that introduces *A Portrait*. For this overture, as Hugh Kenner has observed, casts a long shadow over all of Joyce's work that follows ("*Portrait* in Perspective," 142).

Joyce may or may not have been entirely conscious of specific psychoanalytic sources for every detail he uses that echoes one from a psychoanalytic source. And these traces, like Joyce's allusions to more traditional sources, are hardly ever exact parallels; they are often somehow aslant or askew. Perhaps the most obvious nonpsychoanalytic example of this generalization is the fact that the role of Homer's Odysseus in the episodes to which Joyce has assigned Homeric titles is by no means consistently taken by Leopold Bloom, Joyce's designated Ulysses. Indeed, in the one place in *Ulysses* that most clearly evokes a picture of Odysseus— that is, his communication with the dead when he visits Hades in book 11 of the *Odyssey*—it is Stephen who claims Odysseus's power to call the "past and its phantoms . . . into life across the waters of the Lethe." It is Stephen who is "lord and giver of their life" (*U*, 14.1113–16) as is Odysseus when he allows the ghosts to drink the "dark blood" and speak. To be sure, in one of the many parallels between the thinking and speech of the two protagonists of *Ulysses*, Bloom has obliquely alluded to this same Homeric scene when, in "Lestrygonians," he refers to "[f]amished ghosts," licking up "hot fresh blood" (*U*, 8.729–30), though he makes no claim to the power of Homer's hero. Weldon Thornton, in his *Allusions*, lists the Homeric allusion in Stephen's boast (114), but does not identify Bloom's phrase as Odyssean or note the correspondence with Stephen's allusion in "Oxen of the Sun." Of course, the "famished ghosts" of Bloom's vision appear earlier in the novel than Stephen's boast, with no overt Homeric context. But surely we have learned in our three quarters of a century's experience with the nonlinear *Ulysses* that such a separated allusion and such a correspondence is entirely possible, even probable, and I have at times acted on this assumption in the case of psycho-analytic traces.

It has always been difficult to find a neat label for the way Joyce incorporates other texts into his own. Certainly, in any consideration of the interaction between the text of *Ulysses* and the texts of the psychoanalytic movement, the "influence" label should be dismissed. By the time Joyce wrote *Ulysses*, he was all but immune to influence as we commonly understand it, although he was always almost preternaturally aware of analogous relationships and astonishingly sensitive to confirmation, in anything he read, of what he himself had thought or felt or experienced—or read somewhere else. What did not relate he ignored. Stanislaus Joyce recalls that "my brother remembered little or nothing of most of the books he read so voraciously," but "could make good use of the one or two things he did remember from his reading" (*BK*, 79), an observation affirmed by Gillespie in his assertion that "any reading which did not yield data for his own work seems to have had little effect on him" (*Inverted Volumes*, 64).

Since Joyce's work is heavily motivated by the autobiographical impulse, it is not surprising that he assigns the same characteristic to his fictional surrogate, Stephen Dedalus. For Stephen, also an omnivorous reader, "retained nothing of all he read save that which seemed to him an echo or a prophecy of his own state" (*P*, 155). Indeed, like the Coleridge of John Livingston Lowes's classic study of influence, *The Road to Xanadu*, Joyce's mind, equipped, like Coleridge's, with "an almost uncanny power of association," moved "like the passing of a magnet" over his reading and "drew and held fixed whatever was susceptible of imaginative transformation" (40, 32). And even more in Joyce's case, this magnetic attraction was awakened by whatever related to his own life and consequently to his autobiographical fiction.

We cannot seriously call this interaction "borrowing." We may remember Frank Budgen's label for Joyce in relation to his use of literary devices originated by others: "the *larron impénitent*" [the impenitent thief] ("Joyce's Chapters," 343). We may also remember Joyce's admonition to Budgen that "to get the correct contour on me, you ought to allude to me as a Jesuit" (*JJII*, 27), as well as his reminder to August Suter that the principal gain from his Jesuit training was "how to gather, how to order and how to present a given material" (Budgen, "Further Recollec-

tions," 533). This discipline has traditionally involved a habit of "acquisi-
tive adaptation" of texts,[18] and there is no aspect of Joyce's artistic stance
in which he is more truly a child of the Fathers than in the freedom with
which he appropriates insights from any source and adapts them to his
own artistic purposes. Like Cardinal Newman, who claimed for the
church whatever the heathen had said rightly for the purpose of "enlarg-
ing the range and refining the sense of her own teaching" (quoted by
Rahner, 56), Joyce simply takes whatever he may find in any source if he
sees a use for it in his own text. And so skillful is the interweaving that,
unless a reader knows the source, the addition most often goes unnoticed
and is attributed to Joyce or to Stephen's unassisted virtuosity.

In the 1960s, Thornton suggested that Eliot's early label of a "mythical
method" be replaced by the more comprehensive designation of an "allusive method," a label that would recognize the complex effect of the extraordinary range of allusions in the novel, which Thornton himself has
catalogued in his immensely useful *Allusions*.[19] But probably the best
general critical descriptor we now have for Joyce's way of incorporating
other texts into his own is M. M. Bakhtin's notion of "dialogism," or
indeed Julia Kristeva's descriptions of Bakhtin's concept as "intertextuality," a term which she herself coined in her "Word, Dialogue, and
Novel." Bakhtin provides many names for the interaction of texts, a process that he sees as fundamental in the novel, and discusses them in various places and in considerable detail.[20]

In this study I assume that "dialogue" and "intertextuality" are interchangeable terms in relation to Joyce's way with other texts, and both
relate to Bakhtin's description of the process in which the novelist "welcomes the heteroglossia and language diversity of the literary and
extraliterary language into his own work" (298).

Bakhtin insists that this absorption of other texts, not only does not
weaken the texts that thus become a part of the novel, but "even
intensif[ies] them." As for the effect on the novelist's own work, it is "out
of this stratification of language" that the novelist "constructs his style,"
without sacrificing, Bakhtin says, "the unity of his own creative personality and the unity . . . of his own style." Indeed "all these strata" work
together to "become a unique artistic system orchestrating the intentional theme of the author" (298–99). Small wonder that David Lodge,
reviewing Bakhtin's *Dialogic Imagination* for the *James Joyce Broadsheet* in 1983, commented that it was no overstatement "to say that

Bakhtin's theory of the novel needed the work of Joyce to confirm and fulfill it" (1).[21] Like Bakhtin's "prose writer as a novelist," Joyce "does not strip away the intentions of others from the language of his work." Instead, he "makes use of words that are already populated with the social intentions of others and compels them to serve his own new intentions" (299–300).

On a more naive level, I think it is possible, even helpful, to think of the mixture of texts in *Ulysses* as analogous in some degree to the "hidden pictures" puzzles that are a regular feature of children's magazines. In these puzzles, which have entertained generations of children, there is always a large picture, and the puzzle is to find little pictures that are hidden in it. The child-reader is given a list of the hidden pictures, and once the small pictures are named, most children can find the majority of them with consequent delight. The pliers in the list, for example, may be hidden in the branches of a tree; the ice-cream cone is part of some clouds; the sock makes part of the leg of a table; the rabbit is an open space in the foliage of a tree; and so on. All the hidden pictures are an integral part of the large picture, but at the same time, once one of them has been found and identified, it can always be seen as what it is; it is all there. Just so in Joyce's allusive texts. His appropriations from other texts, which often are fragments, fit just where Joyce puts them, but at the same time, once an allusion is identified (like the pliers in the hidden picture) it retains its individual identity, to the delight of the Joyce exegete. The resulting text represents Joyce's unique synthesis, but the "social intentions" of the words he appropriates do not entirely disappear; the allusions retain at least something of the intentions of their originators. What is more, Joyce's allusions often bring significant context with them, and this context almost always enriches the substance of the text.

Over a decade ago Bernard Benstock suggested a distinction between allusions with "literary validity," which "generally support the new text that subsumes them," and those with "narrational validity," which "are absorbed so completely as to expand their original shapes into transformed guise and significance." In the case of the latter, Benstock pointed out, "the lifeline back to a source can only be traced once we suspect that such a source exists" ("Text," 361). But with such a suspicion, which we may also call a hypothesis, the line *can* be traced, and my hypothesis is that psychoanalytic writings provide such a source. Now Joyce often offers assistance in identifying an allusion, providing a signal in the surrounding text, which functions, though generally somewhat obliquely, as a hidden footnote, so that when an allusion is recognized, the exegete will find evidence that Joyce was *also* aware of his source. Thus, Wilde's "cracked lookingglass of a servant" in the opening scene, though not directly attributed to its originator, is preceded in the text by Mulligan's "If Wilde were only alive to see you" (*U*, 1.146, 143–44). There is also a footnote guiding the reader to a source for Stephen's ringing assertion that "a man of genius makes no mistakes. His errors are volitional and are the portals of discovery" (*U*, 9.228–29). The portals of discovery are, so far as I know, Stephen's own invention, but the volitional error has its origins in the *Lesser Hippias*, a minor Socratic dialogue whose sole point is that the better man is the one who errs voluntarily.[22] That Joyce was aware of the Socratic origins of the concept is indicated by the footnote immediately provided by John Eglinton: "What useful discovery did Socrates learn from Xanthippe?" (*U*, 9.233–34).

Likewise, Meredith's misquoted definition of the sentimentalist (*U*, 9.550–51), not immediately attributed, is followed, though pages later, by mention of "a novel by George Meredith" (*U*, 9.994), and the footnote is completed episodes later, hidden in the babble of the end of "Oxen of the Sun": "Mummer's wire. Cribbed out of Meredith" (*U*, 14.1486). This is an example of what Joyce is reported to have called a "chord" in a remembered conversation with a boy who was a pupil of his in Zurich. Claiming that writing a book is very much like writing music, Joyce explained to the young Hans Kraus, who many years later was to become John Kennedy's physician: "Suppose I write in Chapter One about a man who has kidney disease, and sometime later in the book about a person who eats kidneys, and still later about someone who gets a kick in the kidneys. Then you have a chord."[23]

Now, nowhere in *Ulysses* does the name of Oedipus appear, but he is nevertheless recognized in the text through an extended chordlike footnote, whose parts must be reassembled in order for it to be identified. Two of the separate parts of the footnote are found in "Scylla and Charybdis," in which, to a reader on the lookout for them, traces of psychoanalytic texts abound, whether or not they can be called full-fledged allusions. And a reader should be on the lookout since the one psychoanalytic allusion listed by Thornton—Stephen's mention of the "new Viennese school" and its view on incest—is in "Scylla and Charybdis" (*U*, 9.778–80; Thornton, *Allusions*, 199). It is in this episode that Stephen carries on a little dialogue with himself about a pound that AE has lent him, most of which, he reminds himself, he spent "in Georgina Johnson's [a prostitute's] bed" (U, 9.195). Later in the same episode, during his *Hamlet* presentation, Stephen alludes to "the poisoning and the beast with two backs that urged it" (U, 9.469–70), using the phrase from *Othello* to suggest that the adultery between Hamlet's mother and Claudius has motivated the murder of his father (see Thornton, *Allusions*, 182–83).

In "Circe," then, these two originally unconnected allusions are picked up again and associated with each other and with a third to form a chord. As Stephen and Lynch appear in Nighttown, Stephen says they are going to "*la belle dame sans merci*, Georgina Johnson" (U, 15.122), the prostitute mentioned in the library episode, who, he finds later, has married and left the brothel: "And so Georgina Johnson is dead and married. . . . Married. Hm" (U, 15.3620–22). "Hm. Sphinx. The beast that has two backs at midnight" (U, 15.3631–32). The beast, however, that has two backs at midnight, is not the Sphinx, but man, echoing Oedipus's solution to the riddle of the Sphinx—"What has four legs in the morning, two at noon, and three in the evening?"—to which Oedipus provided the correct answer—"man"—and was rewarded by being given his mother, Jocasta, for a wife. And in this fragmented footnote, Joyce has painstakingly put together a chain of associations that links "the beast with two backs" first, through Gertrude, to Hamlet, then, through Georgina Johnson, to Stephen, and finally, through the riddle of the Sphinx, to Oedipus. This chain in turn attaches to the view of "the new Viennese school" (U, 9.780) on incest, which is, after all, a version of "the beast with two backs."

Through this complicated footnote, stretching over both "Scylla and Charybdis" and "Circe," Joyce has put Stephen into a pattern with Hamlet and Oedipus, whose symbolic equivalence had first been suggested by Freud in his *Interpretation of Dreams*. The centrality of the Oedipus complex in Freud's structuring of the new psychology of the twentieth century—psychoanalysis—rests on the legendary figure of Oedipus, even as Joyce's *Ulysses*, a monument of twentieth-century literature, relies for its structure on the legendary figure of Odysseus, and I find no other rationale for the appearance of the Sphinx in this context than to provide a link to Oedipus and hence to Freud. This construction thus may serve as a signal that Joyce has quite consciously given a place in *Ulysses* to Freud's psychoanalysis.

Surely Joyce found much in the early psychoanalytic literature that confirmed his own experience and resonated with the complex symbolic statement of *Ulysses*, as well as much that was analogous to his other reading. But just as surely Joyce's use of these psychoanalytic shards does not necessarily indicate any kind of allegiance to the theories of psychoanalysis. Indeed, any assumption about his intentions in including these shards is a matter of probability only: there is no way to prove it. Joyce was extraordinarily sensitive to individual texts—and even to individual words and phrases of these—that caught his ear, were congruent with his own vision, and fit into his artistic agenda. It is on the basis of such a multipronged fit that he included these echoes in his work. And the two European cities in which he lived in the early years of the century afforded him unusual opportunities to interact with the texts of psychoanalysis.

The Trieste Connection

After bobbing around from Zurich to Trieste to Pola when he and Nora first arrived on the Continent, Joyce, except for a nine-month stay in Rome, lived for ten years in Trieste, a very old Italian city with a complex history of alternating autonomy (as a free port) and foreign domination. Situated on the northeastern border of Italy, and thus subject to influences from Austria, Slovenia, and Croatia, Trieste was the main port of the Austro-Hungarian empire at the time Joyce lived there, with a rich mixture of races and outlooks.[24] This produced an intellectual climate, according to Bollettieri, that was "open to any influences of a stimulating nature," including Freud's psychoanalysis (177). There was no university in Trieste at the time, so that Triestines had to go elsewhere for their professional training, and doctors, lawyers, and scientists gravitated toward Vienna. It might thus be expected, and it was the case, that Freud's ideas, in contrast to the opposition they met with in the rest of Italy, "took root with relative ease" in Trieste (Bollettieri, 178–79).[25] Through Joyce's position as an English teacher he became associated with many of the cultivated Triestines who were acquainted with Freud's theories and interested in discussing psychoanalysis, and, as Bollettieri points out, it is "logical to assume that Joyce came into contact with the early phases of this new adventure in thought" during such discussions (179).[26] One of the most important of these discussants was surely Svevo, who, according to Staley, approached Freud's psychoanalysis between 1910 and 1912 "to introduce it as a literary method in his writings" (208).[27] I thus assume that Joyce knew something about the psychoanalytic context of the pamphlets by Freud, Jung, and Jones before he purchased them some time between 1910 and 1913, and, as I shall develop in detail in the next chapter, he was prompt to incorporate into the opening pages of *A Portrait* relevant bits and pieces from Freud's psychobiography of Leonardo, as well as from Jung's 1909 essay on the father. With these, Joyce embarked on the process of weaving psychoanalytic strands into his texts while he was still in Trieste, a process that continued after his move to Zurich.

The Zurich Connection

In July 1915 Joyce moved to Zurich, a uniquely cosmopolitan city during the period of World War I because of Switzerland's status as a neutral nation. Zurich also has a very special place in the history of psychoanalysis, which is set forth by Freud himself in his summary of "the great services rendered by the Zurich School of Psychiatry in the spread of psycho-analysis" (*History, SE*, 14:27–30). The "Zurich School" had a distinguished history well before Jung became the designated "crown prince" of Freud's movement and before Zurich became "the second capital of psychoanalysis," to borrow a phrase from Frank Budgen ("Joyce's Chapters," 344). The Burghölzli, the public mental hospital with which the School of Psychiatry was associated, was world-famous; indeed, this teaching hospital provided the training for Freud's followers even after Jung's defection from the movement (*SE*, 14:27). The international prestige of the Zurich School, in fact, was so high that John Kerr claims that "it was Jung and Bleuler who put Freud on the scientific map, not the other way around."[28] Jung's advocacy of Freud and psychoanalysis predated the beginning of their correspondence in 1906 and their first meeting in early 1907, and, in fact, a Freud Society had been established in Zurich by 1907.

As the century opened, Jung was beginning his medical career as a resident at the Burghölzli, and even in his 1902 doctoral dissertation on occult phenomena, he alluded to Freud's *Interpretation of Dreams*, which he had read twice and "discovered how it all linked up with my own ideas" (*Memories*, 147). It is startling to realize that the extremely intense and influential relationship between Freud and Jung lasted considerably less than a decade. For during the years between 1906, when the correspondence between the two men began, and 1913, the year it ended and mutual hostility replaced mutual admiration, Freud had come to refer to Jung as his "son and heir" and had designated him editor of the *Yearbook*, the first of the movement's journals, as well as president of the International Psychoanalytic Association.[29] It was Freud's declared intention that Zurich become the center of the new movement, and it was Freud's influence that secured Jung an invitation to the 1909 celebration of the twentieth anniversary of Clark University in Worcester, Massachusetts, a meeting at which prominent scientific figures from all over the world were in attendance (Rosenzweig, 38–39).

Both Freud and Jung were awarded honorary degrees during this celebration, and in effect the two men, as a team, introduced psychoanalysis to the United States. Indeed, in a *New York Times Magazine* interview of 29 September 1912, during Jung's later visit to Fordham, the interviewer declared that it was Jung "who brought Dr. Sigmund Freud to the recognition of the older school of psychology, and together these two men stand at the head of a school of thought which is considered by many students of the subject to give the most radical explanation of the human mind and the most fundamental, since the beginning of its study."[30]

The separation between Freud and Jung was more a gradual disintegration of their mutually sustaining relationship than a "break," as it has often been called. Jung's theoretical disagreements with Freud had been present from the beginning, but somewhat submerged by Jung and overlooked by Freud, in part because of their personal fascination for each other and also in large part because each of them had a great professional stake in the continuation of their personal relationship, and they struggled to maintain it in the face of a variety of conflicts.[31] But by the beginning of 1913, they had ended their personal correspondence; in mid-1913 Jung resigned as editor of the *Yearbook*; and in April 1914 he resigned as president of the International Psychoanalytic Association.[32]

Thus the close connection between Zurich and Vienna was ended by the time Joyce moved his family to Zurich in July 1915, but psychoanalysis was still very much alive in the city. As Budgen has said, "It was like the foehn wind: you couldn't escape it" ("Joyce's Chapters," 344). In addition to the pamphlets in Joyce's Trieste library and Freud's *Psychopathology of Everyday Life*, which he purchased in Zurich, Joyce had access in the public library to much of the early psychoanalytic literature, most important, perhaps, the material that was appearing in the four journals established by the movement between 1909 and 1913. It was in these journals that many of the early writings were first published, and in 1915 the Zurich library was receiving three of the four—the *Yearbook*, the *Central Bulletin*, and *Imago*.[33]

The first article in the first issue of the *Yearbook*, for example, is Freud's "Analysis of a Phobia in a Five-Year-Old Boy," the charming case study of "Little Hans" (1–109).[34] And toward the end of this first issue is a listing of Freud's works from 1893 to 1909, compiled by Karl Abraham (546–94). Articles in one journal were noted in the other journals, and, of course, the psychoanalytic publishers advertised their books, even as publishers do today, but in rather more detail than we now expect. An advertisement for Rank's *Incest-Motif*, for example, appears at the beginning of the 1912 *Yearbook* (volume 4), with a three-page summary of the contents and another three pages devoted to a detailed table of contents, followed by ads for Rank's *Der Künstler*, *Der Mythus von der Geburt des Helden*, and *Die Lohengrinsage*. The following pages of this front material contain advertisements for a collection of articles edited by Freud, with a table of contents, and for fifteen other pieces of varying lengths, many of them apparently the kinds of pamphlets that Joyce had purchased in Trieste. In these early journals, the bibliographical information alone is impressive.

Now, Tom Stoppard was acute enough to see the Zurich library as Joyce's natural habitat in his play *Travesties*. But, despite evidence in both *A Portrait* and *Ulysses* of the importance of the library to the autobiographical Stephen Dedalus, Joyce's library habit has never been given the documented biographical attention that his drinking habit has. The index for Ellmann's 1982 *James Joyce*, for example, includes under a main entry for Joyce's personal characteristics an entry for "drinking habits," with a subentry for Zurich, but nowhere in the index is there mention of the Zurich library.[35]

But libraries were important to Joyce, and he knew how to use them. His report in a letter to Stanislaus (13 November 1906) of a visit to the *Biblioteca Vittorio Emanuele* in Rome is exemplary evidence of this. He reports reading about the Vatican Council of 1870, which declared the infallibility of the pope, information that he needs for validation of details in the *Dubliners* story "Grace." He tells Stanislaus about checking not just one account, but at least "another," and also a life of John MacHale, Archbishop of Tuam in Ireland, who, Ellmann notes, opposed making papal infallibility a dogma. He "had not time to finish" that day, but is planning to return the next day and gives Stanislaus a summary of what he expects to be able to find in "the Bib. Vitt. Eman," including "all the dictionaries I want" (*Letters*, 2:192–93). This is a man who cannot buy every book he wants to look at, but is very knowing about how to find what he wants in a library.[36]

Libraries were also important in Zurich, and the Zurich library had a 600-year history stretching back to the thirteenth century, when the first library was established in the choir loft of the Grossmunster.[37] Over the centuries, various other libraries were established in different locations, and by 1911, *Zürichs Bibliotheken*, a combined history and directory, listed twenty-two individual libraries, some quite small and specialized, to be sure. The two largest were the *Stadtsbibliothek* [City Library] and the *Kantonsbibliothek* [Canton Library], which also served the University of Zurich.[38] In 1911 the *Stadtsbibliothek* was housed in the building complex of the Wasserkirche, the Helmhaus, and the adjoining Wasserhaus, at the Limmatquai, while the *Kantonsbibliothek* was located at the Predigerkirche, near the University of Zurich. By the time Joyce arrived in Zurich in 1915, however, the *Kantonsbibliothek* had moved to the location at the Limmatquai, since construction had begun in January on a new library, which was actually built around the Predigerkirche.

Thus in 1915 a major part of the library collections were located at the Limmatquai, quite close to Joyce's residences from 1915 to 1918.[39] Indeed, Ellmann reports that Claud Sykes often saw Joyce reading English newspapers at the *Museumgesellschaft* (*JJII*, 411), one of the libraries on the 1911 list, which was also located at the Limmatquai. This library had been founded in 1834 as a reading room, and even in 1911 was receiving "not less than 136 newspapers and 751 journals." It had also developed as a library with a collection of approximately 85,000 volumes "in the areas of *belle-lettres*, geography and history, and biography and memoirs" (Wyss, 50–51). And it was here that Joyce might well have discovered Otto Rank's psychoanalytic study of the artist, since the 1907 edition of *Der Künstler* in the library's collection bears the stamp of the *Museumsgesellschaft Zürich*.[40]

A movement to consolidate the collections in one building under one administration had been in process since the end of the nineteenth century, with the intermediate step of a "Central Catalogue of the Library of the City of Zurich" accomplished in 1901. And on 28 June 1914, the day that the Archduke Franz Ferdinand was shot in Sarajevo, touching off World War I, a referendum, by a large majority, authorized the establishment of the Zentralbibliothek Zürich. Most of the funding for the project was supplied by private donation, and despite wartime problems, construction on the new library began in 1915, shortly after the beginning of the year, and was completed in April 1917, when the new Zentralbibliothek opened on the site of the present library. Again, this location was easily accessed, by foot or by tram, from Joyce's residences in 1918 and 1919 on Universitätsstrasse. The present Zentralbibliothek, completely restructured in 1994, except for the entrance and the outer rooms that were a part of the 1917 Zentralbibliothek, is still identifiable from a distance by the spire of the Predigerkirche.

During his years in Zurich, from July 1915 to October 1919, Joyce, for the first time in his life, was subsidized by patrons outside his family. Early in Joyce's stay in the city, Ezra Pound, with great energy, arranged for a pension from the Civil List in England, as well as a small monthly subsidy from the Society of Authors (*JJII*, 405), and later Harriet Shaw Weaver provided an anonymous monthly subsidy, as did Edith Rockefeller McCormick (*JJII*, 413–15, 422). The amounts were generous enough that Joyce had time to be a full-time writer, which, we surely recognize by now, always involved a measure of research, much of it in libraries. His German, which Frank Budgen pronounced "fluent" during the Zurich period (*James Joyce*, 178), was good enough that he was paid as a translator, and thus it was surely adequate for the kind of selective appropriation from the psychoanalytic texts that is characteristic of Joyce's way with allusions.[41] And finally, he had access in Zurich's public library to a remarkable collection of the essential literature of the psychoanalytic movement. It seems inevitable that traces of this literature should have entered *Ulysses*, and in this study, which, as I have noted, is representative rather than exhaustive, based on probabilities rather than proof, I am following a variety of such traces.

2

Freud's *Leonardo*

Childhood and Beyond

The evidence I offer for correspondences between Joyce's fiction and psychoanalytic texts produced before 1922 is basically internal, a matter of Joyce's text paralleling or echoing a psychoanalytic text. These echoes may be verbal or situational or both, and I make no claim to "prove" that Joyce deliberately wove psychoanalytic texts into his fiction or even that he read them. I see no way to do this. The cumulative effect of the parallels I present, however, becomes something to deal with. And since psychoanalytic literature, with its focus on sexual matters, would have had a particular appeal for Joyce, I am assuming that he dipped into these texts during the years of patronage in Zurich and in some quite complicated way remembered and used selected fragments from them. Some of the broader similarities between Joyce's later fiction and psychoanalytic speculation are presumably connected with living in roughly the same place at roughly the same time as the psychoanalytic pioneers. In addition, some psychoanalytic hypotheses that appear to find an echo in *Ulysses* duplicate insights of classical writers, but are fitted into a different frame. When such perceptions enter Joyce's fiction, it is my assumption that they carry both contexts with them, but it is also my assumption that, in some way, such insights were Joyce's insights *first*, that they buttress his own thinking.

My identifications are thus based on probability rather than proof, but the probability is strong. In this chapter I start with the only psychoanalytic writings with which Joyce had a provable acquaintance: the pamphlets that he purchased in Trieste. And, although this study focuses on *Ulysses*, it begins with *A Portrait of the Artist as a Young Man*, which is a prerequisite for understanding the larger and greater book. Joyce himself implied this when he identified *Ulysses* as a "sequel" to *A Portrait* (*JJII*, 416). And the status of *A Portrait* as an essential preliminary for *Ulysses* is underscored by Joyce's reminder to Stanislaus in a 1925 letter that "I never give [translation rights for *Ulysses*] till *A Portrait* is first translated" (*Letters*, 3:128).[1] Thus, when Adolf Hoffmeister, the noted Czech artist and writer, presented Joyce with the first copy of the Czech translation of *Ulysses*, it was bound in four volumes, the first being a translation of *A Portrait of the Artist as a Young Man* (See Hoffmeister, 128 n. 14).

The published *Portrait*, of course, was itself the outgrowth of two preliminary unpublished autobiographical works: *Stephen Hero* and the odd little essay/manifesto that Joyce wrote in 1904 and titled "A Portrait of the Artist." This short piece, rejected for publication by the editors of *Dana*, was, Ellmann says, "the extraordinary beginning of Joyce's mature work" and the revelation to Joyce that "he could become an artist by writing about the process of becoming an artist" (*JJII*, 144).

"The features of infancy," this first portrait begins, "are not commonly reproduced in the adolescent portrait," and Joyce's 1904 essay is no exception, for the first glimpse the reader has of its subject is his praying in the wood as a boy of fifteen (*FP*, 60). By 1913, however, when the manuscript of *A Portrait of the Artist as a Young Man* was ready to be set in type,[2] the "features of infancy" had been expanded into a dramatic overture, opening with the meeting of "baby tuckoo" and "the moocow," and throwing a symbolic shadow not only over the whole of *A Portrait*, but, as Hugh Kenner claims, over "the entire lifework of James Joyce" ("*Portrait* in Perspective," 137, 142.)

Between 1904 and 1913, of course, infancy had assumed a more powerful significance for a growing portion of the intellectual world of the twentieth century with the publication in 1905 of Freud's *Three Essays on the Theory of Sexuality*, which focused on the crucial effect of infant sexuality on the psychological destiny of the adult.[3] But more directly relevant, I think, to Joyce's vision of Stephen Dedalus as an infant and a small child in the first pages of *A Portrait* was Freud's *Leonardo da Vinci and a Memory of His Childhood*, published in 1910 and purchased by Joyce in Trieste (hereafter abbreviated *L*).

The certainty that Joyce was directly acquainted with psychoanalytic writings well before the publication of *Ulysses* and probably even before the completion of *A Portrait* clears the way for a revised perspective on

Freudian motifs in both novels, motifs that have been identified and discussed from the beginnings of Joyce criticism.[4] But there has been almost
no attempt to trace these motifs to specific sources in the body of Freud's
writings.[5] With the discovery, however, that as early as 1911 or 1912
Joyce owned Freud's essay on Leonardo, which highlights the artist's relationship with his mother, a relationship also central in *Ulysses*, an examination of the links between Joyce's text and Freud's could contribute
to something quite different from another "Freudian" reading. For
Joyce's great and unique gift is his uncanny ability to recognize and appropriate insights and ambiences not his own and to transform them into
an integral part of his own symbolic statement without sacrificing their
original integrity. He has so transformed the work of still uncounted
thinkers and artists, and he has so transformed Sigmund Freud and his
Leonardo da Vinci. For the congruences between Freud's picture of this
supreme artist and Joyce's fictional portrait of the artist, which arises out
of his own life, bear witness to Joyce's probably conscious—though undoubtedly complicated—use of what he has found in Freud. To be sure,
since Joyce's portrait is always subject to the constraints of autobiography, he has adapted these insights to conform to his own artistic needs.
Still, distinctive features of Freud's portrait of both the child Leonardo,
whom he reconstructs, and the adult Leonardo of history, whose portrait
Freud at least retouches, appear to be integrated into Joyce's portrait, as
his artist develops from infancy to adulthood.[6]

Leonardo, as Freud pointed out when he presented his proposed study
to the Vienna Psychoanalytic Society at their meeting of 1 December
1909, "is esteemed as one of the greatest artists" (Nunberg and Federn,
2:338), and this preeminence probably furnishes motive enough for
Joyce's purchase of Freud's monograph. In addition, the "childhood
memory" of Freud's title promised further material that would be perti-
nent to Joyce's autobiographical project, still in its beginning stages in
1910. Richard Ellmann, discussing the nature of Joyce's identification
with great figures who appealed to his imagination, speculates that it was
not so much that Joyce "wanted to become them," but rather that "he
wanted them to become him . . . he wanted an interplay among their
images and his own" (*JJII*, 47). And the authors of *The Workshop of
Daedalus* have concluded that he deliberately designed *A Portrait* so that
material relating to other artists was interwoven with the events of his
own life, making it "both a self-portrait of the author and a portrait of the

artist in general" (xiii). This is a design that carries over into *Ulysses* and of which Freud's Leonardo is a part.

At any rate, Joyce has crafted a childhood memory for Stephen Dedalus in the opening section of *A Portrait* that reveals remarkable parallels with Freud's interpretation of the childhood memory that he makes the focus of his study of Leonardo. To be sure, Joyce has adapted features of the memory to autobiographical fact, but without losing touch with the Freudian context. And the resulting symbolic construct prefigures themes that deepen and darken from *A Portrait* to *Ulysses*, where the central importance of the artist's resolution of his radical ambivalence toward the simultaneously supportive and menacing tie with his mother—drawn from Leonardo's memory by Freud—is complicated by his need to define his relationship with his father, a figure significant in Freud's interpretation only through his absence. This characteristic combination of appropriation and transformation operates in both novels, but in *A Portrait* implications of the Freudian portrait of Leonardo are more or less superimposed on a form already substantially complete, whereas in *Ulysses* this portrait fuses with Joyce's own perspective and becomes an integral part of the symbolic pattern of the novel.

Leonardo's Memory and Stephen's

It is in the second chapter of *Leonardo da Vinci and a Memory of His Childhood* that Freud quotes the brief memory with which Leonardo interrupts his discussion of the flight of vultures:[7] "I recall as one of my very earliest memories that while I was in my cradle a vulture came down to me, and opened my mouth with its tail, and struck me many times with its tail against my lips" (*L*, 82). Recognizing that this almost certainly does not describe an actual memory, but rather a later fantasy transposed back to earliest childhood, Freud identifies it as Leonardo's reminiscence of being suckled at his mother's breast (*L*, 84, 87). But he finds it odd that the fantasy, in contrast to the active nature of a baby's nursing, is "so completely passive in character" (*L*, 86) and that the mother has been "replaced by—a vulture" (*L*, 87–88). In fact, Freud says, what Leonardo describes, with the vulture "opening the child's mouth and beating about inside vigorously with its tail, corresponds to the idea of *fellatio.*" This is a fantasy, Freud points out, which resembles dreams and fantasies produced not only by passive homosexuals but also by women who have no awareness of the sexual practice itself (*L*, 86–87). And Freud hypothesizes that the universally pleasurable "organic impression" of sucking on a nipple merges with the "repellant sexual phantasy" through the homely intermediary figure of the cow. For every cow has a visible udder, "whose function is that of a nipple, but whose shape and position under the belly makes it resemble a penis" (*L*, 87).

Joyce's *Portrait* opens with the story told to Stephen by his father about a "moocow coming down along the road" that "met a nicens little boy named baby tuckoo" (*P*, 7), a childhood memory authenticated by John Joyce's birthday greeting to his son in 1931: "I wonder do you recollect the old days in Brighton Square, when you were Babie Tuckoo, and I used to . . . tell you all about the moo-cow that used to come down from the mountain and take little boys across?" (*Letters*, 3:212). Chester Anderson sets the stage for his Freudian reading of this memory with a series of autobiographical assumptions about the connections between the story and the arrival of more Joyce babies,[8] which may well be true but which are not necessary to establish the textual fact that Stephen's memory, like Leonardo's, arises out of the suckling period. We have, after all, the cow, and we also have the lemon platt, a "tit-bit" made of lemon-flavored barley sugar, which also requires sucking (Gifford and Seidman, 86).

But from the beginning, Stephen's memory departs significantly from Leonardo's because it starts from the father, whereas a significant factor in Freud's analysis of Leonardo is that Leonardo, an illegitimate son, was separated from his father in his earliest years (*L*, 81, 91–92). Stephen's father "looked at him through a glass; he had a hairy face," an image which Kenner sees as "a traditional infantile analogue of God the Father," linking at the same time the phrase "through a glass" with Paul's "through a glass darkly" ("Perspective," 137–38), and the link may well be intended. But the hairy face and the glass are also found in Freud's 1909 "Analysis of a Phobia of a Five-Year-Old Boy," to which he refers in his discussion of Leonardo's early "sexual researches" (*L*, 79).[9] And in Freud's early study of "Little Hans," the hairy face and the glass are found together in a context that brings both mother and father into the picture.

The five-year-old Hans had developed a phobic fear of horses, and his father, an early adherent of psychoanalysis, had been working with his son—and Freud—along the lines of Freud's hypothesis that intellectual enlightenment was the avenue to freedom from neurotic fear. They had already established that somehow the horses Hans was afraid of were connected with "affectionate feelings towards his mother" and that "he was particularly bothered by what horses wear in front of their eyes and by the black round their mouths" (*SE*, 10:41). Then Freud relates:

> As I saw the two of them sitting in front of me and at the same time heard Hans's description of his anxiety-horses, a further piece of the solution shot through my mind. . . . I asked Hans jokingly whether his horses wore eyeglasses, to which he replied that they did not. I then asked him whether his father wore eyeglasses, to which, against all evidence, he once more said no. Finally I asked him whether by "the black round the mouth" he meant a moustache; and I then disclosed to him that he was afraid of his father, precisely because he was so fond of his mother (*SE*, 10:42).

Freud then reassured Hans that he had known long before Hans was born that "he would be so fond of his mother that he would be bound to feel afraid of his father because of it." Still, Freud assured the boy that his father was fond of him in spite of his great affection for his mother, and the happy ending is signaled by the father's recognition of Hans's phobia about horses as "an expression of the little boy's hostile disposition towards him, and perhaps also as a manifestation of a need for getting punished for it" (*SE*, 10:42).

The case study of Little Hans could thus provide Joyce with a bridge between the exclusive maternal relationship that Freud posits for the child Leonardo and his own more normal family constellation, which in turn defines Stephen's memory. His father, who, like Hans's father, has a "hairy face,"[10] looks at Stephen "through a glass" because, unlike Hans's father, Simon Dedalus wears a monocle, which he is shown using at the Christmas dinner and later at the Whitsuntide play (*P*, 29, 77). Stephen's memory then, through association with Freud's explanation of Hans's phobia, becomes colored with a repressed hostility and fear toward the father that is connected with excessive affection for the mother, the essential configuration of the Oedipus complex. And the mother appears in her proper person (assuming the cow to be a symbol for the boy's earliest relationship with her) only after the father's place in his babyhood has been acknowledged.

When Stephen's mother does appear, she is putting on the oilsheet after Stephen has wet the bed, and Joyce is surely aware of the Freudian attribution of sexual connotations to this typical happening. In Jung's 1909 essay, also purchased in Trieste, Joyce could find the flat statement: "Bed-wetting must be regarded as an infantile sexual substitute," a statement that was removed, along with many other expressions of the "Freudian standpoint," in a later revision (*CW*, 4:319). But the pamphlet that found a place on Joyce's bookshelf was written firmly from a Freudian point of view. Jung's essay depends on four case studies, of which Joyce has used details from only one, that of "an eight-year-old boy, intelligent, rather delicate-looking, brought to [Jung] by his mother on account of enuresis." This eight year old, who may remind us of the six-year-old schoolboy Stephen, "never played with his school-fellows" and "feared the boys' roughness and violence" (*CW*, 4:317), even as Stephen takes to heart his mother's advice "not to speak with the rough boys in the college" and, "in the whirl of a scrimmage," is "fearful of the flashing eyes and muddy boots" of the other boys (*P*, 9). Like the younger Stephen of the beginning of *A Portrait*, the boy is a bed-wetter. Also like Stephen, "every time he wet his bed he called to his mother, who would then have to change the bedclothes" (*CW*, 4:318).

Now when Stephen's childhood memory moves from the "queer smell" of the oilsheet to the observation that "his mother had a nicer smell than his father," Joyce is carefully setting up an associational progression that is also sexually tinged. When he rounds this off by producing the memory of Stephen's mother as she played "the sailor's hornpipe for him to dance," the chain of sexual associations is subtly continued. For "horn" is one of the battery of phallic synonyms that Joyce uses in the notorious pornographic letters written to Nora (for example, 3 December 1909, *SL*, 181), and the "hornpipe" is not, I think, used neutrally here, but rather points to the image of the "phallic mother," which is also the source for the vulture-mother of Leonardo's fantasy.[11]

Freud links the appearance of the mother figure as a vulture in Leonardo's fantasy to an association between the vulture and motherhood, originating in ancient Egypt, but familiar to Leonardo, Freud says, through the writings of the church fathers, a familiarity that Freud carefully documents. The vulture, he writes, is found in Egyptian hieroglyphics as the symbol for motherhood, an association explained in certain classical sources cited by Freud by the fact that "only female vultures were believed to exist." This belief was in turn useful to the church fathers because of the correlative belief, "mentioned by almost all of them," that vultures were impregnated by the wind with no assistance from a male, a natural-history fable of obvious relevance to the dogma of the Virgin Birth (*L*, 88–90). Furthermore, Freud points out, the association of the mother with the vulture is also found in the ancient Egyptian mother goddess Mut, a woman with vulture's head (*L*, 88), who "was usually represented with a phallus; her body was female, as the breasts indicated, but it also had a male organ in a state of erection." Thus in this figure "we find the same combination of maternal and masculine characteristics as in Leonardo's phantasy of the vulture" (*L*, 94) and may identify the "common source" of both images as the infantile theory of the mother with a penis (*L*, 97). The prominence of the vulture's tail in Leonardo's fantasy may then be translated: "That was a time when my fond curiosity was directed to my mother, and when I still believed she had a genital organ like my own" (*L*, 98). Just so, Stephen's association of his mother with the "hornpipe" may well veil the repressed memory of this theoretical construct which, according to Freud, is common to most boys.

For it is the mother who is the central figure motivating the small boy toward his earliest investigations into the two great sexual problems: the problem of birth, including the obscure part played by the father, and the problem of the differences between the sexes.[12] For though a boy may or may not have a sister, he necessarily is close to a mother or mother-surrogate. "Most children," Freud explains in his discussion of Leonardo's overdeveloped instinct for research, "or at least the most gifted ones, pass through a period of infantile sexual researches" (*L*, 78). It is to be expected that Joyce would have Stephen participate in this process, although Joyce's sensitivity to the reality of the psychoanalytic concept of repression is such that he veils the most significant of Stephen's researches and discoveries behind screen memories.

Thus, what Stephen does remember of his sexual research is only the episode with Eileen (*P*, 8), a shadowy memory at best. It appears to be an early research into the difference between boys and girls, whose general outlines could be supplied by most adults from their own childhood memories, and its nature may be indicated by the parallel in *Finnegans Wake* (*FW*, 327): "playing house of ivary dower of gould and gift you soil me peepat my prize." The terrible threat that the episode brings down on Stephen's childish head of the eagles' pulling out his eyes seems monstrously disproportionate, but this "childish naughtiness" almost certainly screens, as Ruth von Phul has asserted, "a greater guilt," the spying on the parents (121, 126).[13] Though the memory has been repressed below the level of consciousness, Stephen's mother has presumably been the object of the same kind of investigation, a prototype of the episode with Eileen. And the punishment of blindness suggests the Oedipal nature of the offense, as Stephen's researches are brought to an end, as is typically the case, Freud points out, by "a wave of energetic sexual repression" (*L*, 79).

Although it is Mrs. Dedalus herself who promises that Stephen will apologize, a promise that prefigures her cry of "Repent!" in "Circe" (*U*, 15.4198), it is Stephen's aunt, Mrs. Riordon ("Dante"), "the terrible mother" of Anderson's reading ("Baby Tuckoo," 149), who threatens that "the eagles will come and pull out his eyes" (*P*, 8), a punishment of extraordinary resonance. The designation of the eagle as the instrument of punishment may point obliquely to Prometheus, as Kenner has suggested ("Perspective," 141), but Dante's threat calls on eagles much closer to Stephen's actual world, the imperial eagles of Rome, symbols of her church and the sexual repression it represents for Stephen's future. And if the threat of blindness recalls the legendary figure of Oedipus, it also represents an acutely personal threat to Stephen as well as to Joyce himself. The link between blindness and punishment is, of course, involved in the boy Stephen's first questioning of the authority of the Church at Clongowes. Excused from the writing lesson because he has broken his glasses and truly cannot see, we may remember, Stephen is nevertheless punished with the pandybat by the prefect of studies and protests the unjust punishment to the rector (*P*, 50–59). And the punishment of the pandybat echoes throughout *Ulysses* until, in "Circe," it attaches again to blindness and to Oedipus. For Stephen's reference to breaking his glasses "sixteen years ago" is juxtaposed to the final term of the complicated allusion to Oedipus that I have outlined earlier. Here Stephen, borrowing from *Othello*, adds to the riddle of the Sphinx a sexual component of his own: "The beast that has two backs at midnight" (*U*, 15.3629–32), through which Oedipus is linked to Hamlet and to Stephen himself.[14]

Now the self-inflicted blindness of Oedipus as punishment for his transgression against the parental bond relates in turn to Freud's version of blindness as self-inflicted punishment in neurotic disturbances of vision, which he presented in "The Psycho-Analytic View of Psychogenic Disturbances of Vision" (*SE*, 11:314–21), published in 1910 and hence possibly available to Joyce in Trieste. This essay is not cited in the Leonardo study, to which it has no relevance, and we have no external evidence that Joyce had seen it, but the title indicates content of considerable interest to Joyce, with his continuing eye problems. We may remember Stanislaus Joyce's comment that if Joyce read a book that appealed to him, "he tried to read as many by the same author as he could lay his hands on" (*BK*, 79), and the practice, already noted, of publishing individual psychoanalytic essays in pamphlet form obviously increases the likelihood of their being available. Certainly the content is extremely relevant to Stephen's memory, since in it Freud introduces the idea of "talion punishment" by the ego when the sexual instinct makes excessive demands on the eyes.[15]

In the "obscure psychical processes concerned in the repression of sexual scopophilia and in the development of the psychogenic disturbance of vision," Freud writes, it is "as though a punishing voice was speaking from within the subject, and saying: 'Because you sought to misuse your organ of sight for evil sensual pleasures, it is fitting that you should not see anything at all any more'" (*SE*, 11:216–17). And it is significant that, though Dante defines the punishment, it is Stephen himself, hiding under the table, who makes a litany of it. Literally, as the small boy repeats the rhyme to himself, the "punishing voice" of Freud's reconstruction is "speaking from within the subject," and the lifelong punishment of the fear of blindness is indeed, in true Oedipal fashion, self-inflicted.

The Homosexual Threat

Thus, Joyce keeps intact the lines to Leonardo's fantasy, which includes no hint of blindness or punishment, even as he adapts its implications to the facts of his own historical and spiritual autobiography. The vulture is replaced by another bird of prey, the eagle, which pulls the church into the orbit of the multifaceted allusion, while the menace of the phallic mother remains strong through her association with the fear of blindness. But there is another fear, present as a hidden threat in *A Portrait*, but made thematically explicit in *Ulysses*, where it dominates Stephen's Bloomsday choices and is identified with his mother: the fear of homosexuality as a life pattern. And the "causal connection between Leonardo's relationship with his mother in childhood and his later manifest, if ideal, homosexuality" (*L*, 98) is the most significant implication that Freud draws from Leonardo's fantasy of the vulture-mother: "It was through this erotic relation with my mother that I became a homosexual" (*L*, 106).

Any erotic relationship with the mother in Stephen's childhood memory must be deduced from sexual connotations attaching to the chain of associations it presents, and Stephen's repressed memory is a far cry from Freud's reconstruction of Leonardo's infancy, for the mother as a menacing seductress does not appear directly in either *A Portrait* or *Ulysses*. True, Freud's comments on "a mother's love for the infant she suckles and cares for" as "a completely satisfying love-relation, which not only fulfills every mental wish but also every physical need" (*L*, 117) are echoed in Cranly's paean to motherhood in *A Portrait* (*P*, 241–42). And Cranly's ardent observations in turn prefigure Stephen's thematically significant musings in *Ulysses* about "*amor matris*" as "the only true thing in life" (*U*, 2.143, 165; 9.842–43). Freud's further reminder that some of the satisfactions may be considered perverse,[16] however, finds no echo. Nevertheless, Freud's picture of the "fateful" consequences for Leonardo of his mother's tenderness in his discussion of the "double meaning" of Mona Lisa's smile (*L*, 115) resonates in Stephen's Shakespeare discussion in *Ulysses*.

"Like all unsatisfied mothers," Freud hypothesizes of Leonardo's mother, "she took her little son in place of her husband, and by the too early maturing of his erotism robbed him of a part of his masculinity" (*L*, 117), and the cause-and-effect situation is paralleled by what Stephen proposes for Shakespeare. The mother, to be sure, is replaced by the wife, Ann Hathaway, "who tumbles in a cornfield a lover younger than herself" (*U*, 9.260), but Freud's tracing of a causal connection between the too-early arousal of erotic feelings and the later sexual disability is echoed in Stephen's assertion that through Shakespeare's seduction by an older woman, "Belief in himself has been untimely killed. He was overborne . . . and he will never . . . play victoriously the game of laugh and lie down. . . . No later undoing will undo the first undoing" (*U*, 9.454–59).

And a reader may well be reminded that the implications of the "too-early maturing of his erotism" and of being "overborne" have appeared earlier in *A Portrait*, though without the threat of consequences, in the teenage Stephen's sexual initiation by the prostitute, which concludes part 2 of *A Portrait*, as Stephen "close[s] his eyes, surrendering himself to her" (*P*, 101). If we then read the microcosmic description from the childhood memory in *A Portrait*—"She played on the piano the sailor's hornpipe for him to dance. He danced" (*P*, 7)—in the light of Stephen's attack on Ann Hathaway, which Mark Shechner sees as "significantly related" to Stephen's "maternal obsession,"[17] there are darker shadows in the innocent picture of the mother encouraging her son.

And the darker shadows, specifically the connection between mother love and homosexuality that Freud highlights in his reconstruction of Leonardo's childhood, are suggested even in the early pages of *A Portrait*. The "erotic attraction" of his mother for the very young boy "soon culminates," Freud says, "in a longing for her genital organ, which he takes to be a penis," and his later discovery that women are not so equipped often turns this longing to disgust, which may lead to permanent homosexuality. "The fixation on the object that was once so strongly desired," however, may well persist in "fetishistic reverence for a woman's foot and shoe" as a "substitutive symbol" (*L*, 96). And the picture of himself before the fire at home, which the homesick boy at Clongowes conjures up to ward off the memory of the "cold slimy water" of the ditch into which Wells has pushed him, focuses on his mother's feet on the fender, "and her jewelly slippers were so hot and they had such a lovely warm smell" (*P*, 10), a picture whose fetishistic overtones are emphasized by the appeal to the senses of touch and smell.

This picture, then, is followed almost immediately by the introduction of Simon Moonan as "McGlade's suck," the homosexual connotations of which are reinforced by the association with the "cocks" of the lavatory at the Wicklow Hotel (*P*, 11). And the combination of the dirty water in the white lavatory and his own feelings of being "cold and then a little hot" repeats the antithesis of the cold, slimy water and the hearth fire in the earlier picture, an antithesis that is first set up in the boy's earliest memory of his mother as she changes his bed, which first "is warm then it gets cold" (*P*, 7).[18] The juxtaposition of the memory of the comforting mother with the dimly grasped implications of the relationship between Simon Moonan and McGlade points to the same contradictory mixture in the "queer word" *suck* (*P*, 11) that is found in Leonardo's memory of being suckled at his mother's breast as it combines with the homosexual fantasy of fellatio.

In *A Portrait*, as the scene shifts from playground to classroom to refectory, the boy's longing "to be at home and lay his head on his mother's lap" (P, 13) is set off against his relationship to other males, again in the context of Simon Moonan and the prefect of studies, for as Wells teases Stephen about kissing his mother goodnight, Simon is knotting the false sleeves of the prefect (P, 14), a practice that in the earlier scene has been identified with his being "McGlade's suck," and Stephen once again experiences heat and cold—the heat of embarrassment alternating with the memory of the cold slime of the ditch water—as he tries to determine whether it is right or wrong to kiss his mother, examining the idea of *kiss* as he has earlier examined the idea of *suck*, and again there is a sound, but only "a tiny little noise" (P, 14–15). And we might remember that a nursing baby also makes a tiny little noise. The comforting mother fades out of the early pages with that kiss, but the inner conflict that her image sets off is picked up again much later in Stephen's response to "the unspoken speech behind the words" of Cranly's outburst about mother love: "Pascal, if I remember rightly, would not suffer his mother to kiss him as he feared the contact of her sex" (P, 242), and we have returned to Freud's question of the "causal connection" between Leonardo's relationship with his mother and his homosexuality.

This is the question that broods over the opening pages of *Ulysses* and is picked up again in distorted form in "Scylla and Charybdis," where the question attaches itself to Stephen's Shakespeare discussion. For in both these episodes Stephen's obsession with his dead mother is played against his relationship with Buck Mulligan, a relationship that is shadowed by the ghost of Oscar Wilde's "love that dare not speak its name." Mulligan's assurance as the novel opens that Stephen has "the real Oxford manner" (U, 1.53–54) surfaces in "Scylla and Charybdis" as "Manner of Oxenford" (U, 9.1212) in a context that identifies it explicitly with homosexuality. Mulligan's laughing taunt, "If Wilde were only alive to see you" (U, 1.143–44), is sandwiched between allusions to Wilde's *Dorian Gray* and "The Decay of Lying" (Thornton, *Allusions*, 14), one of the "Platonic dialogues Wilde wrote" (U, 9.1069), to which Best refers in the library scene. Mulligan's response to Stephen's question about Haines—"Yes, my love?" (U, 1.48)—is echoed in Stephen's reference to Shakespeare's "dearmylove," followed by his inner association: "Love that dare not speak its name" (U, 9.658–59). This phrase also comes into his mind in "Proteus" as he contemplates "his broadtoed boots, a buck's castoffs" (U, 3.446)—Mulligan's discarded boots, which he wears on

Bloomsday, and which replace the fetishistic symbol of the mother's slippers in *A Portrait*.

The mother appears in death, both in "Telemachus" and in "Scylla and Charybdis," but in the later episode her living influence is projected onto Ann Hathaway, whom Stephen charges with responsibility for Shakespeare's sexual malaise, a charge that includes an allusion to a passage in Wilde's *De Profundis* about his mother's death while he was in Reading Gaol (Thornton, *Allusions*, 181). And the terms of Stephen's charge suggest the submerged, unconscious character of the early maternal influence: "The soul has been before stricken mortally, a poison poured in the porch of a sleeping ear" (*U*, 9.466–67).[19] Buck Mulligan appears as Stephen winds up this charge, and the ensuing discussion of the Sonnets throws the shadow of the homosexual threat over the remainder of the episode, regularly associated with Mulligan, most explicitly in Stephen's unspoken "Catamite" (*U*, 9.734). But as Stephen follows Mulligan down the stairs and prepares to leave the library with him, "about to pass through the doorway, feeling one behind, he stood aside" (*U*, 9.1197–98). And the "one behind" is Leopold Bloom, who embodies the alternative to Mulligan.

"Part," Stephen tells himself, "The moment is now" (*U*, 9:1199), confirming his vow of the morning to leave Mulligan and the Tower (*U*, 1.739–40). But asking himself, "Where then?," his answer is allusive and involved: "If Socrates leave his house today, if Judas go forth tonight" (*U*, 9.1199–200). He is alluding to the line from Maeterlinck that he has earlier paraphrased: "*If Socrates leave his house today he will find the sage seated on his doorstep. If Judas go forth tonight it is to Judas his steps will tend*" (*U*, 9.1042–44; Thornton, *Allusions*, 213–14, 217). Earlier Stephen has followed this paraphrase with his observation that "we walk through ourselves . . . meeting [all kinds of people], but always meeting ourselves" (*U*, 9.1044–46). All this, then, becomes a part of his foreshortened answer to the question of "Where?"[20] And when Stephen concludes, "That lies in space which I in time must come to, ineluctably," he is referring, in this expanded context, to a meeting with himself, and at this moment Bloom passes out between Stephen and Mulligan, "bowing, greeting" (*U*, 9.1200–3).

Bloom has arrived at the library in pursuit of information for his ad just after Mulligan joins the group in the librarians' office; he is in the library throughout the discussion of the Sonnets and homosexuality, a shadowy presence at the edges of the action—"a patient silhouette," "a bowing dark figure" (*U*, 9.597, 602–3). Like Mulligan, he has come to the library from the museum, and it is Mulligan who announces his presence: "The sheeny!" "What's his name? Ikey Moses? Bloom" (*U*, 9.605, 607). It is also Mulligan who links Bloom with a homosexual threat to Stephen, first, in his initial identification of Bloom—"O, I fear me, he is Greeker than the Greeks" (*U*, 9.614–15)—and then as Bloom precedes them through the gate—"He looked upon you to lust after you. . . . O, Kinch, thou art in peril. Get thee a breechpad" (*U*, 9.1210–11).

But as the episode closes and Stephen stands at the doorway, he acknowledges the conflict between himself and Mulligan—"My will: his will that fronts me. Seas between" (*U*, 9.1202)—providing an almost irresistible image for "Scylla and Charybdis," the title assigned to this episode and the great Homeric choice point.[21] And Bloom, the outsider and the family man, comes between Stephen and Mulligan, textually offering himself as a choice to replace Mulligan, the insider, who is textually associated with the "love that dare not speak its name." That Stephen makes the choice that is offered him is explicitly and characteristically confirmed through a textual correspondence. In "Hades," that is, Bloom, riding in the carriage with Simon Dedalus, sees Stephen near the tramlines and tells Simon that his "son and heir" has just gone by. Simon asks, "—Was that Mulligan cad with him? His *fidus Achates!*—No, Mr Bloom said. He was alone" (*U*, 6.39–50). Achates, Thornton reminds us, was the faithful friend of Achilles (*Allusions*, 90), and in "Eumaeus," this same designation has become assigned to Bloom, who in the early morning hours is "acting as [Stephen's] *fidus Achates*" (*U*, 16.54–55). He warns Stephen that "he wouldn't personally repose much trust in that boon companion of yours" (*U*, 16.279–80), who "is what they call picking your brains" (*U*, 16.298–99), and plans to advise Stephen "to sever his connection with [that] budding practitioner" (*U*, 16.1868–69).

The Identity of Bloom

If Stephen accepts Bloom as his "faithful friend," his alter ego, the question arises, "Who is Bloom?" And the answer, even after three-quarters of a century of critical investigation, is not clearly established. Even in the text of *Ulysses*, we may remember, Bloom himself has no answer to his self-addressed question about his past and present identity—"Was that I? Or am I now I?" (*U*, 8.608). Nor is he able to complete his message in the sand that starts, "I." "AM. A." (*U*, 13.1258, 1264). Early in the critical history of *Ulysses*, Oliver St. John Gogarty dismissed Bloom's connection to the real world of Dublin, so faithfully reproduced in the novel: "The Bloom that never was on sea or land. . . . A mere chorus to Joyce."[22] And later generations of critics have come to accept the autobiographical nature of the portrait of Bloom.

But clearly, as Robert Scholes pointed out in the early 1970s, we are dealing in *Ulysses* with two different kinds of autobiography, not just two stages of the artist's life, the young and the mature—although that too—but two quite different kinds of self-portrait, which Scholes labels "bioenergetic" and "cybernetic." Only the "bioenergetic" portrait of Stephen is clearly recognizable as "Joyce in his skin, with all the significant features that would make him recognizable," whereas "the cybernetic self-portrait" of Bloom "contains large elements of Joyce's neural circuitry without being recognizable as Joyce," even though he may be "at some important levels of experience . . . a 'truer' representation of Joyce than Stephen."[23] Thus, Stephen, the "bioenergetic self-portrait," quite literally has "a shape that can't be changed," as Joyce told Frank Budgen (*James Joyce*, 105). He comes into *Ulysses* out of a fictional world that has been specified in detail in *A Portrait*, a world that is in addition subject to the constraints of the facts of Joyce's own life. Stephen in *Ulysses* represents a piece of Joyce's history, a chaotic time in 1904 when Joyce was living in Dublin and grieving in his own fashion over the death of his mother, and the character is thus very strictly bound to that time. In traditional autobiographical fashion, Stephen duplicates his creator's chronology, up to and through the historical date of 16 June 1904, the fictional day of *Ulysses*. Probably we could all agree with William Noon that, so far as Stephen is concerned, despite minor anachronistic details from Joyce's return trips to Dublin in 1909 and 1912 (Owen, 50), Joyce in effect "stopped his own clock somewhere between 1902 and 1904" (274), while Kenner observes that with Joyce "we are always in 1904" (*Joyce's Voices*, 47).

For Bloom, however, Joyce's clock started after 16 June 1904 and kept running—right up to the final page proofs for *Ulysses*, according to Danis Rose (129). Bloom has no fictional history before he appears in *Ulysses*, and although he is provided a history of sorts in the text of the novel, much of it does not quite fit together. Robert M. Adams, for example, points to a string of "inconsistencies . . . which create a tangled image of Bloom's personal history" with regard to his residences and his "muddled" employment record, as well as a peculiar selectivity in his memory (186, 187, 188–89). Nor is Bloom rigidly tied to any actual time in Joyce's life. On the fictional 16 June 1904, he is given his creator's actual age in 1922: he is a "gent about 40" (*U*, 17.2002), as Joyce was when he was writing *Ulysses*. But he belongs neither to the actual, somewhat elastic, present of the writing of *Ulysses* nor to the actual, very restricted, past that is represented in the work. Certainly there was no "real" Bloom in Dublin on the real 16 June, or before that, and Joyce honors his absence from the Dublin scene in various ways. Adams has pointed out, for example, that Bloom's residence at Number 7 Eccles Street was vacant in 1904 (61), while Clive Hart and Leo Knuth, in their detailed examination of space and time in *Ulysses*, note that there are no house numbers for any of Bloom's residences prior to 1904, concluding that Joyce intended "a certain haziness . . . to surround the remembered past" (16).

Neither do we really know what Bloom looks like. He is always referred to as dark, though it is not always possible to be sure whether *dark* describes his coloring or his mourning clothes, since this is the day of Paddy Dignam's funeral, and, as Molly says, "hed go into mourning for the cat" (*U*, 18.1310). However, his daughter Milly is described in "Ithaca" as "blond, born of two dark" (*U*, 17.868), which, like many of the facts in that episode, is reasonably reliable. Certainly he has dark eyes— "dark thinking eyes," as described by the reliable narrator of "Hades" (*U*, 6.533), a description that agrees with Gerty MacDowell's somewhat less reliable twilight vision of the stranger on the strand, with his "dark eyes" and "pale intellectual face" (*U*, 13.415–16), with possibly a moustache, though this is ambiguous, and she cannot see "whether he had an acquiline nose or a slightly *retroussé* from where he was sitting" (*U*, 13.417–21).

As he and Stephen walk away from the cabman's shelter, Bloom's figure is said to be "full" in contrast to Stephen's "lean" figure (*U*, 16.1887), and this characterization is confirmed in "Ithaca," where he is described in a hypothetical ad with a height of "5 ft 9 1/2 inches," and "a full build" (*U*, 17.2003). But even though he has earlier removed a size 17 collar that is exerting "inhibitory pressure" (*U*, 17.1431), which might be expected for a man of "full build," his weight has even earlier been given as "eleven stone and four pounds" (*U*, 17.91), or 158 pounds, which surely is not heavy for the height. The height and weight, in fact, are exactly those for John Francis Byrne in August 1909, when he and Joyce, before returning to Number 7 Eccles Street (Byrne's residence in 1909), weighed themselves on what Byrne calls "a penny-in-the-slot weighing machine" (157) and the narrator of "Ithaca" describes as a "graduated machine for periodic selfweighing" (*U*, 17.92). And the familiar picture of Byrne with Joyce and George Clancy (*JJII*, 110, plate 5) shows Byrne to be the epitome of trim youth, hardly one who would find a size 17 collar too tight.

The oddities in Bloom's physical description go beyond these scattered figures. The most dramatic collection of anomalies is found in the absolutely zany before-and-after chart connected with Bloom's "use of Sandow-Whiteley's pulley exerciser" (*U*, 17.1815–19), in which Bloom is given, among other equally absurd measurements, a 28-inch chest, which is wildly disproportionate to his size 17 collar.[24] Indeed, as Adams has pointed out, Joyce is here imputing "a physical impossibility to Bloom as a physical organism," and he speculates that in assigning the impossible dimensions to Bloom, Joyce may have "wished to emphasize the extent to which he must be seen from within" (184).

Adams's suggestion that Bloom is created in a different dimension from that which underlies the creation of Stephen harmonizes with Hart and Knuth's conclusion that Joyce's handling of Bloom exhibits a "difference not merely of working method but also of conceptual approach" (16), a conclusion that is reinforced by Scholes's recognition that "Stephen 'is' Joyce in a different way from the way Bloom 'is' Joyce" (164). It is surely relevant to this difference that although Bloom has his origins in James Joyce's world after 1904, this world—the world of Joyce's Europe—has no counterpart in Joyce's fiction. With no constraints of time or place, Joyce has had almost complete freedom in his collection and development of the elements that go into the portrait of Bloom. Indeed, his method of composition in the creation of Leopold Bloom has much in common with the cubist technique of collage, in which a variety of materials are pasted onto the canvas and painted into the picture. The textual elements that Joyce pastes onto the canvas of Bloom's portrait appear to follow a selection principle of more or less free association without necessarily fitting into any organic whole, and the result is described by Adams as "a wonderful sense of Bloom himself as a malleable, formless, indeterminate piece of human clay" (99). This indeterminacy applies even to his Jewishness, which has been vigorously debated for some time now.[25] Bloom is a marvelously synthetic character, who is formed and reformed before a reader's eyes as he moves through the day of *Ulysses*, his identity determined, at least in part, by the textual *trouvés* or "found" texts that are highlighted. And Bloom's psychic characteristics, whatever their autobiographical bases, owe something to the texts of psychoanalysis, starting with Freud's portrait of the adult Leonardo da Vinci.

The picture of the historical Leonardo presented by Freud exhibits curious affinities with the fictional surrogate of Joyce's middle years, which can hardly be accidental, especially as they relate to Freud's emphasis on "Leonardo's double nature as an artist and as a scientific investigator" (*L*, 73). Freud pictures this two-pronged drive as a serious conflict for Leonardo and a threat to his achievement as an artist. In *Ulysses*, then, Bloom embodies the scientific half of the double nature, which is explicitly assigned by the catechizer of "Ithaca" to Bloom and Stephen: "What two temperaments did they individually represent? The scientific. The artistic" (*U*, 17.559–60). And the "proofs" then offered by Bloom of his aptitude for science (*U*, 17.563–75) read like a parody of Leonardo's notebooks, which, as Freud comments, "not only deal with the greatest scientific problems but also contain trivialities that strike us as scarcely worthy of so great a mind" (*L*, 69–70).

The affinities between Leonardo and Bloom, however, extend beyond shared scientific propensities to certain "unusual traits and apparent contradictions" that they also share. In a society characterized, Freud says, by "energetic aggressiveness towards other people," and in that respect no different from the Dublin milieu in *Ulysses*, Leonardo, like the "prudent member" in Dublin, "was notable for his quiet peaceableness and his avoidance of all antagonism and controversy" (*L*, 68). Seemingly "indifferent to good and evil," he nevertheless had such feeling for birds that he was said to have made a habit of buying them in the market in order to set them free (*L*, 69), and Bloom cites his own feeding of the gulls (*U*, 8.74–79) as evidence of "doing good to others" (*U*, 15.681–86) and having a "good heart" (*U*, 15.1188). Leonardo, Freud relates, "condemned war and bloodshed," though "this feminine delicacy of feeling did not deter him from accompanying condemned criminals on their way to execution in order to study their features distorted by fear" and sketch them (*L*, 69). And Bloom, who rises to eloquence in his rejection of "Force, hatred, history, all that" in "Cyclops" (*U*, 12.1481), has earlier in the episode as "Herr Professor Luitpold Blumenduft," expanded at length and with great comic effect, on the "codology" of the anomalous effect on a hanged man of having his neck broken (*U*, 12.468–78).

Beyond these contradictions, however, what points most clearly to the kinship between Leonardo da Vinci and Leopold Bloom is the "peculiarity of [their] emotional and sexual life." For "in an age which saw a struggle between sensuality without restraint and gloomy asceticism, Leonardo represented the cool repudiation of sexuality" (*L*, 69). Freud includes in this repudiation the active homosexuality of which Leonardo was once accused (*L*, 72), an accusation that Joyce attaches to Bloom through Mulligan's mock warnings to Stephen.[26] In Leonardo, in fact, "love and hate threw off their positive or negative signs and were both alike transformed into intellectual interest," and as Leonardo "converted his passion into a thirst for knowledge," investigating took the place of "acting and creating as well" (*L*, 74, 75). Indeed, Freud says, the drive toward investigation may become "sufficiently powerful to sexualize thinking itself and to colour intellectual operations with the pleasure and anxiety that belong to sexual processes proper," so that "the feeling that comes from settling things in one's mind and explaining them replaces sexual satisfaction," and research becomes "a substitute for sexual activity" (*L*, 79–80). Bloom's day is filled with this kind of substitution, but two obviously paired examples will serve as a kind of synecdoche. At two o'clock, when Bloom sees Blazes Boylan, who is scheduled to cuckold him in a couple of hours, he seizes in his panic on the memory of his project of examining the anatomy of the statues of the goddesses in the National Museum: "Cold statues: quiet there. Safe in a minute" (*U*, 8.1176–77). Again, at the end of Bloomsday, as he enters the bed Boylan has shared with Molly, he systematically nullifies all passion through a succession of "scientific" reveries (*U*, 17.2126–226).

Stephen's Flight

The resemblance, then, between Joyce's mature creation of Bloom and the Leonardo recreated by Freud gives striking confirmation to the "scientific" designation conferred on Bloom by the catechizer of "Ithaca," even though the reader has also been assured that Bloom is "a bit of an artist in his spare time" (*U*, 16.1448–49). And for the adult Stephen of *Ulysses*, who is the "artistic temperament" of the dual identification in "Ithaca," Leonardo's childhood memory yields a hopeful sign as "Scylla and Charybdis" closes. For as Stephen and Mulligan separate at the steps of the library to make way for Bloom, Stephen sees the beginnings of a solution of his problem with Mulligan and his hope for the future. To be sure, as *Ulysses* moves toward its close, it provides no clear solutions, for the straightforward narrative of the first half of the book is abandoned, and meaning begins to depend on multiple associations of words. The word *becomes* the event, a peculiarity also of dreams, and it is a dream that points the way for Stephen. Remembering that before his departure from Dublin the year before, he had "watched the birds for augury" from these same steps, he recognizes a development from that time to his dream of the night before: "Last night I flew" (*U*, 9.1206–7), a flight whose significance *as* a solution is clarified by reference to Freud's analysis of Leonardo.

Leonardo links his memory of the vulture with his being destined to study the flight of birds, and "in admitting to us that ever since his childhood he felt bound up in a special and personal way with the problem of flight," Freud says, "Leonardo gives us confirmation that his childhood researches were directed to sexual matters." For in dreams "to fly or to be a bird" regularly disguises "a longing to be capable of sexual performance" (*L*, 126). The symbolic importance of bird imagery in Joyce's *Portrait* has received considerable attention, and Stephen's own determination to fly complements this imagery, reaching an impassioned climax in his vision of "the winged form of . . . a hawklike man" as "a prophecy of the end he had been born to serve," a climax which is sustained through the companion vision of the wading girl (*P*, 169–72)—all of it emotionally charged. This climax is then followed by Stephen's more intellectually determined declaration that he will "fly by [the] nets" of "nationality, language, religion" (*P*, 203). And finally, the diversion of emotional energy into research, which Freud points to in Leonardo, is highlighted in Stephen. For when Stephen watches the birds outside the library in *A Portrait*, it is to escape the raw emotion of his mother's "sobs and reproaches" in the cool contemplation of the flight of birds, which, he reminds himself, Swedenborg links to "things of the intellect." And he turns finally from this soothing contemplation back to the "calmly lit" library (*P*, 224, 226).

But in *Ulysses*, the matching scene on the library steps ends with Stephen's departure from the library, the home of "Coffined thoughts" with "an itch of death . . . in them" (*U*, 9.352–57). On Bloomsday there are "no birds,"[27] and Stephen's vision is dominated by his own flight in the context of his sensual dream of the gift of Haroun al Raschid, a dream that confronts and competes with the dream of his dead mother throughout Bloomsday: "Last night I flew. Easily flew" (*U*, 9.1207). And unlike his unuttered "cry of triumph" in *A Portrait*, which exults in "the freedom and power of his soul" (*P*, 170), Stephen's cry of "Free!" at the renewed memory of this dream in "Circe" (*U*, 15.3936) is a response to the physical, sensual solution the dream contains to his inner cry of the morning to his dead mother: "Let me be and let me live" (*U*, 1.279), a cry that Leonardo da Vinci, as Freud reconstructs his development, never knew how to make.

But then, Stephen's cry—"Free!"—is addressed to his father, who represents a feature of infancy missing from Leonardo's early childhood.[28] In addition, the vulture, which doubles as the mother in Leonardo's fantasy and that, according to legend, has no male counterpart, is absent from *A Portrait* and appears in *Ulysses* as an exclusively male symbol associated with the father-son relationship. In "Circe" Rudolph Virag feels Bloom's face *"With feeble vulture talons"* (*U*, 15.259–60), and Stephen, as he declares his freedom, cries to his father, *"his vulture talons sharpened,"* while Simon, answering him, *"swoops uncertainly through the air . . . on strong ponderous buzzard wings"* (*U*, 15.3940–47). The fable of the vulture's impregnation by the wind is, to be sure, included in Stephen's list of primitive beliefs about conception in "Oxen of the Sun" as "bigness wrought by wind," followed closely by "potency of vampires mouth to mouth" (*U*, 14.242–44), a figure that is explicitly, if obscurely, associated with Stephen's obsession with his mother.[29] But this is in turn followed by his assertion that the female power of creation in the flesh is superseded by the preeminent creative power of the male artist to build "eternity's mansions" from "time's ruins" (*U*, 14.289–90): "In woman's womb word is made flesh but in the spirit of the maker all flesh that passes becomes the word that shall not pass away. This is the postcreation" (*U*, 14.292–94).

And in "Circe" this bridge to eternity is—verbally at least—guaranteed by the father. For, confronted by the apparition of his dead mother, who reaches for his heart with the crab's claws (*U*, 15.4216–21), Stephen, denying the power of her memory to paralyze him, smashes the chandelier with his ashplant, which for this purpose he transforms verbally into "*Nothung!*" (*U*, 15.4242), Siegfried's mystical sword handed down from father to son (Thornton, *Allusions*, 418). In the ensuing darkness—"ruin of all space" (*U*, 15.4242–45) and time's ruin as well—the way is cleared for the building of eternity's mansions, the postcreation, and Joyce, through a dreamlike word magic, has affirmed his artist's release from the dominance of the maternal fixation that Freud pictures as Leonardo's fate.

The release of the son from the power of the mother is further signaled by the replacement of Mut, the vulture-headed goddess of Freud's analysis of Leonardo, by the bird-headed Egyptian god Thoth, who, with his "narrow ibis head," is "the god of writers" in *A Portrait* (*P*, 225) and in *Ulysses* "god of libraries, a birdgod, moony-crowned" (*U*, 9.353). And in E. A. Wallis Budge's *Gods of the Egyptians*, which Joyce almost certainly knew,[30] Thoth is credited with powers not inferior to those of the Word in St. John's Prologue. For it is Thoth who in the beginning "spoke the words which resulted in the creation of the heavens and the earth" and, "as the personification of the mind of God," is "the all-pervading, and governing, and directing power of heaven and of earth" (Budge, 1:407, 415). Like Mut, "who giveth birth, but was herself not born of any" (2:30), Thoth was "self-begotten and self-produced" (1:401). Though Mut gives birth, Thoth creates a world, and the Egyptian connection suggested by Freud is thus used by Joyce to affirm the freedom and the power of the artist as self-created creator.

Thus Freud's Leonardo becomes a part of Joyce's portrait of the artist, from early childhood through to the artist's maturity, from Stephen to Bloom. Along with contributions from other sources, attributes reconstructed for Leonardo by Freud are blended with Joyce's memories of his own childhood and youth, as well as his developing understandings of his maturity in the light of his artistic vocation. Joyce has also included in the childhood memory provided for Stephen specific details from Jung's 1909 essay, which Jung characterized in a December 1908 letter to Freud as "no great shakes," but still a work whose "staunchness to the cause leaves nothing to be desired" (McGuire, 117J, 185).

Even as Jung here expresses concern with his essay's "staunchness" to Freud's cause, Ernest Jones in his essay on Hamlet and Oedipus, the third psychoanalytic pamphlet purchased in Trieste (hereinafter cited as *H*), identifies its aim in terms of Freud's writing: "to expound on an hypothesis which Freud . . . suggested in one of the footnotes to his *Traumdeutung*" (*H*, 75). He is referring, of course, to Freud's hypothesis about the common roots of Shakespeare's *Hamlet* and the *Oedipus Rex* (*SE*, 4:264). In these early days psychoanalysis *was* a cause, and Freud's followers shared in the master's feeling that it was a beleaguered cause. In much the same way that the master artist Leonardo gave direction to the apprentices who worked under him, Freud provided the insights that were the inspiration for the literature of the movement.

Jones begins his essay by acknowledging "the luminous writings of Professor Freud, who has laid bare some of the fundamental mechanisms by which artistic and poetic creativeness proceeds" (*H*, 72). And significant traces of Jones's essay on Hamlet and Oedipus surface in the ninth episode of *Ulysses*—"the Hamlet chapter" in Joyce's words (*Letters*, 1:101) and "Scylla and Charybdis" in the Odyssean table of contents—whose central topic is this same "artistic and poetic creativeness," with Shakespeare as the grand exemplar of the artist.

Freud's *Hamlet* and Stephen's

Play-Within-a-Play

"Psychoanalysis" does not appear in the index for Weldon Thornton's *Allusions in "Ulysses,"* and the single item listed under "Freud"— Stephen's reference to the view of "the new Viennese school" on incest (*U*, 9.779–80; Thornton, *Allusions*, 199)—contrasts with over a page of entries under "Shakespeare." But had Thornton allowed himself the same kind of range for psychoanalytic allusion that he has for Shakespearean allusion in "Scylla and Charybdis," that is, had he been "willing to see phrases, or even individual words" as allusions (150), his list would surely be different. For it is in "Scylla and Charybdis" that psychoanalysis enters *Ulysses* and makes its greatest impact. This episode is saturated with echoes from psychoanalytic texts, synthesized, in a way that is distinctively Joyce's, with echoes from Shakespeare, from the church fathers, and from a range of other texts of the past. Many of these texts were also hunting grounds for the early psychoanalysts, who, in the absence of adequate case studies, turned to literature for confirmation of their hypotheses. Characteristically, though, the psychoanalysts sexualized the texts in their interpretations and assumed the universality of these interpretations. Possibly the psychoanalytic echoes in "Scylla and Charybdis" do not all qualify as narrowly defined allusions, but certainly Joyce's text in this episode is in a lively, though complicated, dialogue with Sigmund Freud's psychoanalysis at the same time that it is engaged with a battery of classical texts.

The Nature of the Dialogue

In the first extended study of *Ulysses*, at the beginning of the 1930s, Stuart Gilbert opined that this episode was "the subtlest and hardest to epitomize of all the eighteen episodes of *Ulysses*," characterizing it as a "quasi-Platonic dialogue, in which Stephen plays the role of a Socrates" and, like a "young symposiarch," leads "his reluctant elders along a dialectic tightrope" (212, 216). Later, at the half-century mark in *Ulysses* criticism, Robert Kellogg labels the discussion a "mock-Socratic dialogue, with something of the Quaker meeting and theosophic seance added," reinforcing Gilbert's note of uncertainty about labels (147). In her 1981 *Odyssey of Style*, Karen Lawrence notes that the episode, after the interrupted narrative of "Aeolus," returns, as does "Lestrygonians" before it, to the "novelistic form of the book's first half," in that the primary concern is "developing our knowledge of the two main characters." And she too accepts the analogy to a Socratic dialogue, which Stephen "carefully orchestrates" (80, 130).

The "technic" for the episode is listed in the Gilbert schema as "dialectic" (30), but Gilbert's later reference to this "symposium of Dublin *litterateurs*, rapt in the pure ecstasy of literary exhibitionism" (213) suggests—as do many details in the episode—that the participants in this discussion are not engaged in genuine dialectic at all, but rather, as I have argued elsewhere, eristic, that is, "competitive and contentious argument," which is distinguished from dialectic by Aristotle and is the focus of his treatise *On Sophistical Refutations* (ch. 2, sec. 165b, lines 11–12; ch. 11, sec. 171b, lines 25–32). Stanislaus Joyce's diary comment that "the Sophists will never be extinct while Jim is alive" (*CDD*, 5) is abundantly confirmed in this eristic exchange, in which Jim's fictional surrogate, Stephen Dedalus, is the chief Sophist, employing most of the sophistical tricks identified by Aristotle in his treatise.[1]

Certainly "Scylla and Charybdis" is a mix. The episode is larded with allusions; it regularly mixes Stephen's announced lecture on Shakespeare with his internal commentary on this discourse, as well as asides and even question-and-answer dialogue with himself, paralleling the asides and soliloquies that characterize Shakespeare's dramas. Added to this mix are entrances and exits and interpolated conversations, sometimes focused on Shakespeare, sometimes not. Examined closely, the talk is largely nonresponsive, and not very much of it can legitimately be called dialogue, let alone dialectic. There is an announced "Entr'acte" (*U,* 9.484), a bit of poetry in a mixed meter (*U,* 9.684–707), and a section of the episode that is presented in play form (*U,* 9.892–934). In a chapter focusing on Shakespeare, it should not be surprising to discover indications of a play structure, and indeed the speech and action in "Scylla and Charybdis" can be roughly mapped out as a three-act drama, divided into scenes, with the "Entr'acte" coming between act 1 and act 2. Below, I have indicated in abbreviated form the action of the episode divided into acts and scenes (part 1), followed by a separate synopsis of Stephen's internal speech and observations, similarly divided and similarly abbreviated as well (part 2).

Part 1: External action and speech

Act 1:	Scene 1 (1–143)	Prologue.
	Scene 2 (144–268)	Stephen's presentation: Shakespeare in *Hamlet.*
	Scene 3 (269–375)	Exit of AE. General conversation, returning to Shakespeare.
	Scene 4 (376–482)	Stephen's presentation: late plays.
	Entr'acte (483–617)	Mulligan's entrance, dialogue with Stephen. Bloom's entrance and exit, identification by Mulligan.
Act 2:	Scene 1 (618–731)	Stephen's presentation: triangle in Sonnets compared to triangle in *Hamlet.*
	Scene 2 (732–810)	Stephen's presentation: incest and "Viennese school," Ann's last days.
	Scene 3 (811–74)	Stephen's presentation: fatherhood, *amor matris,* brothers.
	Scene 4 (875–996)	Mulligan's announcement of his play. Stephen's presentation: Shakespeare's family in works, brother-relationship.

Act 3:	Scene 1 (997–1052)	Stephen's presentation: conclusion and epilogue, Shakespeare in all his characters—"all in all."
	Scene 2 (1053–152)	Exit of Stephen and Mulligan through reading room.
	Scene 3 (1153–225)	Exit of Stephen and Mulligan from the library, Bloom coming between them. Mulligan's charge of homosexuality applied to Bloom.

Part 2: Stephen's asides and soliloquies

Act 1:	Scene 1 (34–141)	Relationship with Cranly and Mulligan. AE identified with Theosophy and as master poet of Irish revival.
	Scene 2 (144–268)	Affirmation of stable identity. Grief for mother. Need for a woman.
	Scene 3 (271–358)	Recognition of isolation from Irish revival. Thoughts about Shakespeare and Ann, Lyster, the library.
	Scene 4 (390–483)	Commentary on presentation, on other participants. "Love passage." Reaction to Mulligan.
	Entr'acte (491–580)	Sabellian Apostle's Creed. Need for a woman. Reminder of drinking with newsmen. "W. H." as "William Himself."
Act 2:	Scene 1 (641–62)	Memory of Paris prostitutes.
	Scene 2 (734–71)	Recognition of dubiety of argument—mixture of "theolologicophilolological."

continued

	Scene 3 (817–74)	Thoughts of Magee's father and of his own, of his mother's last illness. Agitated inner colloquy about purpose of his argument. Question about himself as father.
	Scene 4 (889–982)	Deception in argument acknowledged. Problem of *sua donna,* "his woman." Reflections on brothers and "whetstones," "What's more to speak?"
Act 3:	Scene 1 (1016–26)	Acknowledgment of mind's bondage. Impression of audience as reflector, giving back and confirming thought.
	Scene 2 (1062–141)	Ambiguous statement of belief in argument. Resentment of Mulligan and mistrust of his influence. Question of revelation of himself and his companions through discussion. Glimpses of lunatic, priest, and girl in reading room.
	Scene 3 (1153–54)	Perception of Mulligan as homosexual. Reaffirmation of separation from Mulligan. Question of his future, recollection of his Arabian Nights dream, acceptance of what is—"cease to strive."

This outline represents a bare-bones summary of what happens in "Scylla and Charybdis," as well as Stephen's inner responses, and it is significant, as Kellogg reminds us, that this episode, "perhaps more than any other, embodies an essential quality of Joyce's art: its interpenetration with his life." For, Kellogg points out, the discussion in the library fictionalizes an actual event in Joyce's life, his construction of a theory about Shakespeare that he "also told to Gogarty, Best, and Magee" (147, 151–52).[2] The setting of this episode, the National Library of Dublin, is real and describable, as are the speaking characters, all of whom had their counterparts in living citizens of Dublin in 1904 (Bloom does not speak). Joyce, however, is notably deficient in description, although his references to a person or a place, once the reader has his own picture from some other source, are accurate and telling. The following brief descriptions of the scene and the characters are intended to illuminate some of the dark corners, providing a clearer picture of the people and the place that, if not absolutely indispensable, is helpful for an integrated understanding of what is happening.

All the action takes place at the National Library, which Eugene Sheehy recalls as "the real Alma Mater at this time" for students like Joyce (quoted by Kellogg, 148). Patricia Hutchins has identified the "discreet vaulted cell" (*U*, 9.345), the scene of the discussion, as probably "based on the room used by Mr. Lyster, 'John Eglinton' and Dr. Best, which lies behind the counter and was only lit by a roof light at the time." This would explain the references throughout the episode to shadows and darkness. The office was approached through a corridor behind the main counter in the reading room (Hutchins, 77). Acts 1 and 2 take place in this room, while act 3 moves through the reading room to the portico of the library, which extends in a curve around the middle portion of the building with broad shallow steps (78).

Only two of the six men who take part in the discussion are important characters in *Ulysses:* Stephen Dedalus and Buck Mulligan, the fictional surrogates for James Joyce and Oliver St. John Gogarty. Stephen Dedalus (James Joyce) is twenty-two years old, of medium height and very slender.[3] The publication of his article on Ibsen at the age of eighteen resulted, according to his friend John Francis Byrne, in an impairment of his relationship with his fellow students "by either their jealousy or their sycophancy" (63). His mother has died the previous August, after which he has given himself over to uncharacteristic dissipation, which threatens his artistic vocation. Indeed, Stanislaus Joyce, writing in his memoir about the living model for Stephen, the young James Joyce, records his conviction that "a poet . . . was drowned in those carousals" (*BK*, 249), while his 1903–1904 diary entries testify to his concern about his

brother's forsaking his artistic vocation in order to "live."[4] Stephen has
come to the library after drinking with the newsmen and may well fit the
description given by Stanislaus of his brother when drunk:

> limp and pale, with shadows under his watery eyes, loose wet lips
> and dank hair . . . talking in an exhausted husky voice, as if to show
> how well he can act when drunk, talking about philosophy or poetry
> not because he likes them at the time but because he remembers
> that he has a certain character to maintain, that he has to show that
> he is clever even when drunk, and because he likes to hear himself
> talk. (CDD, 101)

Buck Mulligan (Oliver St. John Gogarty), as Stanislaus describes him, is
"a stoutly built young fellow, a student of medicine at Trinity College . . .
full of bustling energy, wit, and profanity. Slightly older than Stephen
and "in loquacious revolt against the drabness and smugness of Dublin
Life," he too is a poet (BK, 174–75). He and Stephen are living at the
Martello Tower at Sandycove, and Stephen is wearing Mulligan's cast-off
boots.

The other participants are the three librarians—Lyster, Best, and
Magee—and George Russell (AE), all of whom are designated by their
own names. T. W. Lyster, the director of the National Library, is described
by Padraic Colum as a man of "about fifty," with "a closely cropped
beard, rather liquid eyes, and a rich, one might even say an unctuous,
voice,"[5] while Byrne considered him "mentally quick as a flash," as well
as "highly educated and cultured," and "a paragon of courtesy" (162). W.
K. Magee, whose pen name was John Eglinton, was an "Ulster Scot."
"Low-sized, with a fine head, his thoughtfulness . . . expressed in brown
eyes," he was a "distantly companionable, rather estranged person." Dr.
Richard Best, "the youngest of the triumvirate of the National Library,"
was "more continental than either Mr. Lyster or Mr. Magee, having studied in Paris." He was "tall, blond, ruddy-complexioned . . . scholarly, en-
thusiastic, sociable." George Russell (AE), the poet, active with Yeats in
the Irish literary revival and in the activities of the Theosophists, has a
"golden-brown beard," a "full, fresh-cheeked face," and "a sonorous
voice" (Gogarty, As I Was Going, 292).

These are the Dublin literati who are present in the National Library
between two and three o'clock in the afternoon of 16 June 1904 to hear
Stephen Dedalus talk about Shakespeare's Hamlet, a favorite topic for

men of letters. And Stephen's discourse exhibits traces of psychoanalytic material relating to *Hamlet* that was not available to anyone in 1904. For by 1918 when Joyce was composing "Scylla and Charybdis," he had owned for probably five years the German translation of Ernest Jones's 1910 essay on Hamlet and Oedipus, which he had purchased in Trieste. In addition, Otto Rank's *The Myth of the Birth of the Hero*, which Jones acknowledged as an important source for parts of his study, was available in Zurich's public library, as was Rank's *Incest Motif*, with its chapters on "*Hamlet* as an Incest Drama" and "Shakespeare's Father Complex." All these find a place in Stephen's presentation, as does Rank's 1915 essay on the play-within-a-play in *Hamlet*, published in *Imago*, a "journal for the application of psychoanalysis to the arts," which was received by the library.[6] And all of them assume as a base the view of *Hamlet* that Freud first presented at the beginning of the twentieth century.

The Psychoanalytic View of *Hamlet*

The dialogue between *Ulysses* and Freud thus starts, as perhaps all psychoanalytic literary criticism has, from the footnote about *Hamlet* in the first edition of *The Interpretation of Dreams*. In his discussion of Sophocles' *Oedipus Rex* Freud asserts that the effect of the ancient tragedy on modern audiences is to be explained by the universality of the underlying situation in the drama. "His destiny moves us only because it might have been ours," Freud writes, and then elaborates: "It is the fate of all of us, perhaps, to direct our first sexual impulse towards our mother and our first hatred and our first murderous wish against our father. . . . King Oedipus, who slew his father Laius and married his mother Jocasta, merely shows us the fulfillment of our own childhood wishes" (*SE,* 4:262). And after a discussion of typical masculine dreams of intercourse with the mother, as well as dreams of the dead father, Freud inserted the *Hamlet* footnote—incorporated into the text from 1914 on—recording his speculation that Shakespeare's *Hamlet* "has its roots in the same soil as *Oedipus Rex*" (*SE,* 4:264). In 1910, then, Jones's "Oedipus-Complex as an Explanation of Hamlet's Mystery" was published in America to "expound" Freud's hypothesis in the original footnote; in 1911 it was translated into German and published separately as a pamphlet; and not long after that Joyce added the essay to his library.

Simply as a matter of chronology, it is reasonable to assume that

Jones's essay was Joyce's introduction to the psychoanalytic view of *Hamlet*, but I begin this examination of psychoanalytic traces in "Scylla and Charybdis" with the latest published of the four works I have mentioned. Rank's 1915 psychoanalytic interpretation of the play-within-a-play in *Hamlet* was quite probably Joyce's most recent contact with the Freudian *Hamlet* when he was composing "Scylla and Charybdis" in 1918, at which time, Ellmann notes, he supplemented the notes he had gathered for the Trieste *Hamlet* lectures "by a good deal of further reading" (*JJII*, 452). Echoes from Rank in Stephen's lecture suggest that this essay on the play-within-a-play was a part of that reading. Details in Stephen's lecture are amplified and even clarified by the arguments in Rank's essay that they echo. Rank, for example, elaborates at some length on the method of murder pantomimed in the dumb-show (*Hamlet*, 3.2), interpreting the scene "psychoanalytically" as a "distorted" version of the "primal infantile fantasy" of spying on the parents. He thus emphasizes the sexual overtones in the scene, especially the poison that is poured into the King's ears, identifying the poison as a "universally human symbol" whose significance "as sperm (conception = poisoning)" is validated "through folklore and also through the analysis of individual patients." He further notes that the ear is a "symbolic receptor organ in popular psychology," citing Jones's 1914 essay on "The Conception of the Virgin Mary Through the Ear." And finally, Rank connects the whole scene with "the Fall of Man and original sin" ("Play," 17).

Now the "primal scene" aspect of Rank's analysis is of no immediately apparent interest to Stephen, but the sexual significance of the poison is. To be sure, Stephen's first allusion to the murder scene in *Hamlet* is an inner commentary that appears to be an acknowledgment of the dubious nature of his whole argument: "They list. And in the porches of their ears I pour" (*U*, 9.465)—what else but poison? Stephen then introduces the "poison poured in the porch of a sleeping ear" (*U*, 9.466–67) into his lecture, but here it is not connected to the murder in *Hamlet* either. Rather, by an equivocation on the word *murder*, Stephen relates the poison to his own rhetorical invention of the "murder" of Shakespeare's soul, "stricken mortally" when "belief in himself has been untimely killed" as "he was overborne in a cornfield" by Ann Hathaway (*U*, 9.466–67, 455–56). Stephen equates this psychic "murder" with the murder of King Hamlet through the sexual overtones common to both. Stephen then identifies the consequences of the psychic murder for Shakespeare as a "darkening of his own understanding of himself" (*U,* 9.463–64), a charge that he repeats as he concludes his lecture. Here he connects this "darkened understanding" with "original sin" (*U,* 9.1006), echoing Rank's suggestion that the "poison" in the players' drama is related to "the Fall of Man and original sin."

In addition, Stephen brings into his discussion a circumstance about the King's murder that Rank also notes as "unusual"—that "the murdered man was done away with as he slept" ("Play," 18). Stephen points out that "those who are done to death in sleep cannot know the manner of their quell unless their Creator endow their souls with that knowledge in the life to come" (*U,* 9.467–69). Here, of course, the Creator of the murdered King is Shakespeare, and Stephen is returning to his basic premise that Shakespeare's art depends upon his life: his characters can know nothing that the artist has not experienced himself. And this premise has obvious implications for Stephen's own ambition to be a creator/artist like Shakespeare.

Beyond these details, Stephen picks up on Rank's insistence that Hamlet's prime psychological motivation for arranging the play-within-a-play is not to trap Claudius, but to prod himself to take "decisive action" ("Play," 8). Like Hamlet, who knows he must avenge his father but cannot act, Stephen knows that he must, in the colloquial phrase, "get a life," but he talks instead, apparently using his lecture, deformed as it is by deception and sophistry,[7] as Hamlet uses the play-within-a-play, to push himself to act, to "Do" (*U,* 9.651). And even as Hamlet's intervention with his little play forces him to realize, according to Rank, that he is contenting himself with "the merely 'stage' murder of his uncle instead of creating out of it a stimulus to action" ("Play," 10), Stephen recognizes that he is *not* doing, *not* acting, but rather substituting speech for action—"Speech, speech. But act" (*U,* 9.978–79). Stephen's self-chastisement echoes Hamlet's recognition that instead of moving ahead with his task of vengeance, he "Must, like a whore, unpack my heart with words" (2.2.611; "Play," 7), a phrase that is remarkably apt for Stephen's presentation in this episode.

In addition to this psychological parallel, Rank's view of the function of Hamlet's mini-drama is suggestively reflected in the structural function of "Scylla and Charybdis" in *Ulysses.* For Rank identifies the play-within-a-play as "the climax and the turning point of the dramatic and psychological development" of Shakespeare's *Hamlet* ("Play," 6), and

"Scylla and Charybdis," whatever the differences, serves a similar function in *Ulysses*. Identified by Joyce as the "end of the first part of *Ulysses*" (*JJII*, 442 n), the episode is a stylistic turning point in the novel, the final chapter written in what Karen Lawrence calls the "signature style" characteristic of the first half of *Ulysses*. It marks the end of novelistic character development, after which the "rhetorical masks" of the rest of the novel take over the narrative (8).

Certainly this ninth episode marks the apex of Stephen's development in *Ulysses*, giving us the last clear picture of him as a "novelistic" character. Even as Hamlet directs the players in the play-within-a-play, Stephen is the moving force in the dramatic dialogue of the episode: not since *A Portrait* has his point of view been so clearly dominant, nor will it be again in the novel. Indeed, as Stanley Sultan has pointed out, Stephen takes the role of Ulysses in this episode (149): the choice symbolized by Scylla and Charybdis is his to make, and his consciousness rules the action—internal and external—throughout. It is one of the rare anachronisms in *Ulysses* that Stephen is somehow conscious of "the new Viennese school," and it is Stephen in this episode who initiates the dialogue between the text of *Ulysses* and the texts of psychoanalysis.

A major component in this dialogue appears to be the essay by Jones that presumably introduced Joyce to the psychoanalytic link between Hamlet and Oedipus. Unlike the works by Freud and Jung that were purchased at approximately the same time and immediately put to use, Jones's essay has left no discernible traces in *A Portrait*, but we may speculate that Joyce's interest in the pamphlet was in some way connected with the series of twelve lectures on "Amletto di G. Shakespeare," which he delivered at the Università Popolare in Trieste between November 1912 and February 1913 (*JJII*, 345 and 776 n. 9). These lectures, the text of which has been lost, represent "Joyce's only sustained public confrontation with any of Shakespeare's plays," according to William H. Quillian's commentary on Joyce's notes for the lectures.[8] Although Joyce drew on the Trieste lectures in preparation for writing the "Scylla and Charybdis" episode for *Ulysses* (*JJII*, 452), the notes themselves contain no indication of a psychoanalytic perspective and in their pedantic flatness give no hint of the intricate, inward-looking mosaic of Stephen's Shakespeare lecture in *Ulysses*.

Ellmann, however, provides English translations for reports about the lectures from the *Piccolo della Sera*, Trieste (*JJII*, 775–76 n. 9), and the report of the first lecture credits Joyce with "wit and vivacity" through which he "achieved a genuine brilliance." Moreover, it is suggestive, even if not definitive, that the report of the first lecture records that Joyce paid "particular attention to the psychological moment when [Shakespeare] wrote *Hamlet*," an emphasis that is not in any way indicated in Joyce's notes. But Jones's essay, like Freud's original footnote, links the composition of *Hamlet* to the death of Shakespeare's father, with the "awakening effect on old 'repressed' memories" of his childhood jealousy of his father, which might well have given Shakespeare a sharpened understanding of the "psychical conflict" at the heart of *Hamlet* (*H*, 103; *SE*, 4:265–66). We have no way of knowing the nature of the "psychological moment" to which the *Piccolo* piece refers, but it seems possible, even likely, that in this Trieste lecture Joyce also connected the creation of *Hamlet* with the death of Shakespeare's father. Certainly he makes the connection in Stephen's discussion of fatherhood in "Scylla and Charybdis" (*U*, 9.829).

Jones assures his reader that "throughout this essay, I closely follow Freud's interpretation given in the footnote" (*H*, 98 n. 1). In Freud's long note, he points to the attempts of generations of critics to account for the central mystery of Shakespeare's tragedy—Hamlet's apparent inability to act—and provides the psychoanalytic solution: "Hamlet is able to do anything—except take vengeance on the man who did away with his father and took the father's place with his mother, the man who shows him the repressed wishes of his own childhood realized," all of which, Freud reminds his reader, "remain[s] unconscious in Hamlet's mind"—and also, Freud asserts, in the mind of Shakespeare. "For it can of course only be the poet's own mind which confronts us in *Hamlet*" (*SE*, 4:265).[9] And we may well be reminded of Joyce's response to Arthur Power's question about his intentions in *Ulysses:* "What do we know about what we put into anything? . . . Do any of us know what we are creating? Did Shakespeare know what he was creating when he wrote *Hamlet;* or Leonardo when he painted 'The Last Supper'?" (89).

These are, of course, rhetorical questions, not only suggesting Joyce's understanding of the validity of unconscious motivation but also reminding us of the critical consensus about Joyce as an extraordinarily conscious writer. Constantine Curran remembers Joyce's diligence in "following up clues and the modish allusions to more esoteric writers in what he read" (39), and Jones's essay on Hamlet and Oedipus, as was characteristic of the early psychoanalytic manuscripts, was lavish in its documentation, with frequent citations of both English and German authorities on Shakespeare, as well as psychoanalytic writers. The essay begins with a selective review of the critical literature of the previous fifty years—"mainly German"—that had offered solutions to the mystery of Hamlet's vacillation, and Jones observes that this mystery "has well been called the Sphinx of modern Literature," complimenting Freud in a footnote on having "solved the riddle of this Sphinx, as he has that of the Theban one" (*H*, 74 n. 2).

And in Stephen's discussion of a Shakespeare "made in Germany" (*U*, 9.766), at least two of the echoes of Jones's essay come from the footnotes in this preliminary section, a noticeable majority of which cite German critics, though Stephen's references are not among these. Both allusions are assigned to Eglinton, whose comment, "Vining held that the prince was a woman" (*U*, 9.518–19), condenses information from a footnote in Jones's essay that cites Edward Vining's 1881 "The Mystery of Hamlet" for the view "that Hamlet's weakness is to be explained by the fact that he was a woman wrongly brought up as a man" (*H*, 74 n. 5). And when Eglinton tells Stephen that "Dowden believes there is some mystery in *Hamlet* but will say no more" (*U*, 9.1072–73), he echoes Jones's reference to Edward Dowden's speculation about "a conscious interpolation by Shakespere of some secret," with a footnote citing Dowden's 1875 *Shakespeare: His Development in His Works* (*H*, 81 n. 7). In *Ulysses*, Eglinton's observation in turn has been preceded by Mulligan's suggestion of the nature of Dowden's "secret": "I asked him what he thought of the charge of pederasty brought against the bard. He lifted his hands and said: *All we can say is that life ran very high in those days*" (*U*, 9.731–33).

Considerably more substantial is the echo in "Scylla and Charybdis" of the Freudian view, considerably expanded and elaborated by Jones, that Hamlet's inability to act is attributable to the fact that the two crimes of incest and murder with which he charges his uncle are the realization of Hamlet's own childhood desires. These desires, Jones points out, were operative when the child understood neither sexual intercourse nor death, and they have since been repressed. But they are reanimated in the adult Hamlet's unconscious through his father's death and threaten to erupt into consciousness (*H*, 91–100).[10] The crimes, Jones points out, "are two, Claudius' incest with the Queen [incestuous because she is his sister-in-law], and his murder of his brother" (*H*, 91). It is significant, Jones says, that Claudius is a relative, and even though the relationships are different, these are the same crimes the child Hamlet wanted to commit, and the same persons were the objects of the child Hamlet's desire and hostility.

In effect, Claudius has committed these crimes *for* Hamlet, and in *Ulysses* Stephen's ambiguous identification of the source for Shakespeare's sexual malaise echoes Jones's analysis: "An original sin and, like original sin, *committed by another in whose sin he too has sinned*" (*U*, 9.1008–9; my emphasis). At the same time, however, the theological context that Stephen introduces through his reference to original sin extends Freud's analogy between *Hamlet* and *Oedipus Rex* to the Genesis story of Adam and Eve in the Garden and their sin, which in Christian doctrine blights every Christian—a sin "committed by another in whose sin he too has sinned."

The interweaving of psychoanalytic echoes with echoes of church literature exemplified here is characteristic of Joyce's use of allusion, as he combines analogous strands from a variety of sources to add density and resonance to his text.[11] And, in addition to names already familiar to Joyce, Jones cites a substantial number of the early psychoanalysts, starting with Freud, who is represented by much of what he had written by 1910. And it was upon Freud's insights, I stress again, that these early writings openly—even conscientiously—depended. Jones gives the page number for Freud's *Hamlet* footnote in the *Traumdeutung* and also cites Jung's 1909 essay on the father. Moreover, in the course of his preliminary remarks about the nature of the artist's creative impulse, Jones also identifies Otto Rank as the author of *The Artist* and *The Myth of the Birth of the Hero* (*H*, 73), titles with peculiar resonance for Joyce, whose *Portrait of the Artist* had at one time been titled *Stephen Hero*. Furthermore, as Jones launches into the heart of the "Freudian" interpretation of *Hamlet* as one of a "vast group of myths and legends" whose common theme is "the success of a young hero in displacing a rival father," he acknowledges a special indebtedness to Rank's *Myth* as his source for the discussion of these myths (*H*, 104 n. 3).[12]

Stephen on Fatherhood: Myth and Family Romance

In *The Myth of the Birth of the Hero,* Rank, like Jones in the *Hamlet* essay, is elaborating on an insight originally outlined by Freud, that is, the "family romance of neurotics." Rank starts his study with the standard psychoanalytic assumption that myth can be viewed as a kind of mass dream (*MBH,* 9), retelling the birth legends of over a dozen heroes, including Oedipus, Hamlet, and Jesus, and interpreting their common features in psychoanalytic terms. These common features are drawn from an outline of Freud's family romance, the text of which Rank includes in his study with no heading and only a brief acknowledgment of Freud's "kindness" in sharing with Rank his experience with "the psychology of neurosis" (*MBH,* 67–71). Mark Shechner speculates in his Freudian reading of "Stephen's Family Romance" that if Joyce had read Freud on the family romance before or during the writing of *Ulysses,* it was "most likely" in Rank's work (*Joyce in Nighttown,* 43). In fact, Rank's *Myth* is the only place where Joyce could have read this before the publication of *Ulysses* since the section written by Freud was not published separately until 1931 (*SE,* 9:236).[13]

The features of the fantasy portrayed in Freud's family romance, like so many of the patterns described by Freud, though originally revealed through his analysis of neurotics, are presumed to be a repressed part of normal development as well. Noting that "the liberation of an individual, as he grows up, from the authority of his parents is one of the most necessary though one of the most painful results brought about by the course of his development," Freud describes the work of the child's imagination in accomplishing this "task of getting free from the parents" (*FR,* 237–38). In his imagination the child first replaces both parents by others of better birth, and then, as he comes to understand "the difference in the parts played by fathers and mothers in their sexual relations," he alters his wish-fulfilling fantasy by accepting the maternal relation as "unalterable" while "exalting" the father (*FR,* 239).

This pattern is also characteristic of the hero myths, as Rank shows, equating the hero with the ego of the child who originally dreams up the family romance.[14] The mythmaker, that is, credits the hero with his own personal infantile history, with the revolt against the authority of the father that makes the childish ego a hero (*MBH,* 84). Rank outlines the essential features of the myth. The hero is often the son of a king, who is warned that his unborn son will kill him. The father responds to this warning through a life-threatening exposure of the son, who is, however, saved by animals or lowly people, who raise him to adulthood. As an adult, he rejects them and is reunited with his original parents "in a highly versatile fashion," sometimes taking revenge on his father, or at other times, being acknowledged as his exalted father's son.[15] In Rank's tracing of the Oedipus myth, he includes the information that Laius, the father of Oedipus, in order to circumvent this standard warning about the dangerous son, voluntarily "refrains from conjugal relations," but drops his guard while intoxicated and fathers Oedipus. This situation finds an echo of sorts in *Ulysses* in Bloom's avoidance of "complete carnal intercourse" with his wife for over ten years (*MBH*, 20; *U*, 17.2278–82), as well as his notorious prudence about drinking.

The family romance, in fact, becomes a part of the total effect of Joyce's set piece on fatherhood, which starts with the identification of Shakespeare as "made in Germany," a possible psychoanalytic reference, which is reinforced by the allusion to the Viennese school that follows shortly (*U*, 9.766, 780). And beginning with the mingling of this allusion with one to Saint Thomas Aquinas, the section builds through a dense mixture of allusions and epigrams, combined with Stephen's memories and internal dialogue, to his rhetorical question: "Who is the father of any son that any son should love him or he any son?" (*U*, 9.844–45). This question is followed by an internal colloquy, whose heightened intensity has always suggested to readers that the discussion of fatherhood is a vital clue, not only to what Stephen is driving at in his Shakespeare presentation, but even to the meaning of *Ulysses*. And the paternity motif has long been a point of departure for interpretations of *Ulysses*.[16]

Stephen's discourse here, as throughout the episode, is an exhibition of wit and learning, studded with allusions,[17] as he moves quickly from the combined allusion to Saint Thomas and the Viennese school (*U*, 9.478–80) to the topic of jealousy, certainly a corollary to the special view of that "school" on incest (*H*, 107). His casual reference to "Old Nobodaddy," named "Father of Jealousy" in Blake's poem "To Nobodaddy," is mingled with a Shakespearean allusion to the cuckolding "Sir Smile" neighbor of *A Winter's Tale* (*U*, 9.790). His ensuing reference to Ann Hathaway as "the mobled queen," an allusion to the First Player's reference to Hecuba (*Hamlet*, 2.2.520–30), reinforces the Shakespearean context, at the same time linking *Hamlet* with the hero myths, since Hecuba is the mother of Paris, one of the legendary heroes included in Rank's study (*MBH*, 23–24).

Eglinton, then, who has started this dialectical game with his "dare" to "prove" Shakespeare was a Jew (*U*, 9.763), contributes an apparent non sequitur: "But we have it on high authority that a man's worst enemies shall be those of his own house and family" (*U*, 9.812–13). Although Thornton identifies the high authority as biblical, the exact words are Blake's in chapter 2 of *Jerusalem:* "The time will come, when a man's worst enemies / Shall be those of his own house and family,"[18] a warning that comes from the section of *Jerusalem* addressed "To the Jews," thus, by allusion at least, returning to Eglinton's originally suggested topic— Shakespeare as a Jew. But at the same time, the topic that Stephen has added to the agenda—the Viennese school and its view of incest—is also, again by allusion, kept in focus. For the central motivation in the hero myths described by Rank is intrafamily enmity, the reciprocal threat of son to father and father to son, the hostile father being duplicated in various myths by other family members (*MBH*, 77–82, 86–90; *H*, 109).

Eglinton repeats AE Russell's objection to a consideration of the poet's family life, at which Stephen inwardly accuses him of denying, like the hero of the myth, his own humble parentage. He drives home the allusion to the "lowly parents" of the myth with his caricature of Eglinton/Magee's father as a thoroughly uncouth peasant, a characterization that Thornton says contradicts the fact (*U*, 9.820–23; Thornton, *Allusions*, 201–2). The image of Magee's father in turn points Stephen to an almost tender memory of his meeting with his own father upon his return from Paris: "the voice, new warmth, speaking. . . . the eyes that wish me well," followed, however, by the recognition that is the subject of the ensuing fugue on fatherhood: "But do not know me" (*U*, 9.826–27).

Fugue on Fatherhood: A Medley of Intertexts

For this short fugue, beginning with Stephen's "A father . . . is a necessary evil" and ending with Mulligan's "Himself his own father" (*U*, 9.828–75), circles around the "incertitude" of fatherhood, which, of course, makes possible the family romance described by Freud. Complete with an identifiable exposition, middle section, and final section, with two short episodes between, it contains most of the favorite epigrams about fatherhood in *Ulysses*. And all are related to the crucial question, which universalizes Stephen's recognition about his own father: "Who is the father of any son that any son should love him or he any son?" (*U*, 9.844–45).

This question borrows its rhythm from Hamlet's rhetorical question about Hecuba, "the mobled queen," whose near-demented grief at the destruction of Troy and the slaughter of her husband (*Hamlet*, 2.2.513–14) has moved the First Player to theatrical tears, causing Hamlet to wonder: "What's Hecuba to him or he to Hecuba, / That he should weep for her?" (2.2.582–83).[19] But the substance of Stephen's question points to the central fact about paternity, which is restated in different contextual voices throughout this passage: it is never provable, and the question had no certain answer until the advent of DNA-matching in our own time. The wise Telemachus, asked if he were the son of Odysseus, could only answer with an expanded version of Stephen's question: "My mother says I am his son; I know not / surely. Who has known his own engendering?" (*Odyssey*, 1.215–16, trans. Robert Fitzgerald). As Simon Dedalus says in *A Portrait*, "smiling complacently," when one of his friends in Cork teases Stephen about being "his father's son," "I don't know, I'm sure" (*P*, 94).[20]

Freud, explaining the "curious curtailment" of the family romance with the child's more exact knowledge of the roles of mother and father in procreation, says that the child realizes "that '*pater semper incertus est*,' while the mother is '*certissima*'" (*FR*, 239). It is this realization that forces the child to amend his earlier fabrication of complete independence from his actual parents, contenting himself with denying only the father and substituting a more exalted one—a "curtailment" that is also a regular feature of the myths of the hero's birth, including the birth of Jesus, son of God from a virgin, "the most abrupt repudiation of the father [as well as the most extreme exaltation of the "true" father's status], the consummation of the entire myth" (*MBH*, 81). And this biologically based social fact is the theme for the variations in this passage, in which there is no other voice but Stephen's, speaking inwardly or aloud. But in this passage the analogous contexts of creation as biological reproduction (Shakespeare as father and son), creation as artistic begetting (Shakespeare as dramatist, the father of Hamlet), and creation as religious mystery (the Trinitarian relationships) overlap like the voices in a fugue, pulling in a range of allusive contexts, including the psychoanalytic view of the ego as hero, which embraces the others.

Stephen begins this fugue (*U*, 9.828–45), with an allusion to the same biographical fact that Freud attributed to Georg Brandes—also a source for Stephen—in his original footnote about Hamlet and Oedipus: that Shakespeare wrote *Hamlet* "in the months that followed his father's death" (*U*, 9.829; *SE*, 4:265). And the overlapping of the contexts of biological and artistic creation with the psychoanalytic view of *Hamlet* continues with Stephen's capsule outline of the assumptions necessary to identify the middle-aged playwright with his youthful hero. Stephen appears to reject this identification because of the corollary requirement that Shakespeare's elderly mother be identified with "the lustful queen" (*U*, 9.830–33). These identifications, however, fit perfectly with psychoanalytic assumptions about the nature of the unconscious, where time has no meaning and where the elderly mother retains her identity as the "lustful queen."

As Stephen continues with the statement about John Shakespeare, William's father, identified by allusion with King Hamlet, the context of the artist's life and his creation is invaded by the first note of the religious mystery in the reference to the "mystical estate" of fatherhood, "devised" by the father upon the son. This note continues with the reminder that "conscious begetting is unknown to man," and comes out clearly in "an apostolic succession, from only begetter to only begotten." Although in human, biological terms, John Shakespeare's "devising" of the estate of fatherhood upon his son is a genetic fact, echoed in Stephen's earlier line, "*My father gave me seeds to sow*" (*U*, 2.289), the "mystical" paradigm for this devising is the revision of the Genesis story of creation in Saint John's prologue. Here it is said of the Son, the Word: "All things were made by him. Without him was not anything made that was made" (1:3). And this is repeated in the Nicene Creed of the "only begotten Son of God . . . through whom all things were made." But Stephen's statement further overlaps the religious mystery of creation with the "conscious begetting" of the artist, as he introduces an allusion to the ambiguous dedication of Shakespeare's Sonnets to "the onlie begetter of these insuing sonnets," "Mr. W.H.," whom Stephen identifies inwardly as "Mr William Himself" (*U*, 9.526).[21]

All the contexts combine in Stephen's assertion that the church itself is founded, not on the Madonna, but on the mystery of fatherhood: "founded, like the world, macro- and microcosm, upon the void. Upon incertitude, upon unlikelihood" (*U*, 9.841–42). The rationale for founding the Christian Church *depends* upon the absolute "incertitude" of paternity; it is founded on Jesus Christ as the Son of God, who, at the same time, as Martin Cunningham later reminds Bloom, "had no father" (*U*, 12.1806). Since it cannot be proved that Jesus was the son of Joseph, he may indeed be the Son of God. The relationship between Father and Son in the Trinity is analogous to the always uncertain biological relationship between the father and son pointed to by Freud in the Latin phrase "pater semper incertus est." This phrase is echoed by Stephen's Latinate "incertitude," which he contrasts to the Madonna's role, which is not a true mystery, but, like the role of the biological mother, is, as Freud says, "*certissima.*"

In the Old Testament account of the Creation, of course, the macrocosm of the world was literally founded "upon the void," created out of nothing, and the creator remains, as Molly recognizes, a mystery: "who was the first person in the universe before there was anybody that made it all who ah that they dont know neither do I so there you are" (*U*, 18.1569–70). This mystery then is compounded by the New Testament "devising" of creative power upon the Son. Finally, the microcosm, the individual, faces a similar void or "incertitude" as to the author of his being. The mother is unquestionably the vessel, but it is always possible that the named father, though a legal convenience, may be a "fiction."

This episode of the fugue then winds up with a contrast between love of father and love of mother, which brings both Aquinas and Aristotle into the context of Stephen's argument. Stephen declares that "*amor matris*, subjective and objective genitive may be the only true thing in life" (*U*, 9.842–43). He is referring to the son's loving his mother and also being the object of her love, as well as vice versa, that is, the mother's loving her son and being the object of his love. This love is real *because* it is "genitive," which is here not a grammatical description,[22] but a reference to the function of generation, of reproducing, to the link of the flesh between mother and son. When Aquinas takes up the question—"Ought a man love his mother more than his father?"—in the *Summa Theologica* under *Charity* (2:2.26.10)—he replies finally that a father, "precisely as a father," should be loved more than a mother, "precisely as a mother." But the arguments he presents against that conclusion, citing reasons given by Aristotle for loving the mother more than the father, are all presented by Stephen at one time or another in *Ulysses*.

First, Aquinas quotes Aristotle's argument (*Generation of Animals*, 1.20), that a man receives more from his mother, since she "gives the body," while his soul, Aristotle affirms, comes, not from the father, but from God. And in "Nestor," when Stephen spells out the dimensions of *amor matris*—"the only true thing in life" (*U*, 2.143)—he visualizes it almost exclusively in terms of the body. He stresses especially the fact that the mother shares her own flesh with her child, before and after birth (*U*, 2.140–43, 166–67). Aquinas then borrows a second argument from Aristotle, which again reinforces Stephen's conclusion in "Scylla and Charybdis" about *amor matris*. For, Aquinas continues, citing Aristotle (*Ethics*, 9.7), mothers love their children more than fathers, not only because "child-bearing is their more burdensome business," which Stephen has already touched on in "Nestor," but also because "they know better than the father that their children are really theirs" (*Summa Theologica*, 2:2.26.10). And this is a truism that is central to Stephen's unanswerable question, which winds up the first part of the fugue: "Who is the father?"

This is followed by another brief episode, Stephen's impassioned colloquy with himself,[23] beginning with his vehement question—"What the hell are you driving at?"—and ending with another question—Are you condemned to do this?" This internal exchange may well point to the dubiety of much of the argument that follows, punctuated as it is by inner reminders of his own sophistry: "Come, mess" (*U*, 9.892); "Don't tell them" (*U*, 9.936); "Lapwing" (*U*, 9.976)—a traditional symbol of deceit, which Stephen applies to himself four times in rapid succession.[24]

Stephen then presents the middle section of the fugue on fatherhood, beginning with what seems an abrupt non sequitur, that is, an explicit denial of any homosexual tinge to the relationship between father and son. This denial recalls Rank's reminder in the chapter on "Shakespeare's Father Complex" in his *Incest Motif* that in the son's reawakened feelings about the father at his death there is a "latent homosexual component arising from a tender current, which has existed from the beginning and in the unconscious is never surrendered."[25] Stephen, however, claims that father and son are "sundered by a bodily shame so steadfast that the criminal annals . . . hardly record its breach," and the list of "other incests" that he tosses out in the same sentence recalls Jones's comment that there are in the Hamlet legend "ample indications of the working of all forms of incestuous fantasy" (*U*, 9.850–54; *H*, 110). As Stephen then turns to the existential bases for jealousy between father and son, there are echoes of Freud's discussion in his Leonardo study of the effect on the

father of the mother's love for her infant: "In the happiest young marriage the father is aware that the baby, especially if he is a baby son, has
become his rival, and this is the starting point of an antagonism toward
the favourite which is deeply rooted in the unconscious" (*L*, 117).

The episode that follows this middle section is only four lines, but it
brings in, through the doctrine of correspondence which is the law of
Ulysses, contexts from "Proteus," providing a densely figured transition
back to the subject of the original exposition, the "mystery" of fatherhood as begetting, which is again the center of the final section of the
fugue. First, Stephen's answered question—"What links them in nature?
An instant of blind rut" (*U*, 9.859)—brings into the context of the Hamlet discussion his thoughts of the morning about the natural link in his
own life: "They clasped and sundered, did the coupler's will" (*U*, 3.47).
And what follows this acknowledgment of his biological parents is
Stephen's own doctrinally substantiated version of the exaltation of the
father typical of the family romance. "From before the ages He willed me
and now may not will me away or ever. A *lex eterna* stays about him. Is
that then the divine substance wherein Father and Son are consubstantial?" (*U*, 3.47–50). Stephen then applies to his own personal history the
idea of consubstantiality of father and son, *through* the will of the divine
Father, who, as Aquinas has also affirmed, is directly responsible for
Stephen's soul. In addition, God is responsible for the natural procreation
that led to Stephen's birth, in which it is the mother who links father and
son.

For if we take a hard look at Stephen's self-answered question about
this generative link between father and son, we find ourselves face to face
with a physiological fact that is not often taken so literally. The father-
son relationship exists only through their sharing, each in his own exclusive sphere, the complicated, hidden birth apparatus of the woman who is
wife and mother (the father defined as father through conception, the son
through gestation and delivery). And if the father and son are so linked
"in nature," there is also a roughly analogous divine link, which is the
will of God. In his meditation on the Strand, Stephen appears to apply
this conclusion as he refers to "My consubstantial father's voice," which
is unmistakably the voice of Simon, "the man with my voice and my
eyes" (*U*, 3.46).

The identity of the voice of father and son is also part of the substance
of Stephen's memory of the "Shrunken uncertain hand" (*U*, 9.861),

which is not Simon's, but that of another father, Kevin Egan, who said to Stephen in Paris, "You're your father's son. I know the voice" (*U*, 3.229). His "Weak wasting hand on mine" (*U*, 3.263) is a part of Stephen's Paris memories, signaled here by Stephen's mention of "rue Monsieur le Prince" (*U*, 9.858). Paris is also the site of Stephen's conversation with Patrice, "Son of the wild goose, Kevin Egan of Paris. My father's a bird" (*U*, 3.164). And connected in turn with the memory of Patrice is Taxil's *La Vie de Jesus*, from which comes Mary's explanation of her pregnancy: "*C'est le pigeon, Joseph*" (*U*, 3.162). The entire memory thus links the son of the wild goose with the son of "*le pigeon*," later identified as "*le sacre pigeon, ventre de Dieu*" (*U*, 14.307), the Holy Spirit as dove. The religious mystery of the incarnation, discussed as a hero myth by Rank (*MBH*, 50–56), is thus added to a contextual mix that already combines the mystery of the consubstantiality of Father and Son with the everyday puzzle of biological paternity.[26]

Sandwiched between these two references to fathers and sons are Stephen's two related and unanswered questions: "Am I a father? If I were?" (*U*, 9.860). The first is Stephen's personal variant on the rhetorical question he has put to his audience, and like the general question it has no sure answer. But Rank, in his *Myth*, provides a startlingly simple answer for the second. "The conflict with the father," he says, "is nullified at the instant when the grown boy himself becomes a father." For with this natural event, the son effectively puts himself in the place of the father, "just as the hero terminates his revolt against the father"—that is, either through elimination of the father, or, through acknowledgment and inheritance, taking the father's place (*MBH*, 94). Later, in his *Incest Motif*, Rank modified this simplification, at least with reference to Shakespeare, so that the crucial psychological event that nullifies the father-son conflict is not the son's biological fatherhood, but "*Vaterseins*," the feeling of being a father, which came to Shakespeare, Rank says, only with the death of his own father and accounts for Shakespeare's identification with both father and son in *Hamlet* (*Incest Theme*, 179–80), an identification that Stephen also insists on.[27] And Rank's analysis of Shakespeare's psychic situation between dead father and dead son clarifies Stephen's riddling question in the final section of the fugue: "if the father who has not a son be not a father can the son who has not a father be a son?" (*U*, 9.864–65).

In fact, the identity of father and son suggested by Rank is the subject on which the biological, artistic, and religious contexts converge in this final section, which Stephen introduces with a statement of the Sabellian extension of consubstantiality, in which the separation of Persons is lost, and Father and Son become in effect interchangeable: "The Father was Himself His Own Son" (*U*, 9.863).

Now the terms of the Sabellian heresy are in harmony with a group of myths in which the hero realizes *"the fantasy of being one's own son"* (*MBH*, 85; emphasis Rank's). As in the Trinity, so also in *Lohengrin* and in Shakespeare's *Hamlet*, the names of father and son are identical,[28] and this fantasy of self-begetting represents the ambitious final step in the process of the enhancement of the ego, which begins with the exaltation of the father and ends with the ego's taking the place of this exalted father, thus achieving complete autonomy. Stephen's grandiose claims for Shakespeare's procreative power in the "answer" to his question about father and son indicate the creative range that opens up to the artist who is free to beget himself and with this freedom can feel himself "the father of all his race" (*U*, 9.868–69).[29]

Then, as the fugue comes to a close, Mulligan breaks in with what is actually a restatement of this final achievement of the "egoistic and ambitious" wish that motivates the family romance and the analogous myths, the child's need to "establish his personal independence" (*MBH*, 72), to become "Himself his own father" (*U*, 9.875).[30] The three sections of the fugue have elaborated successively on three chronologically ordered human facts about paternity. These facts are at each stage congruent with the analogous psychoanalytic patterns of the family romance described by Freud and the myth of the birth of the hero interpreted by Rank: the radical uncertainty of paternity in conception; the natural competition between father and son, before and after birth; and the eventual displacement of the father by the son. For, in physical fact, the son triumphs simply by becoming himself a father and outliving his own father, only to begin the cycle all over again, a cycle that will end with his own displacement.

But the basic wish of the hero of the myth is to break out of the cycle altogether, to beget and be begotten once for all: both "only begetter" and "only begotten" (*U*, 9.838–39). This self-begetting—biologically impossible, but psychically essential—also motivates the quest of Stephen Dedalus, who embodies the creative ego of the artist/hero of *Ulysses*. For the artist may reproduce himself in a work of art, and obviously the more autobiographical the work the more literally this is true. He may beget a "son of his soul" (*U*, 9.171) and know him as his own and, in the case of an autobiographical fiction, know him as himself, a "conscious begetting" that is otherwise unattainable by a human father.

In his lecture Stephen has presented the case for the legitimacy of this self-begetting as it has been realized by Shakespeare, who, "because loss is his gain . . . passes on towards eternity in undiminished personality" (*U*, 9.476–77). Shakespeare's success defines Stephen's quest in *Ulysses*, which is not significantly different from that specified in the final chapter of *A Portrait:* "to express myself . . . as freely as I can and as wholly as I can" (*P*, 247). But in *Ulysses* the meaning of this quest—the meaning of "myself," in fact—is significantly expanded. And what is added to the creative ego embodied in Stephen is the experience of Bloom, who appears in "Scylla and Charybdis" for the first time in the novel in the same place at the same time as Stephen and comes face to face with him as the episode closes. Bloom does not in any important sense serve as Stephen's father. As Edmund Epstein pointed out some time ago, Stephen is not in fact looking for a father (*Ordeal*, 173), and nothing in his mini-disquisition on the incertitude of biological fatherhood implicates Bloom at all.

What Stephen seeks for himself is the certain, identifiable fatherhood of the artist, and Bloom *is* implicated in this search. A truism that comes out of all the talk in this chapter is that the artist cannot reproduce his life in art unless or until he *has* a life, a requirement that Stephen clearly cannot meet. With the death of his mother, he has lost his only loving connection with the "strandentwining cable of all flesh" (*U*, 3.37), a connection through which he can, as he cries inwardly to his dead mother as‐ the day begins, "live" (*U*, 1.279).

In his telegram to Mulligan, Stephen states his predicament, however obliquely, misquoting Meredith's definition of the sentimentalist as one who "would enjoy without incurring the immense debtorship for a thing done" (*U*, 9.550–51; Thornton, *Allusions*, 186), a definition that may be applied separately to both Stephen and Bloom. For Stephen's sterile, anticreative performance in the library parallels, on an intellectual/artistic level, Bloom's masturbatory "relationship" with Gerty MacDowell in "Nausicaa." Both men reveal themselves in these separate episodes as sentimentalists in the sense of Meredith's epigram, yearning to enjoy a reality that cannot be theirs without taking on "the immense debtorship for a thing done." Bloom, in his rather amorphous way, moons about the son he does not have, but he will not or cannot have intercourse with his wife. Stephen constructs a fantasy about creating a world in his own image, but will not or cannot enter into a living relationship with the created world. An image of their common predicament appears in "Circe," when the two look into a mirror and see reflected a paralyzed Shakespeare (*U*, 15.3821–24).

Potentially, however, if they can come together, there is hope for the "thing done," and as this "Hamlet chapter" comes to a close, the text provides that hope, taking on the prefiguring function that Rank sees in the dumb-show that precedes the players' drama in *Hamlet*, which "anticipates the whole content of what follows in abbreviated form" ("Play," 8). For as Stephen and Mulligan leave the library, amid a flurry of homoerotic chit-chat and Mulligan's recital of the prospectus for his play "Everyman His Own Wife" (*U*, 9.1142–96), Stephen senses "one behind." And the one behind him is Bloom—husband of Molly and father of Milly and the lost Rudy—presenting himself as an alternative for Mulligan and the sterility of the life Mulligan represents. As Stephen stands aside to let Bloom pass between him and Mulligan, the text clearly prefigures Stephen's ultimate acceptance of this fleshly family man as a part of himself: "That lies in space which I in time must come to, ineluctably" (*U*, 9.1200–1201).[31] Stephen must become a complete man before he can achieve the fatherhood of the productive artist; he must have a life before he can immortalize it in a work of art. And it is Bloom, not Mulligan, who can lead him to that life. It is Bloom who completes Stephen, giving him a life and thus opening the gate to the fatherhood that Stephen seeks.

Again Stephen's shift from Mulligan to Bloom is realized textually, whatever questions may remain at the novel's end about his relationship with Bloom. In "Hades," that is, Simon Dedalus characterizes "that Mulligan cad" as Stephen's "*fidus Achates*" (*U*, 6.49; Thornton, *Allusions*, 90), the faithful friend of Aeneus. But by the opening pages of "Eumaeus" this designation has shifted to Bloom (*U*, 16.54–55), as Bloom becomes an alter ego, taking over the immediate management of Stephen's life.

It is *as* father that he completes Joyce's autobiographical portrait of the artist. For Bloom represents, among his many complementary roles in *Ulysses*, the biological father in Joyce—who is, after all, the primary existential model for both Stephen and Bloom—with all the demands and limitations that this role entails, demands and limitations that are in all kinds of ways—psychic and practical—hostile to the demands of the productive artist. To that extent these two protagonists, as projections of conflicting impulses in Joyce's life, are in a relationship analogous to the father-son relationship in life and in myth. They both need to occupy the same psychic space, a conflict that is even more acute because they truly are consubstantial. Like the Hamlet of Rank's analysis of the play-within-a-play, Stephen has exerted himself in this episode—though with dubious success—to move toward the future that is prefigured at its close.

In the morning of Bloomsday, alone on the strand, Stephen has asked himself with some desperation, "She, she, she. What she?" (U, 3.426). And as he and Mulligan leave the library in the afternoon, following Bloom's "dark back" through the gateway to Kildare Street (U, 9.1214–15), the text reveals through allusive indirection that Bloom has the answer to Stephen's question and is the key to Stephen's becoming, like the Shakespeare of his presentation, both father and son, "the ghost and the prince . . . all in all" (U, 9.1018–19). For Stephen recalls his Arabian Nights dream of the night before, featuring Haroun al Raschid: "Last night I flew, easily flew. Men wondered. Street of harlots after. A creamfruit melon he held to me. In. You will see" (U, 9.1207–8). Bloom will later be explicitly identified as Haroun al Raschid (U, 15.4325), and Molly has already been linked with the creamfruit melon (U, 4.206–8). Thus, through his dream Stephen has been promised the woman he needs through a benefactor who is equated with Bloom. And as this episode closes, Stephen's advice to himself to "Cease to strive" signals an acceptance of the promise of the dream, an acceptance that is heightened by the whole context of "the peace of the Druid priests of Cymbeline" and the final quotation from Cymbeline (U, 9.1221–25).

For it was Cymbeline's soothsayer, the "heirophantic priest," to whom Posthumus presented another dream for interpretation: "When as a lion's whelp shall, to himself unknown, without seeking find, and be embraced by a piece of tender air . . . then shall Posthumus end his miseries" (5.5.435–41). As the dream is interpreted, the miseries of Posthumus are at an end because he has found "without seeking" and been "embraced by" Imogen, who, by an etymological analysis that would surely delight Joyce, is "the piece of tender air, thy virtuous daughter, / Which we call 'mollis aer'; and 'mollis aer' / We term it 'mulier': which 'mulier'

I divine / Is this most constant wife" (5.5.446–49; Thornton, *Allusions*, 219). And it is in the "kind air" outside the library (which we may call "tender air" with all that follows) that Stephen remembers his own dream, which is a companion to the one interpreted by the "hiero-phantic" priest, since it promises that he, "without seeking," will be given a "creamfruit melon" by the great and magnanimous Haroun al Raschid, the Caliph of Baghdad in the *Arabian Nights*. He can "cease to strive" because "she" will be given to him. He will fly, but the earth is his element rather than sky and sea. The "crooked smokes" in the final quotation from *Cymbeline* rise from a sacrifice on "wide earth an altar" (*U*, 9.1222).

These "crooked smokes" have appeared before in "Aeolus," as Stephen watches the smoke rising from the cigarettes of the group in the newspaper office. In this setting he recalls the phrase from *Cymbeline*—"And let our crooked smokes"—which is followed shortly, under the heading of "FROM THE FATHERS," by a quotation that brings from Stephen the inner exclamation: "Ah, curse you! That's saint Augustine" (*U*, 7.835–44). For what comes into Stephen's mind is Augustine's great affirmation of the inherent goodness of everything that exists in this world, partially quoted in "Aeolus" but quoted more fully in the 1904 "Portrait of the Artist," where it undergirds the young artist's "conscious[ness] of the beauty of mortal conditions" and is identified as "a philosophy of reconcilement." "It was manifested unto me that those things be good which yet are corrupted; which neither if they were supremely good, nor unless they were good could be corrupted: for had they been supremely good they would have been incorruptible but if they were not good there would be nothing in them which could be corrupted" (*FP*, 65–66).

Thus a prefiguring function, which Rank also sees in the play-within-a-play in *Hamlet*, is accomplished as this "Hamlet chapter" concludes. Through a complex structure of external allusion—to Shakespeare, to Augustine, and to Joyce himself—as well as correspondences within the novel, Stephen is promised a reconcilement to the world of the flesh through Bloom and his gift of the woman Stephen seeks.

4

Psychoanalytic Contexts for "The Mother"

Although "Scylla and Charybdis" concludes with this extended moment of peace for Stephen, the success prefigured for him in his Arabian Nights dream—which surfaces in the text in bits and pieces throughout the day—has not yet been won. For the dream of his dead mother—which also recurs in fragments during the day—competes with the dream of Haroun al Raschid for his allegiance until Stephen himself dispatches "The Mother" in "Circe," making way for the actualization of the Arabian Nights dream. Stephen's apprehension of his mother as a threat bears traces, on the whole and in explicit textual details, of the mother-son relationship envisioned by both Freud and Jung in the early years of the twentieth century.

Stephen's mother enters the text of *Ulysses* with Stephen at the beginning of Bloomsday, and his dream-memory of her in death appears the first time the text shifts to his inner thoughts, in which "pain, that was not yet the pain of love, fretted his heart. Silently, in a dream she had come to him after her death, her wasted body within its loose brown graveclothes giving off an odour of wax and rosewood, her breath, that had bent upon him, mute, reproachful, a faint odour of wetted ashes" (*U*, 1.102–5). Stephen recalls, too, the ugly reality of her dying, "the green sluggish bile which she had torn up from her rotting liver by fits of loud groaning vomiting" (*U*, 1.109–10).

The rhythm of Stephen's prose in the dream-memory itself is strongly reminiscent of another dream-memory, which appears as epiphany 34 in Robert Scholes and Richard Kain's *Workshop of Daedalus*, and in which Stanislaus Joyce detected "the softening influence of Newman's prose" (*BK*, 230):

She comes at night when the city is still; invisible, inaudible, all unsummoned. She comes from her ancient seat to visit the least of her children, mother most venerable, as though he had never been alien to her. She knows the inmost heart; therefore she is gentle, nothing exacting; saying, I am susceptible of change, an imaginative influence in the hearts of my children. Who has pity for you when you are sad among strangers? Years and years I loved you when you lay in my womb. (44)

This dream-epiphany was recorded during Joyce's stay in Paris before his mother's death, a time when he was often "sad among strangers," and Stanislaus suggests that it may have been inspired by a letter from his mother in which "she had spoken comfortingly of her love for him when he was a child" (BK, 230). Whatever the rhetorical similarities between these two descriptive passages, the difference in the subject of the memory is obvious; it is the difference, after all, between life and death. The "mother most venerable" who visits her son in the Paris memory is still a living woman, whereas the specter in the dream recorded in Ulysses comes to him in death. In contrast to the comforting presence of the first dream, who "knows the inmost heart" and is therefore "gentle, nothing exacting," the dead mother of the second brings with her not only the odors of death but also a "mute" reproach. And when the dream recurs moments later in Stephen's mind, this reproach is made more frightening with Stephen's memory of "her glazing eyes, staring out of death, to shake and bend my soul" and "her hoarse loud breath rattling in horror" (U, 1.270–76). Both these dreams—both these mothers—find a place in "Circe" during Stephen's climactic confrontation with the apparition of "The Mother," who reminds him of her love in the words of the Paris epiphany—"Who had pity for you when you were sad among strangers? . . . Years and years I loved you, O, my son, my firstborn, when you lay in my womb" (U, 15.4197, 4204–5)—but who also threatens him with death and "the fire of hell" (U, 15.4182–83, 4212).

Whatever the horror in Stephen's dream or in his recall of the ugliness of his mother's dying, nothing quite prepares a reader for the violence of his response, and nothing in the text quite identifies the addressee for his "Ghoul! Chewer of corpses!" which could be himself or could be his mother, to whom he directs his plea for release: "No, mother! Let me be and let me live" (*U*, 1.278–79). But here in the opening pages of the novel Stephen identifies his fundamental existential problem—to free himself from his entanglement with his mother in order that he may "live."

Joyce's autobiographical impulse demands that the entrapping mother in *Ulysses* be dead, as Joyce's mother was on 16 June 1904, but the threat from the mother, alive or dead, is authenticated, though with different emphases, by both Sigmund Freud and C. G. Jung. Freud first, in his 1910 psychobiography of Leonardo, and then Jung, with his full-scale vision of "the loving and the terrible mother" in his 1912 *Transformations and Symbols of the Libido*, insist that the mother's love is an essential part of her threat to her son.

Freud on Leonardo's Mother

Leonardo was Freud's only full-scale venture into psychobiography, and it is a noteworthy irony that he should have focused in this study on Leonardo's mother as the determining figure in the artist's psychic destiny in the light of his theoretical insistence on the predominance of the father-son relationship. I have earlier examined the oblique echoing through much of *Ulysses* of Freud's identification of a "causal connection" between the excessive maternal tenderness in Leonardo's relationship with his mother in childhood and "his later manifest, if ideal homosexuality" (*L*, 98).[1] Aside from this specific connection between the mother and homosexuality, Freud's vision of Leonardo's mother, as she is reflected in Leonardo's work, blends the mother's loving concern with a half-hidden threat, a blend that prepares the way for Joyce's reception of Jung's "dual mother"—loving and terrible. And both contribute to Joyce's presentation of Stephen's mother.

From Leonardo's childhood memory of the "vulture phantasy," in which the vulture "struck me many times with its tail against my lips," Freud infers that Leonardo is stressing "the intensity of the erotic relations between mother and child." "The phantasy," Freud notes, "is compounded from the memory of being suckled and being kissed by his mother" (*L*, 107), a compound that is, as I have noted in chapter 2, oddly reflected in *A Portrait*. We may remember the child Stephen's anxious debate with himself about whether it was right or wrong to kiss his mother (*P,* 14–15) and his examination of the idea of *kiss,* which parallels his earlier examination of the word *suck.* In both these childish analyses there is a sound—"ugly" in the case of *suck* and "loud" as he hears it in the dirty water draining out of the basin at the Wicklow Hotel (*P,* 11)—but "a tiny little noise" that accompanies a kiss (*P,* 15). A nursing baby also makes a "tiny little noise," so that *kiss* and *suckle* are—with some complexity, to be sure—merged as they are in Freud's *Leonardo.* By the end of *A Portrait,* however, Stephen's response to Cranly's tribute to a mother's love is, by allusion at least, clearly negative: "Pascal, if I remember rightly, would not suffer his mother to kiss him as he feared the contact of her sex" (*P,* 242).

Noting the importance of the mouth in the "vulture phantasy," Freud moves on to the "remarkable smile" in Leonardo's *Mona Lisa,* a smile that "has produced the most powerful and confusing effect on whoever looks at it" (*L,* 107) and one that Leonardo repeated in "all the faces that he painted or drew afterwards" (*L,* 110). Freud quotes Walter Pater, a source that Joyce also found useful in *Ulysses,*[2] who, Freud says, "writes very sensitively of 'the unfathomable smile, always with a touch of something sinister in it, which plays over all Leonardo's work.'" Freud, seeking in Leonardo's life the "deeper reason" for this almost compulsive repetition, not surprisingly finds it there, and he draws again on Pater for confirmation. For Pater speculates that this image springs from Leonardo's childhood, "defining itself on the fabric of his dreams," a supposition that Freud feels "deserves to be taken literally" (*L,* 110–11).

To be sure, Freud has little hard evidence about the facts of Leonardo's childhood, but he speculates that for the "critical first years of his life" Leonardo, an illegitimate child, lived with his mother, Caterina, a "poor peasant woman of Vinci" (*L,* 91, 105), his father having married "a lady of good birth" the same year that Leonardo was born. His father's marriage was childless, and after an unknown length of time Leonardo was taken from Caterina and brought up in his father's household, at least from the age of five, according to Freud's sources. "It fits in best with the interpretation of the vulture phantasy," Freud acknowledges, "if at least three years of Leonardo's life, and perhaps five, had elapsed before he could exchange the solitary person of his mother for a parental couple. And by then," Freud concludes, "it was too late" (*L,* 91). A lifelong pattern had been set for Leonardo.

The "double meaning" of Mona Lisa's smile, which contained, Freud asserts, "the promise of unbounded tenderness and at the same time sinister menace (to quote Pater's phrase)" harks back once again to the "vulture phantasy."

> For his mother's tenderness was fateful for him; it determined his destiny and the privations that were in store for him. The violence of the caresses, to which his phantasy of the vulture points, was only too natural. In her love for her child the poor forsaken mother had to give vent to all her memories of the caresses she had enjoyed as well as her longing for new ones. . . . So, like all unsatisfied mothers, she took her little son in place of her husband, and by the too early maturing of his erotism robbed him of a part of his masculinity. (*L*, 115–17)

Joyce had added Freud's *Leonardo* to his personal library well before he entered into the seven creative years in Trieste, Zurich, and Paris (1914–1921) that produced *Ulysses*. And Freud's vision of this supreme artist's loving mother, as well as the paradoxical threat from that love, must surely have struck a familiar chord in Joyce, the acknowledged favorite of his mother, whose death had left him, like Stephen Dedalus, "alone for ever in the dark ways of my bitterness" (*U*, 14.379). Joyce was thus familiar with the notion of the ambiguity of mother love before he met another version of it in Jung's *Transformations and Symbols of the Libido* some time after he moved to Zurich in 1915.

The Mother in Jung's *Transformations*

Like much of the early psychoanalytic literature, *Transformations* was first published in a journal, the first part in volume 3 of the *Yearbook* (1911) and the second part in volume 4 (1912). Since the Zurich library did not acquire the 1912 volume published by Deuticke until after Joyce had left Zurich in 1919, it was most likely that he saw Jung's *Transformations* as it appeared in the journal.[3] During the period that Jung was writing the book, he was in the midst of the personal and professional upheaval that would lead to his break with Freud and the psychoanalytic movement (See Kimball, *Odyssey*, 24–33). *Transformations* is often identified as a source for that break,[4] although John Kerr has suggested that the work is instead a *result* of the accumulation of disagreements that led finally to the break. Kerr points to the "lack of clarity" in the "hodgepodge of different ideas" as evidence of Jung's emotional upset when he wrote the book ("Beyond the Pleasure Principle," 48). Indeed, in 1950, more than thirty-five years after the first publication of *Transformations*, when Jung finally revised the work and retitled it *Symbols of Transformation*, he acknowledged that the original, "born under such conditions, consisted of larger or smaller fragments which I could only string together in an unsatisfying manner" (*CW*, 5:xxiii–xxiv).

Since Joyce's appropriations from other works tend to be fragments rather than overarching ideas, such lack of scientific rigor and even of basic rhetorical structure could have been no impediment to his response to this emotionally charged work. Indeed quite explicit echoes of *Transformations* can be detected in parts of *Ulysses* written before Joyce left Zurich and his library resources there. I do not mean to claim that Joyce had carefully read and analyzed *Transformations*; I doubt that he had. But his analogical intuition was extraordinary, and he was notably proficient at skimming, so that even fragments that he may select from Jung's work tend to fit where he places them. In "Scylla and Charybdis," for example, Stephen's ambiguous inner comment as he prepares to leave the library with Mulligan at the close of the episode—"My will: his will that fronts me. Seas between" (*U*, 9.1202)—echoes a phrase in Jung's discussion of "coitus play" among primitive peoples, which he interprets as an acting out of "an internal resistance; will opposes will; libido opposes libido" (*PU*, 171).

To be sure, this verbal echo, as I am calling it, is not a direct quotation, and it brings no significant thematic context with it; it is just an attractive phrase that fits where Joyce puts it.[5] But echoes from Jung's development of the threat from "the loving and the terrible mother" have a quite different weight in the thematic structure of the novel. By the time Joyce was working on the climactic encounter between mother and son in "Circe," of course, he had left Zurich and its library for Trieste, which perhaps explains his complaint in a 1919 letter to Frank Budgen that Ottocaro Weiss, whom Joyce already held responsible for Edith Rockefeller McCormick's withdrawal of financial support (*JJII*, 467–69), had reneged on a promise to send him Jung's "Wandlungen der LIBIDO" (*SL*, 244). Joyce's tone is derisive, but his mention of Jung's work is surely not wholly casual. Indeed I know of no other psychoanalytic work that Joyce ever mentioned by title in correspondence or in reported conversation.

The heightened irritation in his mention of Jung's book, in fact, prompted Budgen to record his puzzlement at his friend's "big grouse about not getting that book he was promised—*Wandlungen der Libido*" (*Myselves*, 200).

But "that book," which is an extensively amplified examination of a patient's fantasies, is strikingly relevant to the thematic structures of *Ulysses*. Providing an "archetypal context" for these fantasies, over half its pages are devoted to a mythologically tinged account of the archetypal hero's "battle" to free his creative energy, the "libido," from its entanglement in the mother, an endeavor that is analogous to the struggle of the artist-hero in *Ulysses* to free himself from his dead mother. This psychic project, in fact, which Leonardo, in Freud's reconstruction of his development, was too passive to attempt, defines Stephen's story on Bloomsday, reaching its climax in "Circe" when he confronts the hallucination of The Mother.

Although Joyce does not mention "Circe" in his letter to Budgen, he had already begun to compose the episode before he left Zurich, motivated, according to Budgen, by a visit in the Spring of 1919 to a twentieth-century Circe at Locarno, who gave him "a packet of letters and a valise of books on the theme of erotic perversion" (*James Joyce*, 240–41). And the earliest known draft of the episode, which included the essentials of the encounter with The Mother, was written, according to Phillip Herring, "during Joyce's post-World War I stay in Trieste" (October 1919 to July 1920).[6] It is thus reasonable to suppose that when Joyce wrote to Budgen, the materials for "Circe" were coming together in his mind, both in the way of conscious planning and in whatever mysterious ways the unconscious works in this process. Jung's work on the "mother-complex"[7] has associations that clearly could serve Joyce's purposes, so his irritation at its not being available to him has an understandable basis.

In this work, Jung shifted from the typically Freudian emphasis on the father that characterized his 1909 essay in Joyce's Trieste library to a focus on the mother's influence on the development of her son, an influence that Jung, like Freud before him, pictured as in some ways harmful. The bulk of Jung's melodramatic account of the archetypal hero's psychic struggle with "the loving and the terrible mother" appears in part 2 under chapter headings that signal this focus: "Symbolism of the Mother and Rebirth," "The Battle for Deliverance from the Mother," "The Dual Mother Role," and "The Sacrifice."

Jung, however, announces the thematically significant threat from the mother in his introductory chapter during a discussion of Freud's theoretical use of the Oedipus legend. Even "in the schoolroom," Jung says, "one could scarcely repress a skeptical smile when one indiscreetly reckoned the comfortable matronly age of Penelope and the age of Jocasta, and comically compared the result of the reckoning with the tragic-erotic struggles in the legend and drama."[8] The linking of Penelope with Jocasta is not explained by the context of Jung's discussion, but it should certainly have been noticed by an author who had embarked on a modern epic named *Ulysses*.

The only immediately apparent connection between the two legendary women is that both were mothers, and Jung points out that what the child in the schoolroom did not know was that "the mother can be the all-consuming passion of the son, which perhaps undermines his whole life and tragically destroys it" (*PU*, 4). The dire potentiality suggested by Jung sets up resonances with Freud's outline of Leonardo's destructive relationship with his mother, and we may be reminded that when Jung first read *Leonardo*, he not only pronounced it "wonderful," but admitted to Freud that "it is the first essay of yours with whose inner development I felt perfectly in tune from the start" (McGuire, 198J, 329). And Jung winds up his introductory chapter with a reference to the Leonardo essay and the "masterly manner" of Freud's analysis of Leonardo's individual "psychologic problems" (*PU*, 7).

Freud's analysis, as noted before, presents Leonardo's mother, not as the disputed object of desire in the oedipal triangle, but as a threat to her son's full sexual development, specifically, a threat to his escape from the limitations of homosexuality into a heterosexual relationship. And this threat from the mother echoes and re-echoes in *Ulysses*. Jung's presentation of the maternal threat, on the other hand, ignores the homoerotic aspect of sexual development, highlighting instead the threat that the loving, enveloping mother presents to psychic maturity in a much wider sense. In addition, whereas Freud offers support for his analysis in Leonardo's personal and cultural history, Jung's presentation depends basically on comparative mythology.

He thus provides in his text baleful mythological identifications for the terrible mother, equating her with the Sphinx, the "fear animal" (*PU*, 204); with the "great whore" of Revelation (17.1–5), the "mother of all abominations" (*PU*, 241–42); and with Hecate, who, "as nightmare, appears . . . in a vampire role, or as Lamia, the devourer of men" (*PU*, 405). His descriptions of her are consistently melodramatic, and a number are particularly fearsome in the original German: the mother is not only "terrible" (*furchtbar, schrecklich* [*PU*, 202, 427])[9] but also "devouring" (*verschlingend* [*PU*, 364]), a "malicious pursuer" (*heimtückischen Verfolgerin* [*PU*, 335]), a "death-bringing demon" (*totbringenden Dämon* [*PU*, 388]), and "the mother of death" (*Todesmutter* [*PU*, 396]).

To be sure, the mother has another face: the "nourishing [*ernährend*] mother," the "smiling love- and life-giving mother" (*die lächelnde liebe- und lebenspendende Mutter* [*PU*, 427]). But this loving mother poses an equally drastic threat to the developing son. For his energy, Jung says, is "paralyzed" by the "consuming poison of the stealthy retrospective longing" for the loving mother (*PU*, 427). This is melodramatic language indeed, but the contradictory image of the loving and the terrible mother, the mother of life and the mother of death, is consistently a feature—a melodramatic feature—in the appearances of Stephen's mother throughout the novel. And nowhere is the terrible mother more terrible than in the climactic confrontation between mother and son in "Circe," where identifiable traces from Freud and Jung, as they have already been incorporated in the text of *Ulysses,* come together in Stephen's encounter with The Mother.

Confrontation with The Mother

Like all the encounters in "Circe," the confrontation between Stephen and his mother appears to operate in accord with Freud's outline of the dreamwork, condensing and distorting conscious events of the day. In "Telemachus," as has been said, Stephen's relationship with Mulligan is played against Stephen's obsession with his mother, and in "Circe" it is Mulligan, *"in particoloured jester's dress,"* who *"stands gaping at her"* and announces, "Mulligan meets the afflicted mother" (*U*, 15.4166–70), even as he has introduced Stephen's mother into the novel in the opening pages with his comment, "The aunt thinks you killed your mother" (*U*, 1.88). And the echoes from "Telemachus" are thick as Mulligan repeats his pronouncement, so offensive to Stephen (*U*, 1.198–99, 15.4187) that "She's beastly dead" (*U*, 15.4170) and directly accuses Stephen in her death. He repeats in "Circe" epithets he has used for Stephen in the morning—"Kinch" and "dogsbody" (*U*, 1.55, 112). He also repeats his comment on "the mockery" of Stephen's rejection of his proffered loan of a "lovely pair" of grey trousers because of the bereaved son's insistence on wearing black. And again he produces his figure of the sea as mother (*U*, 1.122, 80). "The mockery of it! Kinch dogsbody killed her bitchbody. . . . Our great sweet mother! *Epi oinopa ponton*" (*U*, 15.4178–80).

These explicit verbal correspondences between "Telemachus" and "Circe" reinforce the pattern throughout the novel that echoes Freud's speculations about the link between Leonardo's mother and his homosexuality. For Stephen's relationship to his mother, like his relationship to Mulligan, is an obstacle to his full development, to his making a life. And the pattern in *Ulysses* of Stephen's obsession with his dead mother, lightened at times by tenderness, but progressively darkened by fear, anger, and guilt about the relationship, clearly picks up on Freud's presentation of the threat from the mother in Leonardo's development even as it parallels Jung's description in *Transformations and Symbols of the Libido* of the archetypal hero's intensely ambivalent relationship with the "loving and the terrible mother," who is introduced in Jung's chapter on "The Unconscious Origins of the Hero" (*PU*, 196, 202).

In his melodramatic recital of the course of this relationship, Jung documents the dangerous power of the mother, making clear that the crucial problem is the son's refusal to give up his infantile personality, his childhood and the loving, nurturing mother at its center. Through this refusal, he cripples himself in his development toward adulthood, at the same time that he shifts all the blame for this failure onto the mother. The mother thus, because of the son's anxiety about his own failure, *becomes* "terrible" for him, "a spectre of anxiety, a nightmare" (*PU*, 267), indeed "the symbol of death" (*PU*, 346).

This same kind of intense ambivalence attaches itself to all of Stephen's memories of his mother, starting in "Telemachus" with the recall of his recurring dream of his mother in her "loose brown graveclothes" (*U*, 1.103–4). This memory, which draws from him his plea for release—"let me live"—reminds us that the mother of the hero in Jung's account, whose "garment is the garment of death" (*PU*, 385), appears to her son as a "malicious pursuer" (*PU*, 335). But the extended image of the mother as the symbol of the terrors of death in the opening episode is set off against the equally extended image of the mother as the giver and sustainer of life in "Nestor," the episode that follows.

Stephen's vision of his dead mother in "Telemachus" brings from him the most dramatic evocation of the terrible mother in *Ulysses*: "Ghoul! Chewer of corpses!" (*U*, 1.278). This cry suggests the "deep animosity" that Jung attributes to the son in the archetypal situation (*PU*, 267), and the rejection expressed in it is emphatically confirmed in "Circe" at the appearance of The Mother. The initial vision of the terrible mother in "Telemachus," however, is immediately counterbalanced in "Nestor" by the case Stephen makes for "*amor matris*," the son's relation to the nurturing mother, as possibly "the only true thing in life." Stephen's interior presentation of the mother who shelters and nourishes her son with her body, her blood, her "wheysour milk," who saves him from "being trampled underfoot" by the outside world (*U*, 2.141–47, 165–66), echoes Jung's emphasis on the nurturing, nourishing, and protecting qualities of the "good" aspect of the dual mother imago (*PU*, 387).

The pattern of alternation between the loving and terrible aspects of the mother, established in the first two episodes of *Ulysses*, is reprised in snatches of memory any time Stephen's mother appears in the text.[10] But in "Oxen of the Sun," the birth chapter, Stephen declares his release from the mother's threat through his proposed appropriation, as an artist, of her creative power: "In woman's womb word is made flesh, but in the spirit of the maker all flesh that passes becomes the word that shall not pass away. This is the postcreation" (*U*, 14.292–94). Like a number of "young Boasthard's" declarations in "Oxen of the Sun," Stephen's arrogant pronouncement has no discernible prospect of immediate realization, but it marks the end of a conscious development. Pursued throughout the day by memories of his mother in death and in life, Stephen has moved from his desolation of the morning, coupled with his inner plea to his mother to release him—"Let me be and let me live"—to this declaration of purpose at the maternity hospital. And this declaration leaps beyond the not-yet-accomplished release to his claim to a creative power that surpasses that of the mother.

In "Circe," then, The Mother confronts Stephen directly, costumed indeed in this "costume episode" (Budgen, *James Joyce*, 228) and lavishly made up as well, *as* the "terrible mother," in her "leper grey," with her "bluecircled hollow eyesockets" in her "noseless" face, "green with gravemould" (*U*, 15.4156–60). And here in the brothel, the release from the mother, which is necessary for him to become the godlike creator of his proclamation, is accomplished in the unconscious, which is the ruling principle of "Circe."

Again in agreement with Freud's insistence on the place of day residues in dream formation, the dialogue between mother and son basically reprises Stephen's encounters with her memory through the day, more or less distorted, but maintaining the same odd balance between the loving and the terrible mother that is characteristic of the conscious memories. For though The Mother delivers a message of death—"All must go through it, Stephen. . . . You too" (*U*, 15.4182–83)—she retains powerful intimations of the loving mother. She answers Stephen's request for "the word known to all men," for example, with a selection from Stephen's own musings about *amor matris:* "Who saved you. . . . Who had pity for you . . . ?" (*U*, 15.4192–96, 2.141–47). But when she calls for Stephen's repentance, she becomes for him "The ghoul! Hyena!" (*U*, 15.4198–200), echoing his cry of the morning and introducing the first animal image associated with The Mother in this "animal episode" (Budgen, *James Joyce*, 228).

"Illustrated Hallucinations"

And here a third psychoanalytic intertext contributes to the effect of the climactic encounter between Stephen and his mother in "Circe": a case study of a schizophrenic young woman reported to the local Psychoanalytic Association by a now obscure Zurich psychiatrist, Dr. H. Bertschinger, and published, with the title "Illustrated Hallucinations," in the 1911 *Yearbook*, volume 3. Appended to the article is an editor's note (100), signed by Jung, referring the reader to his own work in the same issue—part 1 of *Transformations*—for "a complete presentation" of the "half and mixed-beings" in the drawings that illustrate Bertschinger's report (Bertschinger, 100). Part 2 of Jung's *Transformations* appeared in the 1912 issue, volume 4. It seems reasonable to suppose that Joyce came across Jung and Bertschinger at the same time in the 1911 issue and went on to the next issue of the *Jahrbuch* to dip into the second part of Jung's work, in which Jung introduces the contradictory image of "the loving and the terrible mother," a concept already familiar to Joyce through Freud's monograph on Leonardo.

After Joyce had left Zurich, Bertschinger's article, like Jung's *Transformations*, was accessible to him only through memory, though the hallucinations sketched by Bertschinger's patient, with their sadomasochistic tendencies, were surely close enough to the erotic materials given to him by the Locarno Circe to be at least susceptible to unconscious assimilation. These sketches might well have merged also in Joyce's mind with Jung's melodramatic story of the hero and his mother, already mingled with Freud's original suggestion of the threat from the loving mother. They thus contribute a visual dimension to the intertextual mix in the final confrontation with The Mother in "Circe," producing a dreamlike condensation of the psychoanalytic context for Stephen's flight from the mother throughout the novel.

Bertschinger's patient was a twenty-eight-year-old woman, possibly schizophrenic, with a "pronounced fondness for trauma" (82), who regularly fell into "hypnoidal states," during which she "hallucinated vividly." Unwilling or unable to give the psychiatrist any information about the hallucinations, she was prevailed upon to draw what was happening during her trancelike episodes, and she could then explain the drawings when she returned to her more nearly normal condition (70–72). Bertschinger's article in the *Yearbook* was strikingly illustrated with twenty-nine sketches (out of over 100) of the strange animal/human figures that his patient had drawn to illustrate her hallucinations, but Dr. Bertschinger eventually concluded that what the patient related to him as real experiences were an amalgam of "extraordinary sadomasochistic phantasies," drawn from "everything that she might have read or heard of ghastly, strange, gruesome, and bloodthirsty murder and sexual stories" (93).

Among the "illustrated hallucinations" in Bertschinger's 1911 article is the hyena woman in figure 4.1, herself a death-dealing mother, drawn by Bertschinger's patient to illustrate a hallucination whose deepest source was her memory—or pseudomemory—of watching a servant girl in a polka dot blouse (hence the "spotted hyena") bury what appeared to be her newborn child in a coal cellar. Discovered by the maid, the eleven-year-old girl perceived herself threatened by the combination hammer and pickax, which the woman in the drawing holds, and screamed "in deathly fear" (Bertschinger, 79–80). The mother of death, the threat, and the fear that are illustrated in the sketch are all a part of Stephen's encounter with The Mother, whom he acknowledges as "The ghoul! Hy-

Fig. 4.1. Hyena Woman

ena!" (*U*, 15.4200). And as the apparition in "Circe" continues to offer assurances of her loving concern—"Get Dilly to make you that boiled rice. . . . Years and years I loved you" (*U*, 15.4202–3)—her simultaneous threat of the "fire of hell" brings from him the cry, "Corpsechewer!" (*U*, 15.4212–14), completing the echo in "Circe" of his rejection in "Telemachus": "Ghoul! Chewer of corpses!" (*U*, 1.278).

Up to this point in the encounter with The Mother, although mother and son speak to one another, like Odysseus and his mother in Hades, they do not touch. But with Stephen's frantic rejection of The Mother's final demand for repentance, a crab appears, and mother and son touch through the crab. This *"green crab with malignant red eyes,"* though apparently autonomous and freestanding, so to speak, is nevertheless mysteriously, ambiguously attached to The Mother, who *"raises her blackened withered right arm slowly towards Stephen's breast with outstretched finger,"* saying, "Beware God's hand!" as the crab *"sticks deep its grinning claws in Stephen's heart"* (*U*, 15.4218–21). This crab, unlike the earlier animal image, the hyena, is an actual presence for Stephen, and whatever its literal connections with the disease that has killed Stephen's mother—"Cancer did it, not I" (*U*, 15.4187)—it has all the earmarks of an archetypal creature from the murky depths of his unconscious.

And just such a crab appears in a dream reported by Jung in his chapter on "Symbolism of the Mother and of Rebirth," explicitly connected, as is Stephen's, to a strong attachment to a dead mother (*PU*, 275–76). The

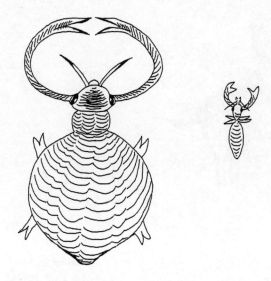

Fig. 4.2. Crab Figures

crab-dream is only briefly explained in the 1912 volume, but Jung's 1917 "Psychology of the Unconscious Processes," also available in the Zurich library, includes a full-scale amplification and interpretation of this same dream—especially of the archetypal crab image[11]—which is significantly relevant to Stephen's hallucination. In Jung's analysis of the crab-dream, he points out that, besides the association with cancer (the cause of death for both mothers and in German, of course, the same word—*Krebs*) the crab is "an animal that walks backwards" (418–19), connecting this characteristic with the dreamer's "overpowering infantile craving" for love (423), naturally associated with the mother, a craving that surely finds an echo in Stephen's remarks about mother love as "the only true thing in life." The crab is thus not a representation of the mother herself or of her memory, but a fact of the dreamer's own psyche, as it is for Stephen, I think: "a symbol of the unconscious contents" (425) that pull the dreamer backwards.

Jung notes the similarity of this crab-dream to "the typical combat of the hero with the monster" (436), which he considers in some detail in *Transformations* in connection with the Siegfried legend (*PU*, 392–410), that is, with Siegfried's combat with Fafnir, the "cave dragon." Not surprisingly Jung equates Fafnir with the terrible mother (*PU*, 396 n. 67,

548) who guards the "incomparable treasure" of the son's libido, so that the son is forced to do battle with the mother-dragon in order to gain this "source of life and power" (*PU,* 397). The crab, in Jung's dream analysis, is thus another manifestation of the "mother-dragon," and so it is for Stephen. As his confrontation with The Mother in "Circe" draws to a close, his hallucinated crab appears to turn into a dragon through an allusion to Siegfried. For, as Stephen lifts his ashplant over his head, he calls out the name of Siegfried's sword—"*Nothung!*" (*U,* 15.4242). This is the sword Siegfried used to slay Fafnir, a sword that Jung, in his discussion of the Siegfried legend, equates with "the word, or the procreative Logos" (*PU,* 393). And with his ashplant-turned-sword, Stephen prepares to slay the mother-crab-turned-dragon, thus acting out his claim in the maternity hospital for the ultimate victory of the artist's word over mortality, the "flesh that passes," which is the domain of the mother.

Stephen's crab is not visible to others, and his dragon is not necessarily visible even to him, but I suspect that both have been visualized by Joyce. For both these creatures were sketched by Bertschinger's patient to illustrate her hallucinations during an extended trancelike state, lasting several days. These hallucinations were connected once again with motherhood and death, since their ultimate source was the patient's "memory" of an abortion, ritualistically performed by gypsies (Bertschinger, 87). During her vision of "a bloody animal battle of death," she saw a "great red crab," which she sketched in two versions (90; figure 4.2). This crab, "quite red with rage, struggled with the snake which lay rolled up on her heart" (89).

To be sure, Stephen's crab is green, possibly a link with the "green rill of bile" associated with his dying mother, though its "malignant" eyes are red. But the locus of the crab's attack—the heart—is the same for Bertschinger's patient as for Stephen. And though the young woman's description of her hallucination includes nothing about the eyes of the crab, they are extraordinarily prominent in both crab drawings, while the "grinning claws," a distinctive detail in Stephen's vision, are also a striking feature of both these sketches.

The "hostile dragon" in figure 4.3, drawn during the same trance that produced the crab, represents a composite of all the animals Bertschinger's patient had seen in the "bloody battle" of her hallucination. A close examination reveals that the dragon has the tongue of a snake, the eyes of a horse or donkey, the head of a bull, the ears of a billy goat,

Fig. 4.3. Dragon Figure

the horns of a ram, the tail of a fish, and the body of a dragon itself. Bertschinger calls this dragon "the sexual animal," which puts together the animals from all the other "sado-masochistic phantasies," which the patient had related to him over the months as real experiences. The patient herself, however, called it "the mother of the devil" (95–96) and provided a sketch of the devil with a snake in his hand (figure 4.4). And even though the dragon that Stephen slays in "Circe" is a creature of his own psyche, it is identified in the text of *Ulysses* in a most literal way with "the mother of the devil."

For the horrible apparition with whom both crab and dragon are associated remains, for the reader and for Stephen himself, Stephen's mother, whatever her textual metamorphoses, and Stephen, not for the first time in *Ulysses* (compare *U*, 3.486), identifies himself with the devil. "Strangled with rage" (*U*, 15.4223) in the wake of the crabmother's attack, he delivers Lucifer's famous line, which he has already made his own in *A Portrait of the Artist as a Young Man*. "*Ah non, par exemple!*" he cries. "The intellectual imagination! With me all or not at all. *Non serviam!*" (*U*, 15.4227–28; *P*, 239).[12] And it is in this Luciferian identity that he slays the dragon-mother. Of course, Stephen's ashplant does not touch crab, dragon, or mother; as it turns out, it hardly even damages the chandelier (*U*, 15.4284–91). But Stephen's blow is followed in the text by the annihilation of time and space (*U*, 15.4243–45) and by the disappearance of the mother from *Ulysses*.

Mulligan, associated throughout with Stephen's mother, also disappears from Stephen's life. He represents throughout the quasi-loving, family-denying relationship of male to male that, like the outgrown relationship of child to mother, Stephen must abandon in order to become a man and an artist. The relationship with Mulligan threatens to nullify the family continuity that Stephen sees as critical for the development of Shakespeare (and, by extension, for himself) as an artist.[13] In "Telemachus" he has vowed, "I will not sleep here tonight" (*U*, 1.739–40). In "Proteus," he has identified the nature of his relationship with Mulligan: "Wilde's love that dare not speak its name. His arm: Cranly's arm. He now will leave me. And the blame? As I am. As I am. All or not at all" (*U*, 3.451–52).[14] And in "Scylla and Charybdis" he has told himself, "Part. The moment is now" (*U*, 9.1199).

Nothing has decisively changed at any of these points, but as Stephen rushes out of the brothel following his "slaying" of The Mother, Mulligan is supplanted by Bloom, who takes over the direction of Stephen's life. Bloom settles with Bella, retrieves Stephen's ashplant, and, "Incog Haroun Al Raschid," follows him out of the brothel and watches over him preparatory to taking him home (*U*, 15.4268–956). Here in "Circe," Stephen has, in Jung's vocabulary, "sacrificed" his mother for his future growth, and when he does, the stage is set for his rebirth.

Fig. 4.4. Devil Figure

For Jung equates the "separation from the mother-imago"—and this does happen for Stephen in "Circe"—with "the birth out of one's self" (*PU*, 337), an event that also occurs in the text of *Ulysses*. Even before his confrontation with The Mother, Stephen has announced his birthday as "Thursday. Today" (*U*, 15.3685). Toward the end of "Circe," then, after he collapses outside the brothel, he first lies with "his face to the sky" (*U*, 15.4748–49), then shifts into a foetal position, "doubling himself together" (*U*, 15.4934), the text says, and "curl[ing] his body" (*U*, 15.4944), as he prepares—in the text at least—for rebirth, a rebirth that is textually accomplished midway through "Ithaca" when he leaves Bloom's garden. For when Bloom unlocks the garden gate for Stephen, Joyce uses an image that suggests the entire birth process, from conception through reproduction: the "male key," that is, is inserted into "an unstable female lock," thus opening "an unhinged door and revealing an aperture for free egress and free ingress" (*U*, 17.1215–19). Stephen's future, as he walks through that door, is, like any newborn's, highly problematic, but he has accomplished a crucial developmental task. Like the archetypal hero of Jung's *Transformations*, he has done battle with the loving and terrible mother, an image that has its roots in Freud's *Leonardo*, and he has won his deliverance.

The "Viennese View" Beyond Oedipus

Rank's *Incest Motif*

The major relationships in Freud's theoretical Oedipus complex—the son's relationship to father and to mother—thus enter *Ulysses* through Joyce's appropriation of textual fragments and even ideas from the two dominant figures in the early psychoanalytic movement, Sigmund Freud and C. G. Jung. These traces are combined, as is characteristic for Joyce, with fragments from a range of other intertexts, and clearly psychoanalytic traces in this lavishly allusive novel extend well beyond the single allusion identified by Thornton to "the new Viennese school Mr Magee spoke of" (*U*, 9.780). This one allusion, however, points to what was a fact, that the incest motif was central to Freud's theory and to the psychoanalytic movement. To be sure, Stephen's contrast between the view of this school on incest and Saint Thomas's view is murky. Thornton (*Allusions*, 199) is unable to locate even a probable source for Stephen's allusion in Saint Thomas's writings, and in 1904 there *was* no "Viennese school." At this time the nearest thing to a school was the small group that met on Wednesday night and called themselves the Psychological Wednesday Society.[1] With this thoroughly questionable and clearly anachronistic allusion, however, Joyce has provided a characteristic footnote, which in all probability points to Otto Rank's 1912 *Das Inzest-motiv in Dichtung und Sage*, surely the most comprehensive exposition imaginable of the application to literature of the early psychoanalytic view of incest—incest as an unconscious impulse rather than as a conscious act.

In this monumental psychoanalytic classic, Rank, one of the earliest, most creative, and most industrious of Freud's disciples, traces variations on the incest motif in literature from Homer and the Old Testament up through Ibsen, focusing primarily on three dramas—Sophocles' *Oedipus*

Rex, William Shakespeare's *Hamlet*, and Friedrich von Schiller's *Don Carlos*—as they exemplify the increasingly strong cultural inhibition against clear expression of the motif. Freud assigned "first place" to Rank's *Incest Motif* "among the strictly scientific applications of analysis to literature" (*SE*, 14:37), a judgment that remains valid today, according to Peter Rudnytsky. Rank's range of reference, Rudnytsky asserts in his introduction to the 1992 English translation of the work, "is so vast as to defy summation"; indeed, "in its encyclopedic erudition, interpretative brilliance, and theoretical cogency," Rank's *Incest Motif* remains "the greatest and most important single work of psychoanalytic literary criticism."[2]

Rivaling *Ulysses* itself in bulk and erudition, *The Incest Motif* is divided into two parts: "The Relationship between Parents and Children" and "The Relationship between Siblings." It is lavishly provided not only with chapter titles and subtitles but also with page headings, and thus it is remarkably adapted to skimming, at which we must assume that Joyce was remarkably adept. In the chapter titled "Shakespeare's Father Complex: On the Psychology of Theatrical Performance," for example, we may cite two successive page headings that are clearly relevant to Stephen's argument in *Ulysses*—"The Significance of the Ghost's Appearance in *Hamlet*" and "The Psychology of the Dramatic Performance." The material under these headings concerns the whole problem of the double identity of son and father as well as Rank's view of the Ghost as a "compromise expression" of the son's ambivalent feelings (*Incest Theme*, 185–88), a significant feature in Stephen's presentation as well.

Joyce and Rank share a tendency toward prolixity, even redundance, so that any comparison between their texts must necessarily be selective if it is to be manageable. The examination of textual parallels in this chapter is thus for the most part limited to the Shakespeare material in Rank's *Incest Motif*, even more specifically to this chapter on Shakespeare's father complex, in which Rank's applications of psychoanalytic theory to specific situations in Shakespeare's life and his dramatic productions are peculiarly congruent with the theory that Stephen proposes in *Ulysses*. Distinctive features of Rank's commentary on Shakespeare are echoed in the *Hamlet* theory that Joyce filters through Stephen in "Scylla and Charybdis," which, like Rank's chapter on Shakespeare, focuses on the relationship between Shakespeare's life and his work. Rank's elaboration of parallel points, in fact, often provides a clarifying context for Stephen's remarks and sometimes completes the thought for a poetically condensed statement.[3]

Over and above such textual parallels, some general observations are in order. Rank's central interest is, like Stephen's, in the psychology of the creator rather than in literary history, and he takes for granted, as does Stephen, that literary creations are intimately connected with the artist's biography. Thus, my examination of parallels between the text in *Ulysses* and Rank's *Incest Motif* rays out into autobiographical connections as well as the Shakespearean material that is the subject of both texts. I recognize the hazard of a diffusion of focus, but this multiplication of connections is almost uniquely characteristic of Joyce, and some such diffusion is possibly inevitable if we are to deal with Joyce's text on his terms.

In the 1912 edition of his *Incest Motif,* Rank accepts absolutely Freud's insistence on the Oedipus complex "as the touchstone of psychoanalytic truth" (Rudnytsky, xii),[4] although his emphases are somewhat different from those of the orthodox pattern. For example, as Norman Holland has pointed out, of the two axiomatic components of the Oedipal wish—first, to kill the father and second, to possess the mother—Rank, especially in his interpretation of *Hamlet,* focuses on the first, with considerably less concern for the other wish to possess the mother (Holland, 167). This emphasis also characterizes Stephen's presentation, especially in his extended commentary on the father-son relationship, which I have examined above in chapter 3.

Underlying Rank's discussion of Shakespeare and *Hamlet* is the assumption that the artist is distinguished from the average man by the intensity, even violence, of his instinctual life, at the center of which is the incest complex. It is this "regular psychic disposition of the poet" that accounts for the ubiquity of the incest theme in the works of the great poets of world literature. The heightened intensity of the artist's unconscious impulses requires correspondingly greater repression to contain them, but leads to much higher possibilities for sublimation—*if* the artist's gifts are great enough. An artistic temperament that cannot produce an art work ends in neurosis; the artist's creation thus saves him from neurosis or paralysis.[5] Shakespeare, who, Rank assumes, experienced serious conflict in his relationship with his father, treats "the father-complex" over and over again, throughout his work (*IM,* 205 n. 1;

Incest Theme, 166). Only in *Hamlet,* however, has he represented the whole range of the incest complex: "along with the son-relationship to the father and mother, also the father-daughter complex (Polonius-Ophelia) and the sister-complex (Laertes-Ophelia)[6] with that of the hostile brother (Hamlet's father and Claudius)" (*IM,* 223 n. 2; *Incest Theme,* 180–81).

It is notable that Stephen mentions all of Shakespeare's family in his *Hamlet* presentation: wife, son, father, mother, sister, brothers, daughters, and granddaughter. William Schutte argues that Stephen "is so anxious to present his thoughts on fatherhood, to him the strongest of family relationships, that he introduces [the other family members] gratuitously into his presentation. They have only a peripheral relationship to his main argument" (90). It would be a mistake, I think, to dismiss any part of the theory out of hand as peripheral, and it must be recognized that fatherhood necessarily implies a range of family relationships. It is generally acknowledged that the incest motif is much more than incidental in *Finnegans Wake,* where it extends beyond the basic Oedipal triangle,[7] but this motif also plays a more varied and significant role in *Ulysses* than has sometimes been supposed, and the correspondences between theoretical observations in Rank's *Incest Motif* and the *Hamlet* theory in *Ulysses* suggest that Joyce may well have been conscious of this role.

Father, Son, and Ghost

Stephen's set-piece on Shakespeare is introduced by John Eglinton's announcement: "He will have it that *Hamlet* is a ghoststory" (*U,* 9.141), and Stephen starts by highlighting the Ghost and the tradition that Shakespeare himself took this part in the first production of *Hamlet.* Proceeding by suggestions and questions rather than by any direct assertions, interchanging Shakespeare's identity as an actor, as a poet, and as a family man, Stephen introduces his major "points" in rapid succession. First, Shakespeare identified himself with the part of the Ghost (*U,* 9.165–68). Second, his dead son, Hamnet, is to be identified with Hamnet's "namesake," Prince Hamlet (*U,* 9.171–73). Third (and this is twice-removed from a positive statement, being posed as a question and in the negative), "the murdered father" in *Hamlet* is to be identified with

Shakespeare, "the dispossessed son" with Hamnet, and "the guilty queen" with Hamnet's mother, Ann Hathaway (U, 9.179–80).

Schutte interprets all this as saying that Shakespeare is not to be identified with the young Hamlet (52), but, as I have earlier pointed out, at no point does Stephen say this; all he says is that Shakespeare *is* the Ghost, "the murdered father," and his acquiescence to Eglinton's summary— "He is the ghost and the prince. He is all in all"—is genuine. Stephen has himself already combined father and son in one image when, talking about the creative work of the artist, he says, "through the ghost of the unquiet father the image of the unliving son looks forth" (U, 9.380–81). It is this mingling of the father and son in the Ghost that Rank sees as the turning point in Shakespeare's inner life and in his creative work (*Incest Theme*, 179), a turning point that was triggered by the death of John Shakespeare.

Rank cites Freud's personally attested observation that the death of the father is the most important event of a man's life (*SE*, 4:xxvi), an event that inevitably revives the childhood feelings toward the father, which are compounded of tender affection and burning hatred (*Incest Theme*, 173–74, 177–78). For Shakespeare, the rearousal of these contradictory feelings, unconscious though they may have been, produced a strong reaction of remorse, and the Ghost represents the projection of an intolerable feeling of guilt over the infantile hatred of the father, which to the mature man seems incomprehensible and unjustified (*Incest Theme*, 174). For the artist's creation, Rank says, is a defense: "all the characters in the drama embody separate psychic drives of the artist, who frees himself from painful inner conflicts through this projection" (*Incest Theme*, 187), a supposition that is paralleled by Stephen's reference to Shakespeare's artistic production as "the creation he has piled up to hide him from himself" (U, 9.475). Thus, through the creation of the Ghost, Shakespeare is, temporarily at least, freed from his half-comprehended feelings of guilt.

Rank emphasizes, however, and Stephen echoes him in this, that Shakespeare went a step beyond the liberating projection of the Ghost and played the role on the stage, gaining even further psychic relief. For "while he himself plays the ghost of the father, the ghost of his own father (his painful thoughts about him) cannot appear to him" (*Incest Theme*, 187). Thus, he plays the role to save himself from an attack of

anxiety. As poet he has defended himself against his anxiety by project-
ing his contradictory feelings outside himself; as actor, he acts them out,
literally puts himself in the place of the father. Thus in the Ghost of
Hamlet's father he can release a range of unconscious and conflicting
impulses all at the same time: his infantile hatred of his father (in the
Ghost's condemnation of Claudius, the father-surrogate) and his erotic
affection for his mother, as well as condemnation for this affection and
fear of future requital through a son of his own (*Incest Theme*, 185–87).

But Rank argues that a son of his own is what Shakespeare did not
have at the time of his father's death. A son had been born to him; Rank
points out that he had been a father for several years before he became a
poet in any important sense. With the long separation from his family,
however, this fatherhood had no psychic reality for him, and his only
son's death appears to have had no continuing effect on him. "Only with
the death of his father, and the awakening of his infantile complexes, focused on his early relations with his parents, did he also awaken to the
memory of his own family, of his dead son, toward whom, because of
his long neglect of him, he felt unconsciously quite as guilty as he did
toward his dead father" (*Incest Theme*, 180). This reconstruction of
Shakespeare's psychic situation at the time he wrote *Hamlet*, giving
equal prominence to his feelings toward father and son, provides a context that puts a foundation under Stephen's "through the ghost of the
unquiet father the image of the unliving son looks forth" (*U*, 9.380–81),
which otherwise appears to be some obscurely motivated paradox.

The character of the Ghost, in which "the son-feeling appears side by
side with the father-feeling" (*Incest Theme*, 185), signals, according to
Rank, a fundamental upheaval in Shakespeare's inner life; for the first
time, with the death of his father, he recognizes in himself the feeling of
being a father (*Vatersein*). This is a "purely psychological" event, Rank
says, which may or may not coincide with the biological fact of fatherhood, but is of the greatest significance in the life of a man. *Vatersein*,
Rank affirms, "is psychically what motherhood is organically" (*Incest
Theme*, 180). Many productions of the artist, Rank points out, are written
exclusively from the one-sided point of view of the son and are understandable only through the "son-psychology." When the artist truly realizes that he himself is a father, however, the "father-psychology" is
added, and everything is "psychically reassessed" (*Incest Theme*, 180).[8]

In *Ulysses*, immediately following his interpolation about the uncertainty of fatherhood, Stephen asks himself, "Am I a father? If I were?" a set of questions which appears to be more relevant to Joyce's agenda than to Stephen's, as does the riddle that follows: "If the father who has not a son be not a father can the son who has not a father be a son?" Stephen's negative response is implicit in his assertion that the creator of *Hamlet* was "no more a son" (*U*, 9.864–68), but this is not quite so. When the son recognizes his own fatherhood, the father-feeling does not substitute for the son-feeling; it is added to it. "I," Stephen has earlier assured himself, "am I by memory" (*U*, 9.208), and psychoanalysis, with its validation of the unconscious, has invested memory with powerful new dimensions, with a degree of autonomy that is reflected in Joyce's provision of two protagonists for *Ulysses*. His *Portrait* is as pure an expression of son-psychology as can be imagined, even though Joyce had been a father twice-over when he wrote it. Stephen is all son and the unequivocal hero. He comes into *Ulysses* still very much the son, and he remains so at the end of the day. The father-psychology, however, enters *Ulysses* with Bloom, and as Bloomsday wears on, everything is "psychically reassessed"; the point of view becomes literally equivocal, but Bloom *joins* Stephen, he does not eliminate him. Bloom and Stephen may well be father and son, but which takes which role is not entirely clear or consistent, since they are truly "consubstantial," united in the invisible Ulysses, "the mind of Joyce-over-the-novel," which is, as Robert M. Adams has suggested, "the *terminus ad quem*" of the novel.[9]

There is hardly a detail of the fictional life of Joyce's son-figure Stephen that is not, for all practical purposes, identical with Joyce's own, but Joyce's life as a father is not so neatly paralleled by that of his father-figure Bloom. Joyce dated *Ulysses* 1914–1921, which also marks the period when his son and daughter were growing out of childhood into adolescence: at its completion date, Lucia was fourteen and Giorgio sixteen, a male, if we accept Stephen's summary, informed as it is by psychoanalytic assumptions, whose growth "is his father's decline, his youth his father's envy, his friend his father's enemy" (*U*, 9.855–57). In *Ulysses*, Bloom also is given a son and a daughter, but, though his daughter is very nearly of an age with Lucia Joyce, his son is dead and appears only once as "a fairy boy of eleven, a changeling" (*U*, 15.4957), a ghost, and the same age as Hamnet Shakespeare when he died.

Stephen insists that Shakespeare resurrected his dead son and embodied him in Hamlet, a process that Joyce reverses in his presentation of

Bloom's son Rudy as the shade of a preadolescent boy.[10] Stephen's claim that Hamnet, had he lived, "would have been Prince Hamlet's twin" (U, 9.176–77) is a bit off the mark even for the nineteen-year-old Hamlet of the first quarto—who was thereafter thirty (Schutte, 54). For Hamnet Shakespeare would have been sixteen when *Hamlet* was written, too young to be Hamlet's twin, but a match for the sixteen-year-old Giorgio Joyce. Joyce has Stephen proclaim that "his own image," to the man of genius, "is the standard of all experience," and as a kind of negative corollary, that "the images of other males of his blood will repel him. He will see in them grotesque attempts of nature to foretell or repeat himself" (U, 9.432–35). Apparently acting on this insight in *Ulysses*, which is the immortalization of his mortal life, the "postcreation" (U, 14.294), Joyce cuts down the other males of his blood. He relegates his father to the status of a minor character—albeit a strikingly entertaining one—and reduces his son to a ghost.

The "False," "Usurping," "Adulterous" Brother

But what of that other male of his blood, in theory so prominently featured and in person so conspicuously absent from *Ulysses*? What of the brother, given a name and a prominent role in *Stephen Hero*, all but banished from *A Portrait of the Artist as a Young Man*, and briefly mentioned in *Ulysses* when Stephen asks himself, "Where is your brother?" (U, 9.977), echoing God's question to Cain immediately after Cain's murder of Abel (Genesis 4.9). This biblical context then is reinforced by the following skewed reference to the second hostile brother-pair in Genesis, Jacob and Esau. "I am tired of my voice," Stephen says to himself, "the voice of Esau" (U, 9.981).[11] Now in the Genesis story of Jacob's deception of Isaac, though "the hands [were] the hands of Esau," the voice was Jacob's (Genesis 27.22)—a familiar textual fact that not only Joyce but also Stephen, child of the Jesuits, must have known. The blatant reversal of these fraternal roles thus may be one of a number of signals in this section that Stephen is playing fast and loose with fact.[12]

These biblical allusions, however, which together preface Stephen's claim that "the false or the usurping or the adulterous brother" (U, 9.997–98) is a dominant theme in Shakespeare's dramas, echo material in Rank's *Incest Motif* from part 2, "Sibling Relationships."[13] Although Rank, in orthodox Freudian fashion, points to the origin of the rivalry between brothers as an infantile struggle over the mother (*Incest Theme*, 370), his consideration moves beyond the basic Oedipal triangle of father-mother-son.[14] In the first chapter of part 2, on a page headed "*Der inzestuose Wurzel der Kain-Sage*" [The incestuous root of the Cain saga], Rank comments on the frequent appearance of fraternal hostility in the Bible and cites a quotation from Jakob Minor's biography of Schiller that puts a foundation of sorts under Stephen's accusatory remarks about Shakespeare's brothers: "The theme of the hostile brother," Minor writes, "is the oldest tragic conflict [of] saga and poetry. . . . It stems from the Bible, and not the least part of [its] irresistible effect . . . rests on the fact *that this impression belongs to the . . . most primitive stage of our childhood. Our first love and our first hate concern the brother; our first rival is our brother*" (Rank's emphasis).[15] Rank then points out that in the Bible the first murder of all is a brother-murder (*IM*, 451; *Incest Theme*, 370–71), a literary-historical fact that Stephen also puts into play in his remarks about Shakespeare's brothers. He glancingly acknowledges the reality of his own brother, answering his inner question about his brother's whereabouts with "Apothecaries' hall," where Stanislaus Joyce was working. In addition, Stephen includes his brother in a list of his "whetstones" (*U*, 9.977–78).[16] And the context of the primeval biblical brother-murder may well point to Joyce's awareness of the significance of his artistic "murder" of his brother Stanislaus.

For Stanislaus had indeed worked at Apothecaries' Hall as a clerk during the terrible time after May Joyce's death, the time memorialized in *Ulysses* (*BK*, 240–41). He is the brother Joyce refers to in a 1904 letter to Nora, as the only one of his brothers and sisters "capable of understanding me" (*Letters*, 2:48), and he remained important to his brother's survival for many years thereafter.[17] Yet in *Ulysses* he is downsized to a factor in life "as easily forgotten as an umbrella" (*U*, 9.975), duplicating Joyce's removal of "Maurice" from *A Portrait*, in which, as Maurice Beebe noted some time ago, Joyce "combined key aspects of his brother's character with his own and gave Stephen the strength of both young Joyces."[18]

In *Ulysses* it is Bloom who inherits the added dimension from Stanislaus Joyce, for there is a flavor of mind in Leopold Bloom that owes much to the mind revealed in Stanislaus's *Dublin Diary*. Joyce later reproduced this flavor in the stylized brother pairs in *Finnegans Wake* (see Shechner, *Joyce in Nighttown*, 33), but in *Ulysses* it is personalized and goes far toward giving Bloom his distinctive character. The "prudent member" (*U*, 12.211, 437), is quoted as "talking about the Gaelic league and the antitreating league and drink, the curse of Ireland" (*U*, 12.683–84) and remains throughout the day "in complete possession of his faculties . . . disgustingly sober" (*U*, 16.61–62). And he finds a model in Stanislaus, who lists "drunkenness" as an "Irish national vice" and fails to see "the magnificent generosity in standing a drink . . . an idle habit—ballast to fill up empty time and an empty mind" (*CDD*, 36–37), citing both his brother and his father as outstanding examples of the fact that this rite is carried out "at somebody else's expense" (*CDD*, 37). This diary was an important resource for Joyce in the making of *Ulysses* (*CDD*, vii), and like some exotic tropical plant, Joyce absorbed at least a part of the essential Stanislaus he found there into Bloom, his own opposing self.[19]

But whatever details of Bloom's synthesized fictional character may be appropriated from Joyce's brother, Bloom remains at base a specialized kind of self-portrait, and the circumstances of his life as a husband and father—whether real or imagined—are surely attached in some way to Joyce's own life as husband and father, which was centered in the household in Trieste. Basically a ménage à trois—James, Nora, and Stanislaus—this shifting, unstable household expanded to include both Eva and Eileen Joyce for most of two years, then contracted to four adult members when Eva departed in 1911 (*JJII*, 310 n). The fundamental pattern of the household, however, whatever the shifts during the decade before the brothers were separated by the war, was "two brothers, one wife," in Brenda Maddox's phrase, with the brothers splitting between them the husbandly roles of lover and provider. This "psychological triangle" Maddox points out in a notable understatement, was not "a recipe for domestic tranquillity" (67).[20]

Now when Stephen introduces into his Shakespeare presentation what Mr. Best calls "the three brothers Shakespeare" (*U*, 9.894, 957–58) and applies to these brothers the descriptors "false," "usurping," "adulterous," he is suggesting a psychological triangle for Shakespeare that in some measure is drawn from his creator's experience, although the exact nature of the triangle proposed for Shakespeare remains, like the one in the Joyce household, exceedingly indeterminate. Here in "Scylla and Charybdis," Stephen sets in motion a whirligig of words, in which his desultory pursuit of the topic of the brothers, as well as his inward commentary, mingle with apparently aimless contributions from his interlocutors loosely related to brothers and names.[21] But, although Mr. Lyster "understands" that Stephen is suggesting "misconduct with one of the brothers" and asks which brother (*U*, 9.962–63), Stephen never directly accuses Ann or any of Shakespeare's brothers. His implications about Ann's "misconduct" with the brothers, furthermore, have no reasonable historical underpinning, since, as Frank Budgen pointed out many years ago, Shakespeare's brothers were much too young for such dalliance (*James Joyce*, 117–18), and Schutte concludes that, however impressive the evidence Stephen accumulates to buttress his theory—which he never quite states—"its foundations are sand" (53–54). Speculation about an autobiographical base for Stephen's "case" against Ann and an unnamed brother-in-law are probably similarly supported.

Much of the day-to-day material in Richard Ellmann's biographical narrative of the Trieste years was documented through sources that were not available to other critics, chief among them Stanislaus's "diary" for this period, and critics have from time to time pondered the possibility that this diary could provide an autobiographical foundation for the implications of "misconduct" that Joyce filters through Stephen's remarks. But until Ellmann's papers were deposited in the McFarlin Library at the University of Tulsa after his death, the location as well as the nature of what Ellmann cited as "S. Joyce, diary," was a mystery, as were other frequent citations to "Letter from S. Joyce to his father (1910), unsent." Photocopies of both are now in the Ellmann Collection, though, so far as I have been able to discover, information about the location of the originals, as well as the completeness of the journal, is a matter of guesswork.

The photocopied pages of Stanislaus's "Book of Days" for 1907 to 1909 in the Ellmann Collection are, unlike Stanislaus's 1903–1904 *Diary*, unedited—raw material for the kind of diary we have for Dublin. He writes the entries conscientiously, constantly falling behind and catching up on his day-to-day account, which, he reiterates, is for his own edification. He suggests, in fact that it may well serve as a substitute for confession. This journal gives no ready evidence of "misconduct" involving his brother's wife, and there is much in Stanislaus's observations about Nora to cast doubt on such an accusation. Maddox contents herself with noting that Stanislaus was "attracted to Nora and found her indifference hurtful" (86). Of course, it is clear from his "Book of Days" that Stanislaus found his brother's indifference hurtful too, and my own impression is that his brother and sister-in-law were most of the time lumped together as targets of Stanislaus's resentment—as, for example, in his bitter complaint of "the heartless and thankless sweating of me that has been Jim and his wife's chief profit these four years."[22]

Like Stephen's rambling indirections during the library presentation in *Ulysses*, the speculation about an autobiographical source has thus far ended in nothing solid, and an unanswered (and possibly unanswerable) question is one about Joyce's motivation for including this section about the brother in *Ulysses*. My own belief is that Joyce includes these adumbrations about the treacherous brother in his autobiographical fiction for the same reason that he builds up dubious evidence of Molly's promiscuous infidelity with one hand and nullifies that evidence in the text with the other. It is because, despite Joyce's seemingly compulsive devotion to fact, the "hardly controlled itch for deceit" that Stanislaus sees in his brother (*CDD*, 7) is also operative, and furthermore the idea of betrayal and infidelity is obsessively fascinating to him. "Either/or" has no real meaning for Joyce, and so his text includes both the true fact and the obsession.[23]

Mother-Wife-Daughter

Thus the other males of his blood—father, son, and brother—are displaced from their flesh-and-blood relationships to the artist and assigned their places in Joyce's "book of himself." The placing of the women in Joyce's life, as it is revealed in *Ulysses* and implied by Stephen's picture of the women in Shakespeare's life, follows a somewhat different pattern, though a pattern defined no less dominantly in terms of the artist's own needs. As soon as Stephen has thrown out his main points about father and son, he brings Ann Hathaway, "the guilty queen," into the triangle with "the murdered father" and "the dispossessed son" (*U*, 9.178–80), but the question immediately arises as to the reality of this dispossession. Hamlet expresses no feeling that he should have become king instead of Claudius, and as for Hamnet Shakespeare, how would his mother's adultery, if true, dispossess him? The answer is, of course, obvious to a postpsychoanalytic generation: if either of these sons is dispossessed, it is from his presumed place with his mother, a dispossession that is effected by the father or his surrogate.

Ann Hathaway, "the guilty queen," is in Stephen's triangle both wife and mother, as she is in the Oedipal triangle, and the same dual identity is implied in Stephen's description of her relation to Shakespeare. "She saw him into and out of the world," Stephen says, and immediately refers to his own mother in death—"Who brought me into the world lies there" (*U*, 9.217–18, 221–22).[24] We are thus reminded that in *Ulysses* the dead parent is Stephen's mother, and it is her ghost that is appallingly visible to him, not, as in *Hamlet*, the ghost of the father. Stephen refers to the death of Shakespeare's mother in one of his miscellaneous family paragraphs: "Her death brought from him the scene with Volumnia in *Coriolanus*" (*U*, 9.880–81), echoing Rank's assertion that *Coriolanus* represents the poet's reaction to his mother's death, which, he suggests, intensified Shakespeare's reaction to the death of his father seven years before. The withdrawal from the loving mother, which is projected into *Coriolanus*, had originated, says Rank, "in the regression into early infancy right after the death of the father" (*Incest Theme*, 177–78), and the violent hostility that Hamlet expresses toward his mother reflects a not uncommon phenomenon, a disillusionment with the mother, an outraged feeling of betrayal that arises from the discovery of her sexual relationship with the father and boils up again after his death (*Incest Theme*, 175).

Shechner sees Stephen as harboring "a murderous hostility" toward "the mother who had betrayed him" and notes that "in Stephen's mind, the death of his mother and the sexual undoing of Shakespeare are significantly related" (*Joyce in Nighttown*, 31, 27). Schutte also, noting the identification of Ann Hathaway with May Dedalus, suggests that Stephen's close relationship to his mother "has something in it of the relationship between a pair of lovers of whom the older is the woman" (108). If we accept the symbolic equivalence of wife and mother, which Joyce himself offers in the text, we may consider the "undoing" that Stephen proposes to arise ultimately from the son's inevitable failure in the Oedipal rivalry. This failure results, Rank says, in a disillusionment with his mother, "whose consequences we may again recognize in the unhappy marriage of the eighteen-year-old poet with the wife who is about eight years older," a marriage and a discrepancy in ages upon which Stephen leans heavily. Rank goes on to say that this disillusionment may be inflated to hatred and scorn for all women, leading to "complete withdrawal from them and a concomitant reversal of the libido to his own sex," coupling the mother-son relationship with the homosexual tendency, a connection that Freud had exemplified in the psychobiography of Leonardo that Joyce purchased in Trieste.[25] Furthermore, Rank points out, "in the resurgence of Shakespeare's love for his father at the time of his death, there is inevitably a latent homosexual component" (*Incest Theme*, 175), which is intensified when his mother dies, and this homosexual component is reflected in *Coriolanus*.

Rank, under the page heading *"Der Mutterkomplex in 'Coriolan,'"* stresses the relationship of Coriolanus to the enemy general, Tullus Aufidius, quoting passages that are startlingly explicit in their expression of erotic feeling between the two men (*Incest Theme*, 176–78), reminiscent of the relationship that underlies Shakespeare's Sonnets, "the most impressive expression," Rank says, of "the poet's homosexual affection" and rooted in the whole complicated rearousal of infantile feelings at his parents' deaths (*Incest Theme*, 175). In "Scylla and Charybdis," Stephen's first recorded thoughts are of his intense relationship with Cranly (*U*, 9.36–39), and the context of homosexuality dominates the final pas de deux with Mulligan (*U*, 9.1102–225). This context crops up throughout the discussion itself in connection with intermittent digressions about the Sonnets, which, William Empson suggested some time ago, are "dragged in" because Joyce was leading up to the "adventurous treatment of the Eternal Triangle" that he first tried out in *Exiles*,[26] that is, a sexual relationship between men, consummated by their sharing a woman in common, which is what Bloom (obliquely, to be sure) appears to offer Stephen.

Joyce has planted another of his dismembered footnotes in "Scylla and Charybdis" and "Oxen of the Sun," which appears to confirm Empson's suggestion. In the library, Mulligan quotes Dowdon as having said, with reference to "the charge of pederasty brought against the bard," "*All we can say is that life ran very high in those days*," at which Stephen silently brands Mulligan, "Catamite" (*U*, 9.732–34). At the maternity hospital, then, Stephen picks up Dowdon's line, as he alludes to Beaumont and Fletcher, who "had but the one doxy between them . . . to make shift with in delights amorous for life ran very high in those days and the custom of the country approved with it. Greater love than this, he said, no man hath that a man lay down his wife for a friend" (*U*, 14.358–62).[27] Stephen's garbled quotation, which describes the central situation in *Exiles*, prefigures what Empson has labeled the "Bloom Offer" (134), that is, Bloom's offer of Molly to Stephen later in *Ulysses*, and Stephen's use of the Dowdon quotation carries into this context the associations of "pederasty" and "catamite" that have been earlier attached to the quotation, thus identifying the pattern of two males sharing one woman as homosexual.

At the same time, two males sharing one woman also describes the original Oedipal triangle, which is the primeval paradigm for the three-cornered relationship that is promoted by Richard in *Exiles* and by Bloom in *Ulysses*. With the death of his mother, Stephen has lost his place in the familiar and therefore secure Oedipal pattern: the link of the flesh that has united the two males of the triangle not only with the woman but with each other is gone. And if *amor matris* is indeed the only true thing in life, as Stephen says, then with the mother's death, the son is wrenched out of any true relatedness whatsoever. It is this kind of dislocation that Stanislaus pictures as his brother's state at the death of their mother,[28] and Joyce's Stephen is left "alone for ever in the dark ways of my bitterness" (*U*, 14.379), faced with the alternative routes to relatedness represented by Mulligan and Bloom.

"Where there is a reconciliation," Stephen says, referring to Shakespeare, "there must have been first a sundering" (*U*, 9.334–35), and this sundering in his own life from the world and the flesh is very real for him. But there is no authentic reconciliation through Mulligan, for Mulligan offers the prospect of a male-to-male relationship that is partial only. Furthermore, like the priestly vocation, which Stephen has earlier rejected in *A Portrait* (*P*, 161–62), it is a relationship outside the continuity of a biological family. Thus Stephen silently hails Mulligan, who is connected throughout with Wilde's "love that dare not speak its name," as "O mine enemy" (*U*, 9.483). On the other hand, he senses in Bloom the other self, "which I in time must come to, ineluctably" (*U*, 9.1200–1201). As "Scylla and Charybdis" comes to a close, Stephen is thus implicated in Bloom's life, and Stephen's future, textually at least, is identified with Bloom as husband and as father.

In Bloom's life there is an obvious sundering that cries out for reconciliation. This is the split between husband and wife, a life pattern that finds its place in Stephen's Shakespeare presentation and in Rank's *Incest Motif*. Paralleling the culturally mandated separation from the mother, the consequences of which, Rank points out, are resolved by merging mother and wife, the later sundering is from the wife, whom the daughter replaces as the object of desire, and this estrangement is similarly reconciled by identifying the daughter with the wife. In the father-daughter incest complex, which, Rank points out, appears in literature almost entirely from the point of view of the father (*Incest Theme,* 300), the daughter's puberty is a signal for the father to put her in the place of the mother (*Incest Theme,* 308). This transfer of attention and affection can only be resolved finally by putting the mother back in the place that the daughter has unwittingly usurped in her father's sexual world, through a second marriage to the mother.

Rank points out that the father-daughter complex is fundamental in three of Shakespeare's late plays, the same plays that Stephen cites as evidencing "a spirit of reconciliation" in Shakespeare: *Pericles, The Tempest,* and *A Winter's Tale.* Stephen attributes Shakespeare's gentler mood to the birth of his granddaughter, quoting a line from *Pericles:* "*My dearest wife was like this maid*" (*U,* 9.423), and Rank quotes this same line as an example of a typical feature of the father-daughter incest pattern, in which the daughter is a younger image of her mother (*Incest Theme,* 308). For Pericles says this, not about a baby granddaughter, as the sequence of Stephen's discourse suggests, but about his beautiful fourteen-year-old daughter, Marina, who, as Stephen has no way of knowing, is the same age as Bloom's daughter Milly was when she was sent off to Mullingar. And Milly, who celebrates her fifteenth birthday, "her first birthday away from home," the day before Bloomsday (*U,* 4.415–16), is indeed, as Bloom repeats in various contexts, the image of her mother.

Phillip Herring, commenting on Joyce's British Museum notesheets for *Ulysses,* notes "Bloom's fixation on Milly's sexual maturing."[29] Evidences of this fixation are glimpsed over and over again, swathed for the most part in the batting of Bloom's miscellaneous musings, but baldly stated in "Ithaca," where Bloom is said to reflect that "complete mental intercourse between himself and [Molly] had not taken place since the consummation of puberty, indicated by catamenic hemmorrhage, of [their] female issue" (*U,* 17.2285–87). Nor is Molly oblivious to changes in the father-daughter relationship, as well as the threat this changed relationship poses to her own place in the household. She has been aware of Bloom's heightened attention to their daughter, "always talking to her lately at the table explaining things in the paper and she pretending to understand sly of course . . . helping her into her coat. . . . I suppose he thinks Im finished out and laid on the shelf well Im not" (*U,* 18.1017–22). Her thoughts continue to dwell on Milly's development as a sexually appealing adolescent, all of which merge with musings on her own sexual appeal, epitomized in her observation that Milly is "just like me when I was her age" (*U*, 18.1036).

On Bloomsday the Blooms' daughter has been removed from the scene, and Molly says that it is Bloom who has insisted on sending her away, motivated, she claims, by a perverse wish to clear the way for "me and Boylan" (*U*, 18.1007–8). But Bloom's motivation may well be instead—or possibly in addition—a half-conscious wish to remove Milly, who has become a threat to his fidelity to her mother, in order to clear the way for his own return to Molly. For throughout the day Bloom's thoughts about Milly are consistently coupled with thoughts about his relationship with Molly. His perception of the identity of mother and daughter, starting with his "Molly. Milly. Same thing watered down. . . . a woman too" (*U*, 6.87–89), is embodied in the apparition of Milly as Molly's youth in "Circe." Bloom cries, "I see her! It's she! The first night at Mat Dillon's!" and is told, "That's your daughter" (*U*, 15.3162–65). Wife and daughter thus become a composite figure, a typical feature of the father-daughter complex in Rank's view.

Now in Stephen's treatment of the three late plays identified by Rank as centering on the father-daughter complex, the text, through an intertwining of intertextual with intratextual correspondences that is a consistent mark of Joyce's use of allusion, provides the reader with a complex underscoring of the possibilities of father-daughter incest. Stephen's "epilogue" to his presentation includes three names, one from Shakespeare's work and two from his life: "prosperous Prospero, the good man rewarded, Lizzie, grandpa's lump of love, and nuncle Richie, the bad man taken off by poetic justice to the place where the bad niggers go" (*U*, 9.1038–40). Prospero we know from *The Tempest* as the father of Miranda; "Lizzie" can be identified from Stephen's presentation as the daughter of Susanna, Shakespeare's daughter, indeed, the same granddaughter whom Stephen credits with softening Shakespeare's heart (*U*, 9.677–79). And "nuncle Richie" is the name Stephen has assigned to one of Shakespeare's brothers (*U*, 9.973).

Here the intratextual plot thickens, for "nuncle Richie" is also Stephen's uncle, Richie Goulding (*U*, 3.76), whom Stephen has thought about visiting in the morning and whose daughter Crissie he has characterized as "Papa's little bedpal. Lump of love" (*U*, 3.88). This characterization gives love a distinctly more suggestive context. Nor are we at the end of this particular chain of associations. For in "Hades," when Bloom tells Simon Dedalus that his son is passing, Simon assumes that Stephen has been visiting "the Goulding faction, the drunken little costdrawer [nuncle Richie] and Crissie, papa's little lump of dung." And he follows this with an appositive that surely has an intentional double meaning, though with no necessary foundation in fact: "the wise child that knows her own father" (*U*, 6.51–53). All of these associations have been established in the text before Stephen introduces the girl child as a reconciling factor in Shakespeare's life and work, and through them the hint of incest becomes attached to this reference too.

Pericles ends with a reunion between Pericles and the wife whom he has believed dead (that is, says Rank, wished dead), duplicating the outcome in *A Winter's Tale*, and representing in reality, according to Rank, "only a substitute for marriage with the daughter, as it does in the Griselda legend" (*Incest Theme*, 308). Now Rank had considered the Griselda legend as the traditional folk expression of the father-daughter incest pattern in a 1912 essay published in *Imago*,[30] and, oddly enough, Griselda appears in *Ulysses* as "patient Griselda," paired by Eglinton with "Penelope stay-at-home" (*U*, 9.620) as a prototype for Ann Hathaway Shakespeare during the years of Shakespeare's absence in London. It seems reasonable then to consider possible echoes of Rank's essay in Stephen's discourse on Shakespeare. And, though hardly conclusive, they are there. The basic plot of the story concerns a nobleman who marries a "poor farm girl, Griselda." He then snatches from her without any explanation the children born of the marriage and finally casts Griselda herself off and announces his intention of marrying a much younger woman (who is, in most cases, identified as his daughter); in many versions he demands that Griselda oversee the preparations for the wedding, even the dressing of the bride. All this humiliation she cheerfully accepts. At the end, however, it is revealed that the entire sequence of events has taken place "simply to prove her submissive obedience," and the outcome, in most versions, is that the "pretend wedding" with the daughter becomes a remarriage with Griselda, who has passed her testing ("Griselda," 91–95). Rank points out that the motivation for this "testing motif" has always been difficult to assign without making Griselda's husband a kind of monster, but suggests that many poets have attempted in various ways to soften the "shocking" motivation of the basic story.

Thornton identifies the Griselda in *Ulysses* as an allusion to the heroine of Chaucer's "Clerk's Tale," married to Walter, who mistreats her in the traditional unmotivated way (*Allusions*, 188). Rank's list of the poets who have worked with this popular story indeed starts with Chaucer, but extends through names in the literary history of several nations, including the modern German dramatist Gerhart Hauptmann ("Griselda," 92). And Hauptmann is a name with high recognition value for Joyce, who had translated Hauptmann's *Vor Sonnenaufgang* [Before sunrise] when he was nineteen and always retained his admiration for the German dramatist.[31] Rank, whose essay is introduced by an epigraph from Hauptmann's *Griselda,* identifies Hauptmann's dramatization of the traditional material as "the first attempt at a purely inward motive" ("Griselda," 100), and indeed Hauptmann moves a considerable distance from the traditional situation. There is no daughter in his drama, and, unlike the husband of the Griselda tradition, the nobleman of Hauptmann's version of the tale, Margrave Ulrich, is driven to his cruelty by jealousy of his unborn child. Even though the Margrave abandons Griselda in her pregnancy and during the delivery of their son, he remains steadfastly, indeed obsessively, in love with his wife, with whom he is reconciled in a final passionate scene.[32]

In *Ulysses,* too, however strong the evidence is for Bloom's incestuous impulses toward his daughter (in harmony with the Griselda tradition), his attachment to Molly remains at the center of his day, a fact of his emotional biography that is reflected also in Stephen's discourse about the "reconciliation" evidenced in Shakespeare's late plays. Following his own later advice to himself to "mix up a mixture" (*U,* 9.761), Stephen apparently interchanges fathers and daughters in *A Winter's Tale* and *Pericles,* as well as indulging in a bit of wordplay with father-daughter incest. Presumably referring to Perdita in *A Winter's Tale* ("that which was lost"), Stephen says, "What was lost is given back to him: his daughter's child," continuing with the quotation: *"My dearest wife,* Pericles says, *was like this maid* (*U,* 9.422–23). But the daughter of Pericles is Marina ("a child of storm"); Perdita is the daughter of Leontes, the king of Sicily in *A Winter's Tale.* Leontes' response to the appearance of his daughter Perdita replicates that of Pericles to Marina, in that it is a cry for his wife: "O thy mother, thy mother" (*Incest Theme,* 311). And Stephen's question, "Will any man love the daughter if he has not loved the mother?" (*U,* 9.423–24) is relevant to both dramas, as indeed it is to the drama of *Ulysses.*

At this point in the text, following Mr. Best's attempted interpolation about grandfathers, Hans Gabler, in his 1984 *Critical and Synoptic Edition,* restored a "chunk of text," as he described the five-line segment he inserted in Stephen's discourse (*U,* 9.427–31), and this segment makes sense out of a sequence that had not made grammatical sense before. The restored text—forty-three words, nine of them in Latin—had never before appeared in any published edition of *Ulysses:*

> Will he not see reborn in her, with the memory of his youth added, another image?
>
> Do you know what you are talking about? Love, yes. Word known to all men. *Amor vero aliquid alicui bonum vult unde et ea quae concupiscimus.* (*U,* 9.427–31)

Stephen's rhetorical question, which begins the restored passage, is an explication of his earlier question about the dependence of love for a daughter on earlier love for her mother,[33] and in this second question Stephen introduces three images: (1) the image of the daughter; (2) the image of the wife in her youth, which is restored in the daughter; and (3) the image of himself as a youth. Gabler has called this the "link question," and it does indeed provide a necessary link between the first question ("Will any man love the daughter . . .") and Stephen's much quoted pronouncement that "his own image to a man with that queer thing genius is the standard for all experience, material and moral," followed as it is by Stephen's "Such an appeal will touch him" (*U,* 9.432–33).

In the discussion of the restored passage at the 1989 Miami Conference on the *Critical and Synoptic Edition* of *Ulysses,* Arnold Goldman pointed to the rhetorical gap that had been present before the passage was restored. "What is the appeal?" Goldman asked. "I could never understand what's the appeal."[34] Neither could most of us; before Gabler's textual restoration there had never been a grammatical referent for "such an appeal." The link question provides this referent through the introduction of the word *image* and the actual reality of the three images Stephen introduces in the link question: *Image 1,* the daughter,[35] whose image revives "another image" (*U*, 9.428)—*Image 2*—of her mother as a young woman, "*my dearest wife*," who is reborn in the daughter. *Image 2* in turn resurrects for the artist his own image as a young man, "the memory of his own youth"—*Image 3*.

These three images link up with *Image 4*, the "man of genius," whose image is "the standard for all experience." And *Image 4* can be identified in turn with a figure mentioned earlier in Stephen's discourse, "the artist," who "weave[s] and unweave[s] his image" (*U*, 9.377–78), so that "that which I was is that which I am and that which in possibility I may come to be" (*U*, 9.382–83). Nor is this the end of the trail. The identity of past, present, and future in *Image 4* harks back to Stephen's debate with himself even earlier in "Scylla and Charybdis" about the identity of the ego through change, which concludes "I, I and I. I" (*U*, 9.212). At the same time it leads immediately to Stephen's description of the multiple perspectives of the autobiographical artist: "So in the future, the sister of the past, I may see myself as I sit here now but by reflection from that which then I shall be" (*U*, 9.383–85). Thus the restoration of the amplifying question ultimately supplies the necessary links that make it circuitously clear that Stephen's assertion about "his own image" as the "standard of all experience" implies a double image—the man of genius in youth and in middle age—surely a partial gloss on Stephen and Bloom as they relate to their creator.[36]

Rank's discussion of Shakespeare's *A Winter's Tale* introduces a similar combination of images as this late play moves toward a resolution. I borrow from Rank's summary of the plot: Leontes, king of Sicily, unjustly suspects his wife Hermione of adultery with his boyhood friend, Polixenes of Bohemia, and therefore casts her off and commands the exposure of her newborn daughter Perdita, who is saved by a shepherd of Bohemia. Hermione disappears after being exonerated by a Delphic oracle, and Leontes grieves for both wife and daughter. Perdita falls in love with Florizel, son of Polixenes, but their union is thwarted by Polixenes' ban on his son's marriage to a shepherdess (Perdita), and the pair flee to Sicily, where Leontes welcomes Perdita as his daughter and assures their marriage. Hermione reappears and the couples sort out into their separate generations. Rank points again to the typical resemblance of mother and daughter, underlined by Leontes' cry of "Oh, thy mother, thy mother!" when he recognizes Perdita, and continues, "Just as he sees in Perdita the youthful image of his wife, so he sees in her husband

Florizel his own youthful image" (*Incest Theme*, 311), pointing to the same kind of doubling of images that appears in Stephen's link question: "Will he not see reborn in her, with the memory of his own youth added, another image?"

Thus the second question adds considerable substance to the first— "Will any man love the daughter if he has not loved the mother?"—a question that is present to Bloom, just under the surface, throughout Bloomsday. It receives an answer of sorts in "Ithaca," when Bloom considers "a reconciliatory union" that reflects the mixed motivation of the traditional second marriage to the wife proposed by Rank. For Bloom muses that "the way to daughter led through mother, the way to mother through daughter" (*U*, 17.943–44). Such a union could reconcile both men (and their creator, in whom they are united) to the inevitable separation from the females of their blood, which is universally demanded by civilized societies. Molly, that is, can reconcile Stephen to the loss of his mother and Bloom to the necessary renunciation of his daughter. Whether or not the narrative supports this solution, it is realized through another chain of associations that starts with the companion Arabian Nights dreams of Stephen and Bloom.

For both Stephen's dream of Haroun al Raschid (*U*, 3.365–69, 9.1207–8) and Bloom's parallel "Turkish" dream of Molly (*U*, 13.1240–41, 14.508–10) become a part of the action in "Circe." Bloom, following Stephen out of the brothel in "caliph's hood and poncho," is identified as "Haroun al Raschid," the dominant figure in Stephen's dream (*U*, 15.4325), while Molly appears "in Turkish costume" with her wonderful camel (*U*, 15.297–98), though minus the red slippers of Bloom's dream, which are replaced by "jewelled toerings" (*U*, 15.312–13). The red slippers, however, reappear in "Penelope," when Molly imagines herself getting breakfast for Stephen and tells herself, "Id have to get a nice pair of red slippers like those Turks with the fez used to sell" (*U*, 18.1494–95), suggesting that Bloom's dream may come true for Stephen. Thus, like the "compromise figure" of the Ghost in Rank's interpretation of Shakespeare's *Hamlet* as an incest drama, the "consubstantial" protagonists of *Ulysses* merge in their dreams, the constructs that, according to Freud, give access to the unconscious.

6

Ghost Stories in *Ulysses*

The Psychic Origins of Bloom

However Stephen and Bloom seem to merge from time to time—thinking the same thoughts, dreaming similar dreams—it is clear that they separately represent quite different receptors of experience. Late in the 1950s, just before the publication of Richard Ellmann's *James Joyce*, Maurice Beebe, writing about the "problem of autobiography" in Joyce, characterized the question of the relation between Joyce and Stephen Dedalus as "one of the most crucial, if one of the most tired, issues in Joyce criticism" ("Joyce and Stephen," 68). But Ellmann's biography and, even more, his edition of Joyce's *Letters*, which included excerpts from the extraordinary group of pornographic letters written in 1909 and 1912 to Nora,[1] made it abundantly clear for the first time that the problem of autobiography extended beyond Stephen Dedalus to Leopold Bloom. In *Ulysses*, the subject of Joyce's continuing portrait of the artist, intensely singular in *A Portrait*, is, we now recognize, split into two equally autobiographical protagonists, whose separate portraits Robert Scholes has labeled "bioenergetic" (Stephen) and "cybernetic" (Bloom). Scholes's distinction is at least significantly akin to the psychoanalytic distinction between conscious and unconscious contents in the individual psyche.

The Problem of Autobiography

I take seriously the psychoanalytic understanding of the projection of psychic contents onto objects and persons in the external world, including, as a special group, the characters created by the imaginative writer.[2] I also take seriously Joyce's extended commentary on *Ulysses*, as it has been reported by Arthur Power, in which Joyce insistently highlighted the "subterranean" realities as the "modern theme," an insistence that runs all the way through these conversations. He also assured Power that *Ulysses* was "forge[d] out of my own experience" (54, 52). Freud, in his 1908 "Creative Writers and Day-Dreaming," noted the "inclination of the modern writer to split up his ego . . . into many part-egos [in order] to personify the conflicting currents of his own mental life in several heroes" (*SE*, 9:150),[3] and certainly we have such a split in *Ulysses*. I assume a rough correspondence between the "bioenergetic" portrait of Stephen and the conscious ego personality of the artist who is the subject of Joyce's portrait from its beginnings. I also assume the same kind of rough correspondence between the "cybernetic" portrait of Bloom and alien elements of the artist's unconscious personality that, under the pressure of strong emotion, erupt into consciousness in *Ulysses*.[4]

Now the assumption that the two protagonists of *Ulysses* represent opposing ways of being in the world is a fairly solid part of the critical tradition about *Ulysses*. Early on, for example, Rebecca West identified the opposition in Manichaean terms as that between "Ormuz and Ahriman, the dark force of matter . . . and the spirit of light" (18). Twenty years later in 1948 H. E. Rogers saw the two protagonists as "opposing forces of a single personality in search of integration" (325–26), while James Maddox, late in the 1970s, not only expressed the opposition in terms of the predominance of thought in Stephen contrasted with Bloom's domination by "immediate sensory experience" but also pointed to a "complementarity" in this opposition that is "the most essential theme of *Ulysses*" (194–95, 41–43).

My own further assumption, which is in harmony with Sigmund Freud's observation about the writer's splitting up his ego into "part-egos," is not, I think, so widely accepted. I assume, that is, that the opposing characters of Stephen and Bloom embody conflicting psychic forces in Joyce, which have been projected into *Ulysses* as a necessary development in the process of self-exploration, self-definition, and self-revelation through which Joyce created his portrait of the artist, a portrait that is, from the beginning and throughout, a combination of autobiography and myth.[5]

To be sure, there has always been a line in the tradition that views Stephen and Bloom as reflecting some kind of polarity in Joyce, beginning with Gilbert Seldes's 1922 review of *Ulysses*, which has been identified as one of those that "pleased Joyce most." For Seldes, referring to

Yeats's comment that "the poet creates the mask of his opposite," recognized in *Ulysses* "the dual mask—Bloom and Stephen—of James Joyce," extending this recognition to the claim that the two protagonists provided "the mask of a generation" (Deming, 1:235, 238). C. G. Jung, in his much-debated "'Ulysses': A Monologue," also personalized the opposition as the "disintegration" of Joyce's personality into "Bloom, *l'homme moyen sensuel,* and the almost gaseous Stephen Dedalus" (*CW*, 15:114), and Richard Blackmur identified "the true polarity in *Ulysses*" as a polarity "in Joyce himself" (113).

In *A Portrait* Joyce presented the development of the consciousness of the artist—his consciousness of himself and his world, of which he was the center—through the single character of Stephen; and this initial volume of Joyce's autobiographical fiction conforms to the definition of the "lyrical form" in Stephen's aesthetic theory in *A Portrait*, "wherein the artist presents his image in immediate relation to himself" (*P*, 214). But when Joyce determined that the "sequel" to this ego-dominated phase of his ongoing fictional portrait should be modeled on the *Odyssey*, he moved into another form, and this continuation of the autobiographical fiction conforms to Stephen's theoretical definition in *A Portrait* of "the epical form" as "emerging out of lyrical literature when the artist prolongs and broods upon himself as the centre of an epical event . . . till the centre of emotional gravity is equidistant from the artist himself and from others" (*P*, 214–15).

Autobiography as Epic

Ralph Rader has argued convincingly that Joyce intended his readers to take seriously Stephen's aesthetic theory, in both *A Portrait* and *Ulysses*, as a rationale for his own work,[6] and certainly Stephen's definition of the epical form works for *Ulysses*, which Joyce labeled, in a letter to Carlo Linati, "an epic of two races," as well as "a little story of a day (life)" (*Letters*, 1:146). For as Joyce brooded upon himself as the "centre of an epical event," he found himself seeing double; and like the Shakespeare of Stephen's theory, who drew the Jew Shylock "out of his own long pocket" (*U*, 9.741–42), Joyce produced Bloom to take over a part of the burden of self-revelation in his fiction. Bloom was never acknowledged as a surrogate in Joyce's lifetime, but even as *A Portrait* "was the book of my youth," *Ulysses*, which is dominated by Bloom, "is the book of my maturity," forged, Joyce insisted, "out of my own experience" (Power, 36), experience that is revealed through both Stephen and Bloom.

To be sure, the double story in *Ulysses* is no news, but it is worth noting that the relation of the fictional narrative in Joyce's novel to the facts of Joyce's life is subject to different constraints, depending on whether we are looking at Stephen's story or Bloom's. For in *Ulysses*, Stephen "is" Joyce, even as he was in *A Portrait*, in the sense that Scholes has defined as "bioenergetic," with the "cellular integrity which marks [him] as Joyce himself and not any other person" (165), and, as has been noted, he is very strictly bound to the time represented in the novel. The compulsive historicity of *Ulysses* testifies to Joyce's attitude toward his own history as a given not to be lightly evaded. Such an assumption informs his reminder to Grant Richards that "he is a very bold man who dares to alter in the presentment . . . whatever he has seen and heard" (*Letters*, 2:134) as well as the dictum in *Stephen Hero* that "so long as this place in nature is given us it is right that art should do no violence to the gift" (*SH*, 79).[7]

Bloom, however, the "cybernetic self-portrait," is not rigidly tied to any actual time in Joyce's life. As I have detailed earlier, he has no actual place in the Dublin of 1904, which is the historical setting for the novel, and Danis Rose has reminded us that there are always "two distinct time-frames holding together the world of Leopold Bloom," that of the fictional Bloomsday and a second, which "begins some time in 1917 and ends a few days before February 2, 1922 [the date of the publication of *Ulysses*]."[8] I would expand that time frame backwards to cover all the time in Joyce's life after 1904, a "fluid succession of presents" (*FP*, 60) in the self-portrait that, as they appear in *Ulysses*, are almost all represented by Bloom. "Fluid" is the operative word for this representation, for Bloom is not held to actual time and place as is Stephen. At the same time, he is as essential as Stephen to that "expression of myself" that Joyce identified as the motivating force for his work from *Chamber Music* onward (*JJII*, 240), and he arises as surely as does Stephen out of the events of Joyce's life, even though the "epical event" that led to Joyce's recognition of the Bloom in himself had not actually happened on the day that is reconstructed in *Ulysses* with such a wealth of dated naturalistic detail.

Bloom, I am arguing, had his psychic origin in the extraordinary emotional upheaval that Joyce experienced during his first return to Dublin in 1909, five years after his self-imposed exile. For the space of twenty-four hours in 1909, he allowed himself to doubt Nora Barnacle's complete allegiance to him (*JJII*, 279–82) and was consequently all but overcome by a wave of unmanageable jealousy, which was quite possibly beyond anything he had experienced before. The turmoil produced in him by this doubt, I think, had at least two far-reaching consequences, and the first was to confirm beyond any question his bond with Nora, who in 1904 had courageously joined him in his exile. Whatever we may decide about the rationale for Joyce's selection of 16 June 1904 as the historical day of *Ulysses*,[9] most of us would agree that the fictional day of the novel celebrates a crucial event in the true story of Joyce's life of feeling: his commitment to Nora. But this event took place over time. The initial commitment of 1904 represented at least in part the solution for Joyce to the loss of his mother; it is not too simplistic, I think, to say that Nora filled the terrible gap in Joyce's psychic economy that was created by this loss.[10] His bond with Nora, strained during their first five years by the practical inadequacy of both these young people for a stable married life, but deepened by the birth of a son and daughter, was then dramatically confirmed through the experience of jealousy in 1909.

The second consequence of this experience, I believe, was that Joyce discovered the psychic reality in himself that is at the center of his characterization of Bloom, who thus became the autobiographical expression of what Joyce later described to Power as "the modern theme . . . those hidden tides which govern everything and run humanity counter to the apparent flood" (54). Through Bloom Joyce could explore and exploit in his fiction not only the reverberations of the experience of jealousy itself but also aspects of himself not appropriate for Stephen Dedalus as he had been developed through *A Portrait*. Through Bloom, who is detached from time and place, he could include in his autobiographical portrait "those poisonous subtleties which envelop the soul, the ascending fumes of sex" (Power, 54) as he had been forced to recognize them in himself.

The two separate stories of Stephen's day and Bloom's, conspicuously not integrated in the narrative of *Ulysses*, are thematically united in the fiction and in Joyce's life through their common attachment to the loved place, Dublin, and to the loved woman, Nora. For Nora, whose surrogate in *Ulysses* is Molly, opened for the young Joyce the way out of Dublin and its nets, which is Stephen's existential problem in *Ulysses*. And for the mature Joyce, whose surrogate is Bloom, she guaranteed the way home, for, as Joyce wrote of Nora in his Trieste Notebook: "Wherever thou art shall be Erin to me."[11]

The introduction of Bloom, then, marks a significant shift in the "centre of emotional gravity" in Joyce's autobiographical epic, as Joyce moves into his own interior, a direction that continues through *Ulysses* and *Finnegans Wake*, and an arena in which psychoanalytic assumptions become ever more relevant. Autobiography in the twentieth century comes under a different rubric from that which defined the form before Freud. For the validation of the unconscious, which is associated with the development of Freudian psychoanalysis, has effectively blurred the distinctions between fiction and history and altered our notions about the linear progression of time in our lives. That Joyce was aware of the new dimensions opened up by psychoanalysis by the time he wrote *Ulysses* can hardly be questioned, and it seems reasonable to assume, as I do, that Joyce's acquaintance with early psychoanalytic writings, which were easily available to him in Zurich, contributed to a broadening of his understanding of the possibilities, indeed the demands, of truly autobiographical fiction, an expanded conception that is reflected in *Ulysses*.

In 1917, for example, at a time when Joyce was working in a concentrated fashion on his own autobiographical epic, two essays by Otto Rank on Homer and on the folk epic appeared in successive issues of *Imago*.[12] Citing Freud's 1908 "Creative Writers and Day-Dreaming" as the impetus for his study of the epic, Rank examines the manipulation of time by the epic poet as a variant of the "three-time scheme" described by Freud as characteristic of all forms of human fantasy, acknowledging Freud's rule that "every single phantasy is the fulfillment of a wish, a correction of unsatisfying reality" (*SE*, 9:146) and examining how this is accomplished in the epic. *Imago*, of course was received by the Zentralbibliothek during the period of Joyce's residence in Zurich, and, although there is no way to prove that Joyce read any of these essays, it cannot be disproved either, and it is quite possible that he read them all. Certainly Rank's essays on Homer and the folk epic, as well as Freud's early essay on similarities in the origins and construction of creative works and daydreams, offer a clarifying context for Joyce's manipulation of time in *Ulysses*, which can be seen as a variant of Freud's three-time scheme.

Joyce is fully conscious, I think, that he shares with the epic poet both the self-imposed obligation to re-create in realistic detail the historic past—for Joyce the lost world of his youth—and the freedom, within the limits defined by this obligation, to revise and reorder actual events in this re-created past, as Joyce has done in *Ulysses*. Rank points out, citing the great German romantic critic Friedrich Schlegel as his authority, that the epic poet has regularly "fused past, present, and future with one another" because in the epic these times are "quite equal" and are in fact projected in one plane to present what amounts to a new time, the "mixed time" of the epic.[13] Just so, Joyce in his modern epic, without giving up the appearance of a rigid adherence to historic time, has fused Bloom's time with Stephen's to produce, from different times in his own life, a new psychological time, the "day (life)" of *Ulysses*.

The Three-Time Scheme: Stephen, Freud, and Rank

Throughout "Scylla and Charybdis," an episode that he dominates, Stephen thinks and speaks as an artist. His presentation about Shakespeare's transformation of his life into his work, as well as his inner commentary on it, is in the spirit—whatever the actuality may be—of the librarian's opening reference to Goethe's interpretation of Hamlet in *Wilhelm Meister:* "a great poet on a great brother poet" (*U*, 9.2–3). Indeed, before he begins his lecture, Stephen explicitly claims for himself a place among that great brotherhood. To Eglinton's vehement rejection of any comparison between Aristotle and Plato, Stephen responds, "Which of the two . . . would have banished me from his commonwealth?" (*U*, 9.80–83), referring to Socrates' insistence at the beginning of book 10 of Plato's *Republic* that the "imitative tribe" of poets, that "charming tragic company" whose "great captain and teacher" is Homer, should be banished from the ideal republic (521). And Stephen, having declared himself a member of that "charming tragic company," then puts forward, almost as an aside, an equation that announces his kinship with Shakespeare: "Elizabethan London lay as far from Stratford as corrupt Paris lies from virgin Dublin" (*U*, 9.149–50).

We know, as does Stephen's audience in the library, that Shakespeare came to London from Stratford, and we also share with Stephen's audience the knowledge that Stephen has journeyed from Dublin to Paris. But Joyce, I think, knows more. For he has had access to material in the Zentralbibliothek Zürich that proposes a link between wandering, sexuality, and artistic production. Rank, for one, in a chapter of his *Incest*

Motif dealing with the "mechanisms of displacement of emotion [*Affekt-verschiebung*]," provides a footnote in which he points to the flight from home as a "typical reaction" of the writer to "an overpowerful fixation on the family complex," which for Rank, as we have seen, includes much more than the Oedipal triangle. Such an exodus, Rank asserts, "almost always" signals "the beginning of the poetic career," while later wanderings often are concurrent with a "most significant creative period." Rank then gives examples of poets/artists who have exiled themselves from home, including names that had considerable meaning for Joyce: not only Shakespeare, to whom Stephen explicitly links himself in this episode, but also Goethe, Schiller, Wagner, and Ibsen.[14]

Stephen thus presents his credentials as an artist both to his audience and to himself and goes on to make two much-quoted statements about the relation of time to the process of the artist's transformation of his life into his work. Together these statements suggest a typical Joycean footnote, pointing both to Freud's 1908 essay and to its 1917 elaboration by Otto Rank, who included a series of diagrams to illustrate the differing manipulation of time in the daydream, the nightdream, and the construction of memories, as well as the operation of the three-time scheme in the epic. Here in "Scylla and Charybdis" there are significant echoes of Freud and Rank, and we should consider, as in the parallel lecture on aesthetics in *A Portrait*, how Stephen's remarks apply to *Ulysses*.

First, Stephen reminds himself to "hold to the now, the here, through which all future plunges to the past" (*U*, 9.89), an acknowledgment of the shifting definitions of the three time frames of experience as they follow each other in the linear progression of our lives. To be sure, Stephen's mingling of the times presents an echo of Henri Bergson's description of "the past penetrating the present" and "the present eating into the future,"[15] but it also echoes Freud's description in "Creative Writers and Day-Dreaming" of the operation of the three times in the daydream, which "hovers," Freud says, between "the three moments of time which our ideation involves" (*SE*, 9:147). The diagram in figure 6.1, then, translates into English Rank's "schematic picture" of the operation of past, present, and future in the daydream, which was for the early psychoanalysts "the prototype of all the fantasies" (Rank, "Folk Epic," 373–74). As can be seen in the diagram by the direction of the arrows, the psychic work of the daydream starts, as it does in all fantasies, from the present, moving backwards around the past and then forward to the future, so

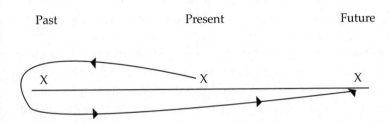

Fig. 6.1. Daydream

that, according to Freud, "past, present and future are strung together, as it were, on the thread of the wish that runs through them" (*SE,* 9:148).[16]

The daydreamer's wish is to correct the reality of the present situation, and what the dreamer does with the fantasy is to project the wished-for situation into the future. But though the action of the fantasy takes place, so to speak, in the future, the wish it fulfills reflects one of the great desires of the past—often an infantile wish that has been fulfilled in the past. The impetus for the fantasy, however, is an occasion in the present that arouses the past wish, and each daydream, in fact every fantasy of any kind, bears what Freud calls a "date-mark" (*SE,* 9:147), determined by the nature of the situation in the present—Stephen's "now" and "here."

Stephen's second statement about the three times is really a double statement, which winds up with an acknowledgment of such a "date-mark" in the portrait of the artist. Delivered to his audience in the context of the artist "weaving and unweaving his image" and couched entirely in the first person, it focuses on the fusion of past, present, and future in the creative act: "In the intense instant of the imagination . . . that which I was is that which I am and that which in possibility I may come to be." And Stephen immediately goes on to spell out what this fusion of times in the artist's consciousness means to him as he reconstructs his experience in the art work: "So in the future, the sister of the past, I may see myself as I sit here now but by reflection from that which then I shall be" (*U,* 9.376–85)—that is, the mature artist who will see his younger self "by reflection" from his own present time and who exists in

Stephen's present time largely as a wish for the future, as does the portrait he will create. What Stephen is putting into words is essentially a recurring daydream, in which he duplicates Shakespeare's achievement in *Hamlet*, writing his own "book of himself" (*U*, 9.115), the "ghost-story" (*U*, 9.141) that will immortalize him.

But from the point of view of the mature artist, the author of *Ulysses*, the situation that Stephen describes involves an act of memory, and in all the shifting of times implied in Stephen's statement, the first person remains: *I was, I am, I may come to be, I shall see myself*, pointing to the assumption that is basic to his Shakespeare presentation and to his own artistic ambitions: the stability of the artist's image through time and thus the validity of the artist's re-creation of that image in his work. Stephen has affirmed this integrity of his own image through the changes wrought by time during his little debate with himself about his identity. The subject of this inner debate is the pound he has borrowed from AE five months before, and he answers his own suggestion that since all the molecules in his body have changed in these months, "I am other I now" with the reminder that "I, entelechy, form of forms, am I by memory. I that sinned and prayed and fasted. A child Conmee saved from pandies. I, I and I. I" (*U*, 9.205–13).

This affirmation echoes Stephen's statement in "Telemachus" about the child he was at Clongowes—"I am another now and yet the same" (*U*, 1.311–12)—as well as his answer to his own half-joking claim in "Proteus" about his activities in Paris—"Other fellow did it: other me"— with the admission that "*Lui c'est moi*" (*U*, 3.182–83). And all these contrast with his response to Cranly's question in *A Portrait* about whether he had been happier as a believing schoolboy: "I was someone else then. . . . I was not myself as I am now, as I had to become" (*P*, 240). It is a significant development of Bloomsday that Stephen can now affirm that there is no "someone else," there is no "other I," because the past remains a living reality in the present, and "that which I was is that which I am and that which in possibility I may come to be"—through memory.

Sigmund Freud, who dealt exhaustively with his own memories in his autobiographical *Interpretation of Dreams* and with other people's memories in the mediated autobiography of his case studies, came to the conclusion, originally to his dismay, that memories are to a degree fantasies,[17] motivated, like the daydream and the nightdream, by a desire to

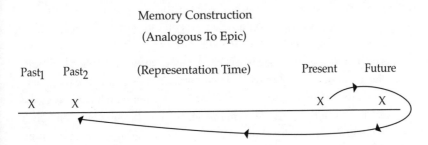

Fig. 6.2. Memory Construction

"correct unsatisfactory reality." But in contrast to the dreamer, who is dissatisfied with the present, the individual who retrieves a memory from past experience wants to correct the past—or at least parts of it. The psychic work involved in memory formation therefore amends, as it can, those elements of the past that do not accord with the individual's present self-image or indeed with the wished-for image of the future.

So, in memory, a new "psychological" past is formed, which Rank labels "representation-time" in the second of the two diagrams he provides for memory-construction (377). And in figure 6.2, a composite modeled on Rank's diagrams, the arrow representing the psychic work of the memory, starts, as it does in the daydream, from the present, goes around the future (in this case very close to the present) and back to an amended past (Past$_2$), the representation time of the memory, which stands between the real past and the present. Thus, the manipulation of time in the psychic construction of memories contrasts to the process in the daydream, in which, Rank says, a man "makes his past into the future." For, through memory construction, he "makes his future into the past" (377).

This does not mean, Rank points out, that memories are made out of whole cloth, for a man is bound to his own memory traces. These he can only "ameliorate, disguise, and rework," so that, even though many memories are historically untrue, they are "composed from true memory-material," through a "complicated working-out process" which, according to Freud, is analogous to epic formation (375–76). Indeed, "'childhood memories' of individuals," Freud recognizes, "come in general to acquire the significance of 'screen memories' and in doing so offer a remarkable analogy with the childhood memories that a nation preserves in its store of legends and myths." And in the epics of a nation, "motivated forgetting" plays an acknowledged role, so that "whatever is distressing to national feeling" is "wipe[d] out."[18]

Freud's analogy may easily be extended to autobiographical fiction, since both epic and autobiography use the materials of a real past, whatever embellishments may be added and whatever deformities may be excised. Both are thus based on memories of actual past events, and both are to a degree limited by those events. At the same time, however, they are significantly motivated by a desire to explain and justify the past in the light of the present and the hoped-for future. Surely this is true of Joyce's autobiographical epic, *Ulysses*, where even the "bioenergetic" portrait of Stephen, seen "by reflection" from his future self, is subject to this kind of mixed motivation. The diagram in figure 6.3—"Stephen's Ghost Story"—represents this situation from the perspective of the author of *Ulysses*, that is, James Joyce in the period from 1914 to 1922, which, for the convenience of the schematic picture, we may label the present.

Ghost Stories in *Ulysses*

From the vantage point of the author who is writing *Ulysses* during this period, Bloomsday, the fictional past that represents the historical 16 June 1904 is peopled with ghosts, thus making good on Stephen's boast in "Oxen of the Sun" about his power over "the past and its phantoms": "If I call them into life across the waters of Lethe will not the poor ghosts troop to my call?" (*U*, 14.1113–14). The power that Stephen boasts about is the power exercised by Homer's Odysseus over the dead in book 11 of the *Odyssey*, so that Stephen is here identified more explicitly than anyone else in the novel with the Ulysses of Joyce's title. To be sure, from the perspective of the Joyce who is re-creating Bloomsday between 1914 and 1922, the fictional Stephen, who stands in for Joyce's twenty-two-year-old self, is one of those ghosts of the past, perhaps the prime ghost. But, if we accept the proposition that "that which I was . . . is that which in possibility I may come to be," then Stephen's claim to be the "lord and giver of their life" (*U*, 14.1116) is also true.

In this "Ghoststory," Stephen is closely tied to the youthful self of 1904, even though Joyce has made some minor changes that have been identified and doubtless others that have not. He himself was not actually

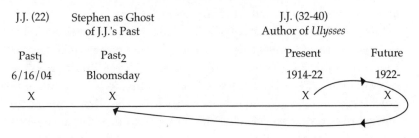

Fig. 6.3. Stephen's Ghost Story: The Artist's Struggle

living at the Martello Tower in June 1904, and his *Hamlet* theory was probably much more rudimentary in 1904 than the theory Stephen offers in *Ulysses*, suggesting a continuation in the later novel of the tendency toward "self-exaltation rather than self-criticism" that Beebe noted as the "surprising thing about the changes from reality" in *A Portrait*. For in the earlier novel, Beebe observed, Joyce, "far from maintaining the ironical attitude of a mature man looking back on the errors of youth, actually gave to Stephen many beliefs and convictions which Joyce did not come by until after 1902." The author thus attributed to his younger self "the learning, the wisdom, the cunning" of the mature Joyce (71). Nevertheless, Stephen is easily recognizable in *Ulysses* as the ghost of Joyce's youth and can clearly be placed in Dublin on 16 June 1904.

Bloom's relation to his creator and to Dublin, however, is not nearly so well defined, as has been earlier noted in some detail (40–45). Although roughly the same age as Joyce in the Present of the diagram in figure 6.4, he does not belong to that actual time. And his presence in the Dublin of 16 June 1904 is made problematic by a variety of details about his history and his living situation on the fictional Bloomsday, typified by his living in a house that was vacant in 1904. Thus he is also alien to Past$_1$ in figure 6.4. Again, his very physical presence is made dubious by the "absurd and impossible dimensions," to use Adams's phrase (184), which are assigned to him in "Ithaca," including, as I have earlier noted, a twenty-eight-inch chest, as well as a ten-inch thigh connected to an eleven-inch calf (*U*, 17.1818–19). Bloom's own uncertainty about his past and present identity, which is reflected in his self-addressed and never answered question, "Was that I? Or am I now I?" (*U*, 8.607), is thus reinforced by otherwise unconnected oddities about him.

His residence on Bloomsday, of course, does have a number, and it is a famous one. For many years it was an actual house on an actual street in Dublin: Number 7 Eccles Street.[19] But Number 7 Eccles Street, we know, was vacant in 1904 (Adams, 61), a temporal fact that accords, I think, with psychic fact. In 1904 Joyce took Nora Barnacle into his life; he committed himself to her, whatever date he chose to give to that crucial commitment. And when he did, Bloom became a possibility: "the manchild in the womb" of the end of "Ithaca" (*U*, 17.2317–18). Bloom was not born on 16 June 1904, though, but rather in August 1909 during Joyce's devastating experience of jealousy in Dublin, the experience that provides the autobiographical base for Bloom's story in *Ulysses*. And he was born at Number 7 Eccles Street.

The Experience of Jealousy

Ellmann tells the story (*JJII*, 278–82), which he has pieced together from John Francis Byrne's account (156), from Joyce's letters of 6 and 7 August 1909 to Nora, and from an interview with Stanislaus Joyce almost half a century later (*JJII*, 282 n. 23). At the end of July 1909, not quite five years after he and Nora had left Ireland for the Continent, Joyce made his first trip back, bringing Giorgio with him and leaving Stanislaus to deal with his chronically unstable household, his wife and daughter, and his creditors in Trieste.[20] Although he had "practical objectives" to justify the trip—a contract with Maunsel and Company for *Dubliners* and the possibility of a professorship at his old university (*JJII*, 276)—his main purpose was to see and be seen by those he had left behind, his family and his friends.

One of the first of these friends to be contacted was Vincent Cosgrave, a schoolmate and longtime fellow idler, memorialized in both *A Portrait* and *Ulysses* as Lynch. Cosgrave in turn told Oliver St. John Gogarty that Joyce was in town, and Gogarty, the model for Buck Mulligan in *Ulysses*, immediately got in touch with Joyce and invited him to his house. Joyce, according to a letter of 4 August 1909 to Stanislaus, told Gogarty that he intended to include in his novel his brief stay with Gogarty at the

Martello Tower, and although Joyce assured Gogarty that he bore him no ill will, he reminded him that "I must write as I have felt" (*Letters*, 2:230–31). Joyce "relished" this meeting, Ellmann says, "as the fulfillment of a daydream, in which he, the lofty, cool, untouchable hero had discomfited his suppliant enemy" (*JJII*, 278).

Joyce also visited John Francis Byrne, the original of Cranly in *A Portrait*, taking with him "in beaming pride" his four-year-old son for a pleasant afternoon. In 1909 Byrne was living at Number 7 Eccles Street, which, of course, is the Blooms' address in *Ulysses*, and Byrne writes in his memoirs: "Joyce had good reason to remember No. 7 Eccles Street, for it was to that house one subsequent afternoon that he came, in a state of utter perturbation, to see me" (155–56). Byrne does not reveal the source of Joyce's distress, but Ellmann does.

Two days before he appeared at Byrne's door on 8 August, Joyce had been told by Vincent Cosgrave that during the time surrounding 16 June 1904, the day of *Ulysses*, Nora was, in Joyce's own words "dividing [her] body" between Cosgrave and Joyce. Apparently Joyce believed him without question, despite the "inherent improbability" of Cosgrave's boast (*JJII*, 279) and despite his own experience of Nora's steadfastness. His assurance to his Aunt Josephine three months into their adventure that "I have not been able to discover any falsehood in this nature which had the courage to trust me" (*JJII*, 189) was temporarily annulled, and he was overwhelmed by a debilitating jealousy he had never experienced before. He was in undiluted agony.

Byrne describes the figure that confronted him on 8 August: "I had never before this afternoon seen anything to approach the frightening condition that convulsed him. He wept and groaned and gesticulated in futile impotence as he sobbed out to me the thing that had occurred. Never in my life have I seen a human being more shattered" (156). This is a far cry from the "lofty, cool, untouchable hero" of the meeting with Gogarty, and we might think Byrne was exaggerating, since the picture of a sobbing, groaning James Joyce does not fit any other picture we have of him, either as a young man—the model, after all, for the cool, detached Stephen Dedalus—or in his middle years, when by all accounts the detachment was even more pronounced.[21] But Ellmann also includes in his account the letters that Joyce wrote to Nora from the irrational depths of his jealous despair (*JJII*, 279–81). An hour after his conversation with Cosgrave, Joyce put his feelings on paper in a letter to Nora that pictured for her his agony, with his eyes full of "tears of sorrow and mortification" and his heart "full of bitterness and despair." He assures her that he will "cry for days" because "my faith in that face I loved is broken," and he has "learnt that the only being I believed in was not loyal to me" (*JJII,* 279–80).

A second letter, written early the next morning, flings questions at Nora about specifics of her sexual past that are reminiscent of Molly's report in *Ulysses* of Bloom's "question and answer would you do this that and the other with the coalman yes with a bishop yes . . . who is in your mind now tell me who are you thinking of who is it tell me his name" (*U,* 18.89–95). Joyce writes to Nora, "Is Georgie my son?" reminding her that "the first night I slept with you in Zurich was October 11th and he was born July 27th. That is nine months and 16 days. I remember that there was very little blood that night. Were you fucked by anyone before you came to me?" He supposes that "the rumour here is circulated that I have taken the leavings of others. Perhaps they laugh when they see me parading '*my*' son in the streets" (*JJII,* 280–81). Indeed, the primitive quality of these letters, which present a startling contrast to any other writing we have from Joyce, entirely confirms the picture presented by Byrne, a picture that is, I think, a candid shot of the Bloom in Joyce, in at least one of his attitudes.

But this picture is by no means identical with the Bloom in *Ulysses* because through Bloom Joyce reworked this particularly humiliating experience of his past at the same time that he systematically worked in traces of the facts of the case in his reconstruction. The diagram in figure 6.4, then—"*Ulysses*: The Experience of Jealousy"—shows Bloom's story as drawn from a second real past, the past of 1909, which is still a part of the Dublin experience, and which Joyce amended and transferred backward to the fictional Bloomsday. The past represented in *Ulysses* is thus to a degree historically untrue, but it is nevertheless composed of "true memory-materials."

We may list among the "true memory-materials" that the twenty-seven-year-old Joyce almost eagerly accepted his wife's unfaithfulness as a fact; that he poured out his unjustified jealousy in wounding letters to her at a great distance; and that he humiliated himself in a blubbering confession to his friend Byrne. None of this could be edifying to contemplate in retrospect. In the depths of his jealousy he had discovered another personality in himself that he had not known about before, and the

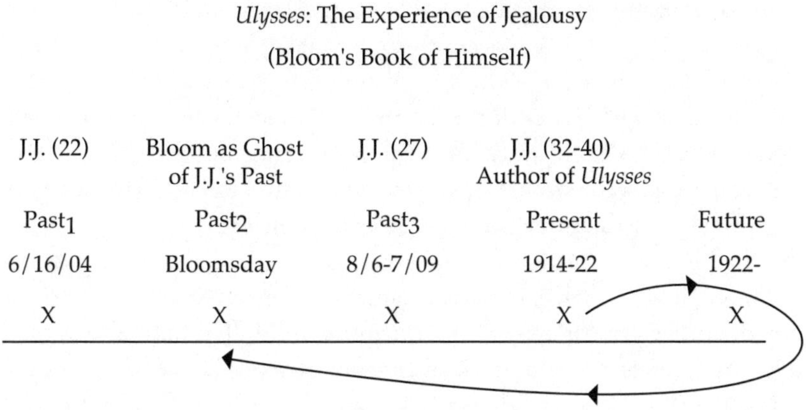

Ulysses: The Experience of Jealousy

(Bloom's Book of Himself)

J.J. (22)	Bloom as Ghost of J.J.'s Past	J.J. (27)	J.J. (32-40) Author of *Ulysses*	
Past$_1$	Past$_2$	Past$_3$	Present	Future
6/16/04	Bloomsday	8/6-7/09	1914-22	1922-
X	X	X	X	X

Fig. 6.4. Bloom's Ghost Story: The Experience of Jealousy

ironic detachment that was his trusted weapon against inner pain vanished as he gave himself over to maudlin self-pity and wailing reproach. This alien personality was not one he could readily acknowledge, but at the same time it was not one that he could absolutely deny or reject or even entirely disapprove. And he had also discovered that the internal uproar he had experienced, painful though it might be, was just about the most exciting thing that had happened to him.[22] In *Ulysses* he merged these true facts of the case with an ameliorating, justifying overlay to create in the fiction a new past, revealing new, "subterranean" aspects of his self-portrait.

The Reconstructed Past

To begin with, although Joyce made Bloom's repressed jealousy the muted center of his day, he also planted throughout the text suggestions of Bloom's complicity in his betrayal, of his promotion of the occasion for jealousy. Bloom appears to be, as Stephen labels Shakespeare, "bawd and cuckold" (*U*, 9.1021), and indeed he is so designated in "Circe" (15.1159), where his compulsive complicity in his own sexual betrayal is dramatized. Bloom is accused, through the Sins of the Past, of "offering his nuptial partner to all strongmembered males" (*U*, 15.3034) as, in fact, he will later offer Stephen access to Molly in "Ithaca" (*U*, 17.929–64).[23] And his eager participation in his cuckolding by Blazes Boylan in "Circe" (U, 15.3756–815), which is a fact of the text, whatever its connection to reality, provides a base for Molly's accusation that Bloom is "trying to make a whore of me" (U, 18.96). Even more it validates her suspicion that Bloom has sent Milly away "on account of me and Boylan" (U, 18.1007–8) and her perception that Bloom "wants me and Boylan" (U, 18.1254), which she leaves unfinished, though hardly unclear.

In his reconstruction of the experience in *Ulysses*, Joyce justifies Bloom's jealousy (an extended and amended version of his own 1909 experience) in a remarkably convincing brief for Molly's insatiable sexuality and promiscuous adultery, certified by Bloom's list of her lovers (U, 17.2133–42). This list was taken literally by early readers and critics; Edmund Wilson's judgment that Molly, a woman "of prodigious sexual appetites," has been "continually and indiscriminately unfaithful to Bloom" (195) represented a critical consensus for many years. But Joyce has also, with great ingenuity, created a point-by-point negation of his own carefully constructed brief, thus acknowledging obliquely the baselessness of his own jealousy in the real-life situation and—also obliquely—destroying in the text the bases for Bloom's list of lovers and exonerating Molly almost completely.

As early as 1951 Murray Godwin pointed to the "negative evidence" in "Penelope" that makes clear that Molly's only adultery "in the literal, physical sense" is with Blazes Boylan on Bloomsday (221–25). It took ten more years for Adams to come to the same conclusion, followed in order by Stanley Sultan and David Hayman.[24] And it has now been established and catalogued in Don Gifford and Robert Seidman's guidebook that Bloom's list of lovers, except for Boylan, is systematically repudiated in the text, name by name, sometimes by Bloom himself (493).

We are left, of course, with that wonderfully named fantasy creature, Blazes Boylan, who does not appear to have had a local habitation or a clear model in the Dublin of 1904, any more than Bloom does,[25] but who, I suspect, is as real as Bloom and just as close to Joyce's heart. Ellmann characterizes "the virile Boylan" as "nothing but a shell," indeed, as Joyce's "villain," although he also acknowledges that Joyce "may have had a sneaking regard for those burly men . . . with whom Boylan belongs" (JJII, 378). I have no quarrel with the ambivalence suggested in Ellmann's judgment, but it seems possible to me that, rather than being a villain, Blazes Boylan may instead be seen as heroic in a special sense. He may well be the projection of a kind of ideal phallic self, a fantasy of unadulterated sexuality, which also comes from the past of 1909. Ellmann charges Boylan with "brutality of animal sensuality without feeling" (*JJII*, 379), but surely it is clear that such one-sided sensuality is what the pornographic letters of the second trip to Dublin in 1909 (*SL*, 181–93) are all about. In virtually every one of these letters, in fact, Joyce himself labels the sexual experiences that he describes as brutal and/or beastly, even as he assures Nora that there is another side to his love. But he also exhibits, it seems to me, a very real pride—coupled, to be sure, with shame—in this aspect of himself, so that Blazes Boylan can be seen as yet another aspect of his self-portrait. And the picture Molly paints of him in her soliloquy[26] may stand as a memorial to Joyce's youthful libido, of which the middle-aged author of *Ulysses* is perhaps more than a little proud, more than a little ashamed, and also more than a little jealous.

Thus, in his fictional reconstruction in *Ulysses* of the experience of jealousy, Joyce has developed with considerable density a far-from-admirable aspect of his internal response, a recognition of which may well have evolved over a period of years. In the telling, however, he has tidied up his own immediate public response, which actually was quite messy and spewed out all over Nora and his friend Byrne. Joyce instead provides for Bloom, also with considerable density, a series of "reflections" about Molly's supposed infidelity that are the absolute opposite of Joyce's own hysterical response to the dubious information that Cosgrave shared with him in 1909. Bloom, that is, responds not only with "envy" and "jealousy" but also with "abnegation" and "equanimity," with, in fact, "more abnegation than jealousy, less envy than equanimity" (*U*, 17.2155–95). He is allowed a certain dignity, almost nobility. Almost, but not quite, for Joyce undercuts the quality of Bloom's feeling through the narrator's comic Latinate elaboration on each of these nouns of feeling, followed by a similar elaboration on Bloom's rejection of retribution and his justification for his "sentiments" (*U*, 17.2200–26). All this leads finally, of course, to the "mellow yellow smellow" kiss that awakens Molly (*U*, 17.2241–43), a passage so beloved by Joyceans as to be virtually a mantra of *Ulysses* criticism that deals with Bloom and Molly.

To be sure, the condensed Latinate diction that is characteristic of "Ithaca" makes any section of the text difficult to paraphrase with certainty, but the text here is worth the effort. A part of its meaning depends on an earlier passage in "Ithaca," in which it is recorded that Bloom has for a guide in all his wanderings, "At sea, septentrional [in the North] by night the polestar" and "On land, meridional [in the South], a bispherical moon, revealed in imperfect varying phases of lunation through the posterior interstice of the imperfectly occluded skirt of a carnose negligent perambulating female, a pillar of the cloud by day" (*U*, 17.1992–99). This complex "celestial phenomenon" looks forward to Bloom's first act after entering the bed he shares with Molly—the preparation for the kiss, the kiss itself, and the response.

Last in the series of reflections that precedes the act is Bloom's consideration of the fact that "posterior female hemispheres, redolent of . . . excretory sanguine and seminal warmth" (*U*, 17.2232–33), are a source of satisfaction everywhere in the world, "in all habitable lands" (*U*, 17.2229–30). By this time, of course, a reader is aware, having followed the course of Bloom's decision—which he carries out—to examine the backsides of the statues in the museum, that Bloom is *always* on the lookout for them, warm *or* cold. In "Ithaca," however, the "posterior female hemispheres" are available in his own bed, and Joyce presents an elaborate before-and-after activity—"antesatisfaction" to "postsatisfaction"—with the kiss, actually a series of kisses, at the center (*U*, 17.2237–46). The essentials of this chiastic structure may be summarized as follows.

As he observes Molly's bottom, which is apparently covered by her nightdress, Bloom becomes aware of the beginnings of an erection ("approximate"). He gradually lifts the nightdress, presumably the "imperfectly occluded" (or not quite closed) skirt referred to earlier, and reveals the "bispherical moon" of the earlier description. He then silently contemplates it, then kisses it. After the kiss, he reverses the order of the activities as he again silently contemplates Molly's bottom, "tentatively" veils it again by gradually lowering her nightdress, and then is aware of a "proximate" erection. Thus Bloom's "guide" in his wanderings is revealed as Molly, who is certainly "carnose," as revealed in the "fleshy charms" of the "faded photo" shown to Stephen by Bloom in "Eumaeus" (*U*, 16.1425–60), and whose "bispherical moon" is certainly a focus for Bloom's husbandly attentions when he enters the bed.

It has been my purpose in this chapter to establish Joyce's experience of jealousy in 1909 as a prime autobiographical base for the portrait of Bloom. In addition I have come to believe that case studies about perversion, with which the early psychoanalytic journals were replete, have also furnished touches in Bloom's portrait that contribute to Joyce's conviction that in *Ulysses* he had indeed successfully explored the "modern theme." For it is through Bloom that Joyce reveals the "pathological and psychological body which our behaviour and thought depend on" (Power, 56). These case studies, though not of any particular significance in themselves, concerned actual people, after all, who were living in Europe at the same time as Joyce. Moreover, the material in them is clearly relevant to Joyce's claim, already noted, that if he "put down a bucket into [his] own soul's well, sexual department," he would "draw up Griffith's and Ibsen's and Skeffington's and Bernard Vaughan's and St. Aloysius' and Shelley's and Renan's water along with my own," as well as his declared intention "to do that in my novel" (*Letters*, 2:191). His interest in the material thus goes well beyond personal prurience, though such prurience surely cannot be ruled out altogether.

Bloom and "*Gesässerotik*"

I shall consider further examples of these studies in the following chapter, but one fairly typical investigation is of particular relevance here: Isidore Sadger's "*Über Gesässerotik*," in which the author examines the behavior of persons whose "principal or exclusive sexual interest" is in the buttocks. He recognizes that what he is calling "buttock- or gluteal-eroticism" is "a part or at least a continuation" of the anal eroticism identified by Freud as a significant stage in the development of sexuality in infants and children (351). But this special form of anal eroticism is characterized by specific symptoms, which Sadger examines (351–52). He notes that "not a few men," when meeting a beautiful girl, "are much less captivated and drawn by her face than by her rearward parts." These men cannot, as Sadger puts it, "resist a splendid backside" (353). And we may be reminded of Bloom's encounter in Dlugacz's butcher shop with the "nextdoor girl," she of the "vigorous hips," whom Bloom remembers "whacking a carpet on the clothesline," her "crooked skirt" swinging. As Bloom watches her in the butcher shop, his paper held "aslant patiently, bending his senses and his will, his soft subject gaze at rest," he sees again in his mind her skirt swinging, "whack by whack by whack" (*U*, 4.145–64). This is language that suggests that Bloom, prudently noncommittal though he is, is sensually stirred by the memory. And he hurries to buy his kidney, hoping to "catch up and walk behind her if she went slowly, behind her moving hams. Pleasant to see first thing in the morning. Hurry up, damn it" (U, 4.171–73).

This evidence of Bloom's fixation on the female bottom is reinforced by Molly's exasperated comments on her husband's habit of embracing "the wrong end of me" as well as her denunciation of "any man thatd kiss a womans bottom" (U, 18.1401–2). But surely the most memorable description of Bloom's enjoyment of Molly's bottom is found in the little bedtime scene that I have summarized above. And here Sadger's report of the manifestations of "Gesässerotik" is clearly relevant.

Sadger points out that "with the normal position in intercourse excluded," the man who is a buttock-erotic has before him during his version—or perversion—of the sex act the desired "globes," and he can, "with great joy, uncover and show the woman" (353).[27] He connects this "show- and uncovering-pleasure" with a variety of perversions and suggests that "the back side of our body serves better for a series of perversions than the actual sex organs, and people with strong buttock-eroticism generally act as if it were the genitals, or, if one will, a form of fetish" (352).[28] Sadger also provides a lengthy footnote, quoting a study titled "The Buttocks in Folk Thinking," which includes the information that "every great brothel must keep at least one broad-buttocked prostitute, who operates, not through her front, but solely through a powerfully developed posterior." This is to accommodate those "festishists who want to know neither normal vaginal nor abnormal anal coitus, but content themselves with the ecstacy which the glimpse of a great woman's buttocks [grossen Frauengesässes] brings to them" (353–54 n. 1). Can this be Bloom?

Certainly it comes very close, and it can further be recalled that Bloom's preparations for bed include "remov[ing] a pillow from the head to the foot of the bed" (U, 17.2112–13) thus echoing another footnote in Sadger's article, elaborating on the case of a twenty-six-year-old patient "with strongly prominent buttock-eroticism," who reported that he had found "a special delight" in turning himself around in bed, putting the pillow at the end where the feet were supposed to lie and lying with his head at the foot of the bed. This position was connected with great pleasure, "a peculiarly comfortable feeling" (357 n. 2). And it is as Bloom settles himself comfortably at the wrong end of the bed that he turns his thoughts to "posterior female hemispheres" and salutes those in his bed,

echoing Sadger's description of the "uncovering" and "showing" so satisfying to the buttock-erotic.

Sadger relates a number of peculiarities of the patient whose case he
describes to his substitutive sexual interest in "the posterior and the anal
crack." To the information that the patient often omits the middle letter
in words, Sadger responds that this gives him "two halves and an empty
space between, i.e., the backside" (357). And we may be reminded that
Bloom's tripartite goodnight kiss salutes the "mellow yellow furrow" as
well as "each plump melonous hemisphere" (*U*, 17.2241–42). When the
patient reports reversing the numbers in a date—1871 becoming 1781—
Sadger assures him that this is another "symptom of your buttock-ero-
tism. You really reversed the genitals, for you are not interested in the
front side, only in the posterior," and through a complicated play with the
relations between the numbers, Sadger comes up with the reminder that
"1 + 7 gives 8, and the lying down 8 (∞) represents the two buttocks with
the *crena ani* in the middle," adding in a footnote that "the buttocks are
called in the vernacular 'the eight back'" (357 n. 1).

The "lying down 8," of course, is familiar to Joyceans as the symbol
used in both the Linati and Gorman schema for the time in "Penelope."
William York Tindall, playing with the significance of the number eight
as it connects with Molly—her birthday is the eighth; there are eight
sentences in her episode—was probably the first to note that "eight lying
down (as Mrs. Bloom commonly is) is a sign of infinity." Tindall thus
connects Molly with the timelessness that fits into his archetypal vision
of her (234). Ellmann, too, identifies the time of "Penelope" as "no
o'clock," pointing out that "it is the time indicated mathematically by the
slightly disproportioned figure oo or lemniscate lying on its side—the
number of eternity and infinity."[29] Any reasonably experienced reader of
Joyce can believe that these connections are intended, but such a reader
would hardly be surprised if the faintly scatological connection to
Sadger's exposition of "*Gesässerotik*" were also in question.

As has been noted, Sadger, apparently something of a specialist in perversion,[30] identifies what he is calling "buttock-eroticism" as a form of
Freud's "anal-eroticism," which, according to orthodox psychoanalysis, is
one of the so-called polymorphous perverse impulses that necessarily
characterize sexual development before puberty. In the adult, however,
acting on such impulses is a regression and a perversion by the Freudian
definition given in Charles Rycroft's current *Critical Dictionary of Psy-*

choanalysis—"any form of adult sexual behaviour in which heterosexual intercourse is not the preferred goal" (129)—or, as stated anatomi-
cally by Richard Brown, anything other than "heterosexual genital love"
(56). Such behavior is also perverse by Catholic definitions, as Brown
documents in his chapter titled *"Emissio seminis inter vas naturale* [the
ejaculation of the semen in the natural vagina]." Thus Brown concludes
that Bloom's sexuality is perverse by either definition, although at the
same time Bloom somehow "retains his precarious normality throughout" (88), an anomaly that Brown attributes to a radical cultural change
in sexual attitudes in the years since the appearance of Bloom. I would
agree with Brown that, in addition to the living autobiographical reality
of his center, it is this shift in social norms that makes Bloom "a proper
hero of sexual modernity" and "saves him in the reader's eyes" (61, 88).[31]

To be sure, when we examine Joyce's uses of allusion, we are more
times than not reminded of Joyce's often quoted comment to Frank
Budgen: "When you get an idea, have you ever noticed what *I* can make
of it?" ("Recollections," 543). This is especially true in his transformation
of psychoanalytic detail as it relates to Bloom. Joyce's description of
Bloom's bedtime kiss, for example, has a certain paradoxical delicacy and
even charm, which the account in the case study it echoes notably lacks.
Of course, like much of the detail about Bloom and his habits, this final
scene in Bloom's day is strongly flavored with the comic, recalling
Budgen's observation that, although Joyce had a "natural awareness of
sexual perversity," this aspect of life was to him "comic" ("Recollections," 186–87).

Indeed, Leopold Bloom is acknowledged as "one of the great comic
characters of all literature,"[32] a "court jester" for Rebecca West and
Charlie Chaplin's "literary twin" for Marshall McLuhan.[33] His sexual
oddities, of which his goodnight kiss is only a particularly dramatic example, are facets of his comic effect. Nothing could be more quin-
tessentially Bloom than Joyce's description of this particular oddity—or
more purely Joyce. The passage is a little miracle of comic prose—perhaps even poetry. If it were not, it might be a little disgusting. But the
comic success of the passage and its surrounding text renders such a
judgment irrelevant, if not impossible. For Bloom is to a large degree
insulated against such a judgment or possibly any judgment, favorable or
unfavorable, through his integrity as a comic character, an identity that
tends to nullify judgment. Lionel Trilling, in fact, in a discussion of the

polymorphous perverse sexual tendencies revealed in Joyce's 1909 letters to Nora, asserts that when Joyce assigned these aspects of his mind to Bloom he rendered them "comic, which is to say morally neutral" because of the "distancing" effect of our laughter (68). And this distancing effect operates as the great corrective for the past in Joyce's translation and transformation of his experience of jealousy in *Ulysses,* as it does, I think, for everything autobiographical assigned to Bloom. Trilling suggests that Joyce's decision to assign his own "perverse fantasies" to Bloom, his refusal to connect them with Stephen, could be seen as "a derogation of Joyce's courage as an artist" or even "a derogation of personal courage" ("Joyce in His Letters," 64). Perhaps.

But Joyce's decision to split his autobiographical subject into two opposite persons, each of whom could reveal a part of the contradictory truth about himself, may instead be seen as the height of artistic wisdom as well as personal honesty. *A Portrait* had traced the development of Stephen, the self-conscious artist of Joyce's original conception of his autobiographical fiction. The 1909 experience, however, including both the unfounded jealousy and its aftermath in the pornographic letters, which wallow in excremental language and mawkish sentimentality at the same time, apparently revealed to Joyce, as an essential part of his true personality, "those poisonous subtleties which envelop the soul, the ascending fumes of sex," which he associated with the "modern theme"[34] and which are at the same time so closely associated with Freud's psychoanalysis. Stephen simply could not encompass the whole, for this realm of Joyce's psyche does not belong to the artist-self that has been developed through Stephen in *A Portrait,* a basic incompatibility that Joyce must have sensed to some degree when he made his first attempt to work through the 1909 experience in *Exiles,* where he attached the jealousy motif to Richard Rowan, with disastrous artistic results.

The writing of *Exiles* appears to follow closely the time scheme that Freud outlines in "Creative Writers and Day-Dreaming" for the imaginative writer's translation of his life into his work: "A strong experience in the present awakens in the creative writer a memory of an earlier experience (usually belonging to his childhood) from which there now proceeds a wish which finds its fulfillment in the creative work. The work itself exhibits elements of the recent provoking occasion as well as of the old memory" (*SE,* 9:151). Although the dates for the composition of *Exiles* are somewhat fuzzy, it appears that Joyce interrupted his work on the beginning episodes of *Ulysses* sometime late in 1913 to write the play (*Letters,* 2:64–65), and the "strong experience" that moved him was apparently his discovery that Roberto Prezioso had propositioned Nora "some time in 1911 or 1912" (*JJII,* 316), reviving in Joyce the memory of the "earlier experience" of 1909 (behind which any good Freudian could surely see the Oedipal triangle of childhood). The play clearly exhibits elements of the Prezioso affair (*JJII,* 317), as well as the mixture of strong and conflicting emotions attached to the earlier experience. And the wish that the creative work tries to fulfill, I think, not only in *Exiles* but also in *Ulysses,* is to bring the extraordinarily violent emotions of the 1909 experience under the control of the intellect and the will.

In *Exiles* Joyce attempted a literal translation of his experience, attributing to Richard Rowan—who is, like Stephen, a bioenergetic self-portrait, recognizable as Joyce—the self-willed jealous doubts that he had come to see in himself in the wake of his ordeal of jealousy. Richard reveals the perverse nature of his motivation in dialogue that is rhetorically akin to the clean parts of the "dirty letters." Speaking, for example, to Robert Hand, a trial version of a second self, Richard admits that "in the very core of my ignoble heart I longed to be betrayed . . . by you, my best friend, and by her . . . passionately and ignobly, to be dishonoured for ever in love and in lust" (*E,* 70). Although the overt sexual perversity that was attached to the 1909 experience in Joyce's life is not revealed, a peculiar miasma of sexual obsession pervades the play, and the writing of *Exiles* may indeed have been a therapeutic success for Joyce, judging from his 1916 comment on Nora's dream about a weeping Prezioso: "the motive from which I liberated myself in art he is unable to liberate himself in life" (*JJII,* 437). As art, however, *Exiles* is widely judged a failure.

But in *Ulysses* Joyce succeeded in bringing the whole of the experience of jealousy under the control of his artistic will, integrating it almost seamlessly into his "epic of two races." He distanced himself from both artist and cuckold, whom he separated into Stephen and Bloom, assigning to each a separate aspect of the total experience, which is mastered for each in a different and appropriate way. To Stephen, the acknowledged artist-surrogate, he assigned the whole question of the "incertitude" of biological paternity that he himself faced in 1909 and immediately communicated to Nora: "Is Georgie my son?" (*JJII,* 280). And Stephen, with access to the fully matured intellectual virtuosity of his creator, rings changes on the "paternity theme" throughout *Ulysses.* He meshes it with Christian dogma and with his artistic ambitions to become the creator of "the word that shall not pass away" (*U*, 14.293–94); the "son consubstantial with the father" (*U*, 9.480–81); the art work that, with its paternity certain, guarantees the personal immortality of the artist.

And through Bloom, the unacknowledged surrogate, Joyce could reveal freely the polymorphous perverse sexual tendencies that are demonstrably an aspect of his mind. Bloom, as Mary Colum recognized in her early review of *Ulysses*, "is the one character whom Joyce really loves" ("Confessions," 332), for, as St. Paul wrote to the Ephesians, "no man ever yet hated his own flesh" (Ephesians 5.29). Joyce combined these revelations with a free translation in the fiction of the experience of jealousy, which had become a significant event in his life and to which these perverse tendencies were apparently drawn as to a magnet. By assigning all this to Bloom, he could bring the factually unacceptable picture of his jealousy and its obsessive fascination for him under the control of his comic genius, which enabled him not only to entertain generations of readers but also to reveal, as an essential part of his autobiographical fiction, his own hidden world and at the same time—at least for his lifetime—*keep* it hidden.[35]

Freudian Contexts Chez Bloom

From the Journals

The psychic core of Leopold Bloom's characterization is thus sunk deep in James Joyce's own experience and personality. The fictional details through which this core is fleshed out, however, are extraordinarily diverse. Many may indeed have their origins in Joyce's life story, but many may not. These fictional details are drawn from a wide variety of models and written sources, of which the psychoanalytic case studies that I consider in this chapter are only one. Unlike Stephen, who, as has been noted, is held closely to actual time and place, the construction of Bloom's shape and circumstances, is entirely flexible, since he exists outside the actual world that *Ulysses* reflects with such factual exactness. Sometimes, in fact, as is true of the details that contribute to the portrait of Molly Bloom, the specifics of Bloom's portrait may be at odds with one another.[1]

At the 1980 Provincetown Joyce Conference, Robert Motherwell, the great American abstractionist painter, declared Joyce "a master of masters of collage, *the* great discovery of twentieth-century modernism," achieving "layer after layer that not even painting can approach."[2] Collage, the third and final stage of cubism, is a technique, we should remember, in which seemingly extraneous materials—"found objects" or *"trouvés"*—are stuck to the canvas and painted into the picture. These attached objects are often in some way associated with the subject of the painting, but not necessarily integrated into the picture. And the external portrait of Bloom is a prime example of Motherwell's accolade: a superb collage, a mix of living and textual found objects, collected and connected through association, but not necessarily parts of an integrated whole.

It is some variation of the fundamental psychoanalytic practice of free association that appears to determine Joyce's selection of the bits and pieces from psychoanalytic texts that become a part of Bloom's portrait. Richard Brown, who examines in his *Joyce and Sexuality* a much broader range of texts than the psychoanalytic literature I am concerned with in this study, points out that Joyce, with "no conclusive allegiance to any single author or theory," drew on a "huge variety of sources for his presentation of Bloomian sexuality" (85, 88). I should like to emphasize this range and also the irrelevance of theoretical conviction, as it applies to the psychoanalytic intertexts I am considering here. I should in addition re-emphasize their fragmentary character. If Joyce finds something he can use in developing his own patterns, he is not concerned with the place of the fragment he finds in its original text. Nor does he have to believe in the principles that lie behind any of the textual shards that he chooses to add to his work. Nevertheless, as I have argued in my introductory chapter, these bits and pieces, once uncovered, retain their identity and something of the intention that produced them in the first place, so that they have an independent impact, which, as they multiply, has a cumulative effect.

Joyce appears not to discriminate according to some predetermined standard of literary or philosophical merit in the work itself. He has commandeered lines not only from Shakespeare and Homer but also from a now largely forgotten novelist, James Lane Allen.[3] Likewise, in the area of psychoanalysis, Joyce may find what he wants among major psychoanalytic pioneers like Sigmund Freud and C. G. Jung and Otto Rank. But he may also appropriate details, as I have suggested in the previous chapter, from writings of no particular significance and from authors like Isidor Sadger, "an insufferable writer," Freud wrote to Jung, and "a congenital fanatic of orthodoxy who happens by mere accident to believe in psychoanalysis rather than in the law given by God on Sinai-Horeb."[4] But the details Joyce chooses for the portrait of Bloom appear in some of the most memorable and most remembered scenes in *Ulysses*—like the scene that includes Bloom's goodnight kiss.

Leopold Bloom and the Case Studies

Like Sadger's essay, the texts I refer to in this section have not been published in English, and there is no reason to think any of them ever will be. They have neither the literary nor the scientific value to warrant translation. As a group, however, they are typical of the material available in the psychoanalytic journals of the period before the publication of *Ulysses*, and material in them is relevant to the Blooms and to the problematic shape of their marriage. Whether or not Joyce read any or all of them is impossible to prove or to disprove, but they were easily available to him in Zurich. Alexander Grinstein, in his *Index*, lists under Sadger's name alone about seventy titles, almost half relating to perversion of one kind or another (1720–23). More than one of these and many other titles in Grinstein's *Index* as well can doubtless be related to Bloom's sexuality as it is revealed or half-revealed in *Ulysses*, but it is not feasible and really not necessary to follow every trace in order to make a case for a pattern of intertextuality. In my consideration of psychoanalytic contexts for Bloom's characterization, therefore, I have selected relevant traces from only three articles in addition to Sadger's article on "buttock-eroticism": Sadger's 1910 article on "urethral eroticism," Karl Abraham's 1912 article on foot- and corset-fetishism, and Hans Oppenheim's 1913 piece on delusional jealousy.[5]

In Sadger's "*Über Urethralerotik*," which appeared in the 1910 *Yearbook*, a number of suggestive parallels of varying weights are discernible. Sadger, for example, discusses at some length the desire of one of his patients to drink urine as well as the various expedients the patient used to satisfy this desire (425–27), and we may remember that we are introduced to Leopold Bloom in the context of his taste for "grilled mutton kidneys which gave to his palate a fine tang of faintly scented urine" (*U*, 4.4–5). In addition, Sadger's account of a patient's memory of a brass chamberpot, which his father called the "musical pot" because urination produced more sound in it than in an earthenware pot (428), is perhaps echoed in Bloom's musings in "Sirens," presumably about the "orange-keyed chamberpot" at 7 Eccles Street (*U*, 4.330, 15.3295, 17.2103): "Chamber music: Could make a kind of pun on that. It is a kind of music I often thought when she. Acoustics that is. Tinkling. Empty vessels make most noise. Because the acoustics, the resonance changes according as the weight of the water is equal to the law of falling water" (*U*, 11.979–83). A "musical pot" indeed.

Sadger in orthodox Freudian fashion takes the reader back to childhood and to the source of the earliest, often quite bitter (and even barbaric in some of Sadger's examples) parent-child conflict during toilet training. As the child learns to control the functions of elimination,

Sadger points out, he[6] discovers the erogenous possibilities of both micturition and defecation, discovering also that retention heightens the
"sensual pleasure" inherent in both processes. And Sadger cites a common complaint of parents "that their youngster wants to use the pot all
the time," which he says is "almost reminiscent of the dog who, for every
cornerstone and every lamppost, has water in readiness to pour over it."
Sadger notes that many children "produce urine and excrement . . . in
repeated small portions, quite like the dog, in order to enjoy the great
pleasure to the full" (411–12).

This observation may well recall for any Joycean the wondrously visualized scene in "Proteus" of the activities of "Tatters," the cockle-
pickers' dog, who smells a rock and pisses against it "from under a cocked
hindleg," then immediately moves on to another and, "lifting again his
hindleg, pisse[s] quick short at an unsmelt rock. The simple pleasures of
the poor" (U, 3.357–59). But more to the point here are echoes in "Calypso," during Bloom's thoroughly enjoyed time in the privy, of the
"sensual pleasure" that Sadger notes in the retention and release of feces,
as Bloom admonishes himself: "No great hurry. Keep it a bit. Our prize
titbit." Later he reads the first column of his paper, "restraining himself,"
then begins the second column, "yielding but resisting," and finally, "his
last resistance yielding," allows "his bowels to ease themselves quietly,"
and pronounces the product "just right. So. Ah!" (U, 4.501–10).

A more complex echoing is apparent in the scene of Stephen and
Bloom's urination in the garden (U, 17.1185–1209), another widely familiar happening in Ulysses. Sadger points to an element of exhibitionism in the fact that many boys and men "perform their business as much
as possible in the open air, on the street or in the grass,"[7] and suggests
that "the powerful wish to perform before another and to be seen doing
so is . . . taken over from childhood" (421). In Ulysses, the mutual urination is "suggested" by Stephen and "instigated" by Bloom, an exchange
that, like much of the reported activity in "Ithaca," presents a difficulty
for convincing paraphrase, since the individually assigned verbs mean
practically the same thing, the second being simply a stronger version of
the first. Stephen proposes, Bloom urges, and both then urinate "in penumbra," defined in the dictionary as "a space of partial illumination (as in
an eclipse) between the perfect shadow on all sides and the full light." In
the textual situation in Ulysses, the "penumbra" is the space between the
darkness of the garden and the light in Molly's window. The two men are

standing side by side, but are keeping their "organs of micturition" out of sight through "manual circumposition."

The path of the urination itself is then described, Bloom's first, then Stephen's. Bloom's "trajectory" is not only "longer" but "less irruent," which is to say less powerful, though this word, like some other Joycean words, does not appear in an English dictionary. The "less irruent" descriptor is followed by the seemingly pictorial description of the trajectory of Bloom's urination as "in the incomplete form of the bifurcated penultimate alphabetical letter"—that is, the Y—but there is no clarification of what is meant by "incomplete," and I at least have been unable to visualize the physical phenomenon that this describes.[8]

A reminiscence from Leopold's senior year in high school follows, which suggests that the present urinary arc at its highest point is considerably lower than it was in 1880 during a pissing contest with "210 scholars," apparently the entire population of the school, urinating "concurrently." Now this really *is* a picture. It is followed by a straightforward description of Stephen's stream, in contrast to the fuzziness of the visualization of Bloom's. Stephen's is higher, the text relates, and more sibilant, since he has a very full bladder from his earlier drinking (*U,* 17.1192–98). This paragraph has echoes of Sadger's account of the competitive element in the development of "infantile urethral eroticism" as the child—always a boy, since he is equipped with a penis, which is what makes this competitive activity possible—moves on into puberty.

Having learned that retention not only increases his pleasure but also results in a stream with a "high arch," the "young rascal" tends to follow the same pattern of retention in his teens and "competes at best in the height of the arch," a competition similar to the slightly zany one Bloom "remembers" from his high school days (*U,* 17.1194–96) One of Sadger's patients reports a memory of a competitive game he and a companion played, during which they would "pee together into a pot," then wait "until we had enough urine to do it again, first one, then the other." The object of the game was to see which was "more potent," which could urinate again, how soon, and how high (431), and Sadger notes more than once the "equal meaning and value" assigned to urine and semen. In the competition that is implied by the textual comparison of Bloom's stream and Stephen's, Stephen thus appears to be the winner.

One other suggestive echo should be noted before leaving Sadger's study. In his extended discussion of the trials of toilet training, Sadger points out that besides the pleasure the child experiences in the action itself, "wetting himself . . . is often an evidence of love for the person who is struggling with him," so that he "pisses on just that person he inwardly loves," almost never on "an unsympathetic person," an observation that Sadger supports with examples of urination "as a warm proof of love" (414) from several of his cases.[9] The circumstances of the scene in Bloom's garden are totally different, to be sure, but the connection between urination and love is, though somewhat circuitously, highlighted.

Prior to the urinary ceremony, Bloom calls Stephen's attention to the lamp behind the window shade "in the second storey (rere)" of his house, the "visible luminous sign" which "denote[s]" the "mystery of an invisible attractive person, his wife Marion (Molly) Bloom" (U, 17.1171–78), at which the two fall silent, "each contemplating the other in both mirrors of the reciprocal flesh of theirhisnothis fellowfaces" (U, 17.1183–84). It is only after this mutual acknowledgment of Molly that the actual ceremony begins, and the ceremonial nature of the activity, involving as it does the basic trinity of Stephen, Bloom, and Molly, is maintained, for during the urination, both men lift their gaze to Molly's lighted window, in much the same way that the participants in certain Christian rituals face the Cross (U, 17.1186–90). The dual urination plus the focus during the activity on the reality of Molly, the loved woman behind the lighted window, thus takes on the color of a rite.

And the whole sense of this rite is reminiscent, whatever the differences, of one of Sadger's examples of the "love-significance of micturition": a patient who remembered that when a beloved sister "took me in her arms, I let it loose. *It is striking that I did it only to her. It was something quite special, destined for her*" (414; emphasis Sadger's). William York Tindall, noting Joyce's habit of implicating "higher things" through the commonplace, speculates on this ritual urination as "celebrating all creation" and observes, "If cocoa is adequate for Eucharistic wine, why not piss for this?" Tindall also suggests allusive connections to Dante and to the Vulgate (225–27), which doubtless are a part of the effect of this scene, but I would suggest that Sadger's much less prestigious work has also made its contribution.

Karl Abraham's psychoanalysis of a case of foot- and corset-fetishism, which was published in the March issue of the 1912 *Yearbook,* also finds echoes in the picture of Bloom. Abraham's aim in his essay was to throw light on the psychogenesis of fetishism through an analysis of the case of

a twenty-two-year-old male student, and echoes of this case, transformed, to be sure, are discernible in Bloom's behavior or remembered
behavior on Bloomsday. Abraham records that the sexual interest of his
patient moved from an early practice of tying himself up whenever he
was alone in the house to a fascination, at fifteen, with "elegant shoes,"
especially the "patent leather boots with high heels" that were worn by
prostitutes (558–59). At this stage looking at elegant shoes became a significant sexual activity for the patient (559).

In *Ulysses* the most extended evidence of the fascination that elegant
footwear exerts on Bloom comes in "Lotus Eaters," when Bloom's attention alternates between his conversation with M'Coy about Paddy Dignam's funeral and the progress of a lady departing from the Grosvenor
(*U*, 5.98–136): "Proud: rich: silk stockings," with "high brown boots" and
a "wellturned foot." Anxious to catch a glimpse of her feet and ankles as
she climbs into the "outsider" that is waiting at the curb—"Watch!
Watch! Silk flash rich stockings white. Watch!"—Bloom is frustrated by
a tramcar that blots out the scene, evoking from him the doubly apropos
comment, "Another gone." But, like Paddy Dignam, she is not forgotten.
In "Lestrygonians," Bloom remembers "that one at the Grosvenor this
morning" as one of the "horsey women" (*U*, 8.347, 345), and a reminder
of the incident appears in "Circe" when Bloom reacts to a close call with a
"Motorman": "Might be the fellow balked me this morning with that
horsey woman" (*U*, 15.205–6).

Like Abraham's patient, who was not only charmed by elegant footwear, but correspondingly offended by "an inelegant shoe" or "awkward,
ugly footwear" (558, 560), Bloom is selective in his response to feet and
footwear, including stockings. When, for example, he glimpses AE with a
young woman in the morning, he notes that "her stockings are loose over
her ankles. I detest that: so tasteless" (*U*, 8.542), a detail that surfaces
twice more—in "Nausicaa" and in "Eumaeus." In "Nausicaa" Bloom
contrasts Gerty, with her "transparent stockings, stretched to breaking
point," to "that frump" with AE and her "rumpled stockings" (*U*, 13.929–
31). And in "Eumaeus," he explains to Stephen that his distaste for
rumpled stockings "possibly is a foible of mine but still it's a thing I simply hate to see" (*U*, 16.897–98). Also repeated is Bloom's comment in
"Lestrygonians" on the "thick feet" of a woman in "white stockings" (*U*,
8.616–18), a sight that he remembers in "Nausicaa": "the one in Grafton
street. White. Wow! Beef to the heel" (*U*, 13.931–32).

Now the subject of Abraham's case study soon expanded his interest in feet and shoes to include a sexual interest in corsets, and when he was sixteen, he took one of his mother's old corsets, laced it up tightly on himself and "wore it repeatedly on the street under his suit" (559). We may note in passing that in the peculiar reality of "Circe," Bloom's "memory" of "dear Gerald," who "converted me to be a true corsetlover," goes back to an age that matches that of Abraham's sixteen-year-old patient: "when I was female impersonator in the High School play *Vice Versa*." Gerald, Bloom notes, "got that kink, fascinated by his sister's stays" (*U,* 15.3009–11), rather than his mother's, as was true in Abraham's case study, but still in the family.

Readers of *Ulysses* may also be reminded of Bloom's experiments with the "old wraps and black underwear" that Mrs. Miriam Dandrade, a "divorced Spanish American," sold him in the Shelbourne hotel. "Didn't take a feather out of her," Bloom observes, "my handling them. As if I was her clotheshorse" (*U,* 8.349–52), and in "Circe," during Bloom's metamorphosis into a woman, "Bello" goes into considerable detail about this handling. Threatening that should he join her crew, he "will be laced with cruel force into vicelike corsets," with his/her figure "restrained in nettight frocks" (*U,* 15.2974–78), "Bello" reminds Bloom of his posturing in "the secondhand black operatop shift and short trunkleg naughties all split up the stitches at her last rape that Mrs Miriam Dandrade sold you from the Shelbourne hotel" (*U,* 15.2990–95). Bloom claims that he "tried her things on only twice, a small prank, in Holles street" (*U,* 15.2986–87), but "Bello" provides details: "You were a nicelooking Miriam when you clipped off your backgate hairs and lay swooning in the thing across the bed as Mrs Dandrade about to be violated by lieutenant Smythe-Smythe [and nine other equally improbable 'lovers']" (*U,* 15.2999–3007). And it may be supposed that "Bello's" reminder of a time "when you took your seat with womanish care, lifting your billowy flounces, on the smoothworn throne" (*U,* 15.3015–17) also harks back to the same "small prank" or another like it.[10]

Abraham reports that looking at elegant shoes and tightly tied bodices "became the chief sexual activity" of his patient, and the same, mutatis mutandis, is true for Bloom, accompanied, as this voyeurism is in both cases, by "the extraordinary *reduction of sexual activity*," which, in the case of Abraham's patient, "never passed beyond the boundaries of *autoeroticism*" (559–60; emphasis Abraham's).[11]

The apparently mutually autoerotic experience with Gerty on the strand is the most explicit example in the novel of a parallel to Abraham's report—and probably the most frequently explicated.[12] The focus on Gerty's underwear—her "transparent stockings" (*U,* 13.426, 499–502, 716, 929–30); her "garters . . . blue to match" (*U,* 13.716); her "nainsook knickers, the fabric that caresses the skin" (*U,* 13.724–25)—fits well into the Homeric correspondence with Nausicaa's washing day, but as these articles provide the stimulus for Bloom's sexual arousal, they also echo Abraham's case of foot- and corset-fetishism, in which he concludes that his patient's "passionate wish to wear women's clothes, corsets and suitable shoes" (559) underlay a wish to *be* a woman, "not in order to fulfill the sexual function of the woman," but simply "to wear laced shoes and corsets and to be able unobtrusively to look at shop windows where they were displayed" (563). And we may be reminded of Bloom on Grafton street, his senses "lured" as he passes, "dallying, the windows of Brown Thomas, silk mercers," with their "cascades of ribbons. Flimsy China silks," as well as "petticoats on slim brass rails, rays of flat silk stockings" (*U,* 8.614, 620–21, 631–32).

Bloom's desire to be a woman, however, goes farther than that of Abraham's patient, for in "Circe," as has been repeatedly expounded upon, not only is Bloom diagnosed as "the new womanly man" (*U,* 15.1798–99), but himself declares: "O, I so want to be a mother" (*U,* 15.1817). To be sure Robert Byrnes has convincingly argued for a reading of the feminization of Bloom "through [Otto Weininger's] *Sex and Character,*" an approach that, he points out, demonstrates a "counterpointing of Homeric archetype with Weiningerian stereotype."[13] But, as I am suggesting throughout this study, such counterpointing is often multiple and may include specific psychoanalytic texts as well. Moreover, Byrnes's reminder that Joyce could borrow from Weininger's work "for comedic purposes without actually believing in it" (276) is a helpful caution that is equally true of these psychoanalytic intertexts.

Abraham and Sadger, in the articles I have been examining, are concerned with examples of perversion. But the last of the articles I discuss here—Hans Oppenheim's "Genesis of the Delusion of Jealousy"— moves into the arena of psychosis, which involves a distortion of reality, as the perversions obviously do not. Oppenheim's 1912 essay is not, strictly speaking, a case study, although his discussion of the characteristics of this delusion, which he limits to the domain of "conjugal faithfulness," obviously depends on case material. Delusional jealousy is slow to develop, Oppenheim says, but once it takes shape in "a systematic crazy notion," it is "extraordinarily resistant to correction" (67). It is to be expected that such delusions generally evoke "angry bitterness or threatening vengefulness," but Oppenheim notes that "in exceptional cases" they may be accompanied by "a more indifferent attitude" (68).

Bloom, of course, is that exceptional case. His indifference, indeed, is demonstrated at length in his reaction to Molly's Bloomsday adulterous encounter with Blazes Boylan, upon which he reflects, as I have noted in the previous chapter and many others have noted before me, with "envy, jealousy, abnegation, equanimity," but with "more abnegation than jealousy, less envy than equanimity" (U, 17.2155, 2195). These reflections, we may remember, follow immediately upon the famous list of Molly's lovers prior to Boylan—twenty-four, "assuming Mulvey to be the first" (U, 17.2133)—all of whom, as I have pointed out earlier, are eventually repudiated by the text. This list is a prime example of a characteristic of delusional jealousy that Oppenheim develops at length.

Although the "mother ground" for the origins of delusional jealousy, Oppenheim notes, is "the drive- and wish-life" rather than any intellectual source (68), the jealous ideas are not "products of pure fantasy." They instead have their origins in "illusional interpretations" of actual marital experiences—"memory distortions" or "memory delusions" similar to hallucinations (67–68). The patient, Oppenheim explains, "'composes,' if I may put it so, outer events, to which he gives his special interpretation," a process that is in no way "to be thought of as playing itself out in the patient's consciousness. . . . Only the end product, the jealous idea, is conscious or, as we say, 'actual'" (69). Furthermore, Oppenheim points out, this "morbid jealousy" is not content with "an adultery with a single strange person," but insists on a "repeated, many-sided faithlessness" (75), such as Bloom's list proclaims, depending, by implication at least, on some extremely "illusional interpretations" of events in the Blooms' lives.

This list is worth looking at in some detail. Every one of the names is cross-referenced in the text, and most of them appear in Molly's concluding monologue. Attempts have been made, with dubious success, to fit them all into some general category that has a relationship to Molly's putative libidinous behavior. Don Gifford and Robert Seidman, for example, recognizing that the list cannot refer to adultery in any "techni-

cal" sense, suggest that Christ's expanded definition of the seventh com-
mandment in the Sermon on the Mount may unite these names, since all
the men named have looked on Molly "to lust after her," which admittedly many have. But what then do we do about number 14 on Bloom's
list, the "Italian organgrinder," identified in "Sirens" as "that hurdy-
gurdy boy," whose song Molly interpreted as meaning that "the monkey
was sick" (*U*, 11.1092–93)?

This is a wonderfully comic list, especially when it is cross-referenced
with Molly's commentary: for example, John Henry Menton, "that big
babbyface . . . of all the big stupoes I ever met and thats called a solicitor"
(*U*, 18.39–44); Val Dillon, "that big heathen" with the "dirty eyes" (*U*,
18.428–29); Ben Dollard, "grinning all over his big Dolly face like a
wellwhipped childs botty didnt he look a balmy ballocks" (*U*, 18.1287–
88); Simon Dedalus, "such a criticiser with his glasses up with his tall hat
on him . . . and a great big hole in his sock one thing laughing at the
other" (*U*, 18.1088–90), who "was always turning up half screwed" and
"always on for flirtyfying too" (*U*, 18.1290–93). As for Andrew (Pisser)
Burke, number 18 on the list, whom Molly identifies as "that other
beauty Burke out of the City Arms Hotel" (*U*, 18.964–65), "youd vomit a
better face there was no love lost between us" (*U*, 18.966–67). In contrast,
Molly remembers "old frostyface Goodwin," number 4, with a certain
fondness as "a real old gent in his way it was impossible to be more re-
spectful" (*U*, 18.335–39).

The one thing all the names have in common is that they are associated with what Oppenheim calls "actual marital experiences." Bloom
knows all these men or knows about them through Molly. Except for
Mulvey, they are all part of the Dublin scene, with not a stranger among
them. Their relationships with Molly are not "products of pure fantasy,"
but the fact that they are all on Bloom's list of the "series" who have
entered Molly's bed means that he has, even unconsciously, "compose[d]
outer events," giving them "his own interpretation" (Oppenheim, 69).
Dwelling on this "systematic crazy notion" of Molly's infidelity, however, appears to produce in Bloom a certain calm pleasure, rather than the
more violent emotions of what Oppenheim calls "mentally sound jealousy" (75).

The man who suffers from "normal jealousy," Oppenheim points out,
discovers the occasion for it "accidentally" and truly "*suffers* under jealous doubt," as Joyce himself suffered during his own experience of jeal-

ousy. The "normal" victim of jealousy thus seeks to arrive at a *"quick conclusion* to the disagreeable circumstance," whatever the "terror" of the consequences of new knowledge. For the man in the grip of delusional jealousy, however, the case is quite opposite. Not only does he "intentionally and longingly *seek*" the occasion for jealousy and indeed *"pleases himself"* in the experience but, far from looking for a solution, "strives after the possibility of *prolonging* it" (75; emphasis Oppenheim's).[14] Bloom's apparent collusion in promoting occasions for jealousy is typified in his exhibiting to Stephen Molly's "slightly soiled photo creased by opulent curves, none the worse for wear" (*U*, 16.1465) and in his extended, mostly inward, commentary not only on the alluring features of the photograph but on adulterous sharing in general (*U*, 16.1437–565). "An awful lot of makebelieve went on about that sort of thing," Bloom muses, "the same old matrimonial tangle alleging misconduct . . . instead of being honest and aboveboard about the whole business," concluding that it is "a case for the two parties themselves" unless, he adds, it turns out "that the legitimate husband happen[s] to be a party to it" (*U*, 16.1480–84, 1532–34), as Bloom certainly is.[15]

Branded "bawd and cuckold," during his trial in "Circe" (*U*, 15.1159), Bloom's vigorous participation in the scene of his own cuckolding by Blazes Boylan (*U*, 15.3765–816) is remarkably explicit evidence of an involvement that goes well beyond Frank Budgen's label of *"mari complaisant"* in his report of a conversation with Joyce during the Paris years ("Further Recollections," 530). In his *James Joyce and the Making of "Ulysses,"* Budgen recalls, he had attributed Bloom's peculiar attitude toward his own cuckolding to his "Jewish and personal masochism" and also to "the homosexual wish to share his wife with other men" (146), a dual motivation that Joyce acknowledged as probably correct, although he added, "But there is another aspect of the matter you seem to have missed."

He then asked Budgen if he knew *Le Cocu Magnifique* (a farce by Fernand Crommelynck that had opened in Paris on 18 December 1920). Reminding Budgen that *Exiles* was to have been put on by Lugné Poë (who was also the director of *Le Cocu*),[16] Joyce said that the project came to nothing because Crommelynck's farce "took the wind out of the sails of *Exiles*. The jealousy motive is the same in kind in both cases. The only difference is that in my play the people act with a certain reserve, whereas in *Le Cocu* the hero, to mention only one, acts like a madman." And Joyce continued, "Make all the necessary allowances, and you'll see that Bloom is of the same family" ("Further Recollections," 531).

It is instructive to look a bit more closely at the plot of Crommelynck's farce. Bruno is passionately in love with his wife Stella, who also loves him and is stubbornly faithful to him despite his insistence on her feeding his jealousy and cuckolding him. He not only praises her physical charms to all comers but forces her to display them and throws her into the arms of other men, sounding like the madman Joyce says he is as he tells her: "I want you impure and I want to be dishonored! Let there be no compromise. I'll be a cuckold this very day or I'll be dead. Horns or cord. Choose for me" (Knapp, 59). Stella to a degree humors him in his madness, thus becoming the object of scandal throughout the village, and finally detaching herself from Bruno, she runs off with an ox-driver.

This synopsis does not do full justice to the craziness or the brutality of the plot, but it is perhaps adequate to indicate what Joyce meant by the similarity in kind between the "jealousy motive" in Crommelynck's play and in his own. Most Joyceans can recognize in Bruno's determination "to be dishonored" an echo of Richard Rowan's "ignoble" longing "to be betrayed . . . by you, my best friend, and by her . . . passionately and ignobly, to be dishonoured for ever in love and in lust" (*E*, 70).[17] And Bloom, though he gives no evidence of recognizing such a motivation in his own behavior, is, as Joyce said, "of the same family" as Richard in *Exiles* and Bruno in *Le Cocu Magnifique*. His jealousy, however, though equally self-willed and delusional, is that of a remarkably passive and gentle madman. He is the exceptional case acknowledged by Oppenheim in his examination of the origins and characteristics of delusional or pathological jealousy: a causelessly jealous husband who is without anger or vindictiveness in his jealousy.

Indeed, whatever the textual evidence of Bloom's delusion as well as his sexual perversities, responses of readers and critics to him—at least in recent times—have been uncommonly nonjudgmental. He somehow, as Richard Brown notes, retains "his precarious normality throughout" (88). In the text of *Ulysses*, however, his wife, who pronounces Bloom "not natural like the rest of the world" (*U*, 18.268), does not so easily let him off the hook.

Molly Bloom and Otto Rank's *Matrone von Ephesus*

Important as case studies were for the exposition and confirmation of psychoanalytic theory, the early psychoanalysts, in the absence of an extensive body of such studies, depended heavily on literature for confirmation of their insights, especially literature that had been reworked over a long period of time. The tale of the Widow of Ephesus, with a history that begins in the obscurity of folklore and extends into contemporary literature, was thus an ideal hunting ground for psychoanalysis.[18] And in 1913 Otto Rank, probably the most industrious and creative researcher in the area of literary psychoanalysis, and editor of two of the psychoanalytic journals, published a psychoanalytic interpretation of the tale of the Widow of Ephesus in the *International Journal for Psychoanalysis*.[19]

When Joyce includes in "Oxen of the Sun" mention of "another Ephesian matron" (*U*, 14.886), Thornton lists it as an allusion to the *Satyricon of Petronius* (*Allusions*, 340), a version of the tale that Petronius inserted into his *Satyricon* in the first century of the Christian era.[20] But it may also be an allusion to Rank's 1913 psychoanalytic interpretation of the tale, a not uncommon Joycean layering of contexts. For the psychoanalytic perspectives explored by Rank in this early essay provide a clarifying context for some of the complications and ambiguities in Joyce's treatment of the triangle—basic to Bloom's story in *Ulysses*—of Molly Bloom, Leopold Bloom, and Blazes Boylan, especially in connection with Molly's motivations, which are oddly congruent with those of the widow of Ephesus.

The Ephesian matron, according to Petronius's story, was so famous for her fidelity to her husband that the women of neighboring towns came to Ephesus merely to stare at this prodigy. Her husband died while she was yet young, and the faithful widow followed him to his tomb, vowing to mourn there, without food or drink, until she, too, died. Meantime, near the tomb where the widow mourned, several thieves were crucified and a young soldier was assigned to guard the bodies so that they could not be removed from the crosses and buried. Noticing a light in the nearby tomb, the soldier investigated, discovered the beautiful widow, and persuaded her, first, to eat and drink, and then to make love—in the tomb—over a period of three nights. During the time of the soldier's absence from his post of duty, one of the corpses was removed and buried by relatives. When the soldier discovered the vacant cross, he returned to the widow in the tomb, told her that he would himself hang for his dereliction of duty, and threatened to commit suicide and join her husband in the tomb. The widow, however, proposed to substitute her husband's body for the stolen corpse and gave orders for the body of her husband to be lifted out of the coffin and fastened upon the vacant cross.

Rank's analysis of "The Woman of Ephesus," like the analysis of a dream, looks beyond the manifest content of the story for vestiges of what has been repressed and distorted in the various reworkings of the old folk tale over time as a clue to the "unconscious motive power," no longer recognizable on the surface (50). The basic building blocks of the tale are three: (1) the extraordinary faithfulness of the wife before the death of her husband; (2) the triangle of the widow, the dead husband, and the young lover; and (3) the hanged man, a complex motif that attaches to both the husband and the lover. Traces of all these motifs are found, though with some odd twists, in Joyce's *Ulysses*.

At first glance, of course, Molly Bloom seems a far cry from the faithful matron of Ephesus, whose reputation for fidelity she has by no means enjoyed, either in the minds of her husband's acquaintances, as they are reflected in the text of the novel, or among the novel's early interpreters. Molly's extraordinary sexual appetites, as well as her indiscriminate adulteries, became a byword of the first fifty years of her critical history, and although Molly, as already noted, has been cleared, textually at least, of the charge of promiscuity, the notion has died hard. For the personality she herself reveals in her final monologue, set against the sexual deprivation in her marriage, as it is spelled out by the catechizer in "Ithaca" under the heading of "inhibitions of conjugal rights" (*U*, 17.2271), makes her sexual loyalty to her husband up to Bloomsday as extraordinary in its way as the fidelity of the Ephesian matron.

Bloom, the text reveals, has not had "complete carnal intercourse," with his wife for "a period of 10 years, 5 months and 18 days" (*U*, 17.2278–84). The fact of the sexual estrangement of the Blooms has been as standard a feature of Joycean interpretation as Bloom's list, but its effect on the reader's judgment of Molly's fidelity has been oddly muted by its placement so late in the novel. The fact that it is Molly whose "conjugal rights" have been "inhibited" has been all but ignored in the text of the novel before this.

True, one of the parodic voices in "Oxen of the Sun" addresses her

plight: "Unhappy woman, she has been too long and too persistently denied her legitimate prerogative" (*U*, 14.918–19), setting up a resonance
with the "conjugal rights" of the later episode. The voice then goes on to
chastise Bloom for his abandonment of the "seedfield that lies fallow for
the want of the ploughshare" (*U*, 14.929–30). But the bewildering succession of voices in this episode of parodies makes it difficult for a reader to
sort out the narrative facts that are revealed throughout the episode but
obscured by the language. And during the day, when Bloom's thinking
turns to the breakdown in his marital relations after Rudy's death, it is
likewise obscure in the text *who* has withdrawn.[21] But Molly's indict-
ment of Bloom in "Penelope" is in no way obscure, as she concludes: "its
all his own fault if I am an adulteress" (*U*, 18.1516). We can hardly quarrel with the conclusion Heather Cook Callow suggests, that "Joyce has
encouraged us to err" in judging Molly (475), but the fact of her steadfast
chastity through the ten-year period of sexual withdrawal by her husband is nevertheless conclusively, if deviously, established in the text.
This chastity is a matter for wonder that rivals the wonder inspired by
the fidelity of the woman of Ephesus. David Hayman labels it "simply
grotesque" ("Empirical Molly," 38).

The second essential element in the old tale, the triangle of the widow,
the dead husband, and the young lover, also retains its form in *Ulysses*.
Molly's marital situation, as she reveals and responds to it in "Penelope,"
establishes her status as widow in the primary sense of Rank's analysis of
the original tale. For Rank sees at the deeper levels of motivation in the
tale an equivalence between the "dead" husband and the "sexually incapacitated" husband (58), and even though Poldy is still alive, still
"plottering about the house" (*U*, 18.507) and still saluting Molly, as he
does on his return from the wanderings of Bloomsday, with "the usual
kissing my bottom" (*U*, 18.53), sexually, he is dead—for Molly. Like the
widow of the tale, Molly is still young, though "its a wonder Im not an
old shrivelled hag before my time living with him so cold never embracing me except sometimes when hes asleep the wrong end of me," a practice for which Molly clearly expresses her abhorrence: "any man thatd
kiss a womans bottom Id throw my hat at him after that hed kiss anything unnatural where we havent 1 atom of any kind of expression in us
all of us the same 2 lumps of lard before ever Id do that to a man pfooh
the dirty brutes the mere thought is enough" (*U*, 18.1399–405).

This practice, of course, is only one item in Molly's widely scattered catalogue of her husband's deviations that support her judgment that "of course hes not natural like the rest of the world" (U, 18.268). Her reaction to the mildly pornographic reading material Bloom provides for her—"sure theres nothing for a woman in that" (U, 18.495)—is paralleled by her distaste for Bloom's incessant "question and answer" about her sexual fantasies, "trying to make a whore of me," a prospect she rejects as "simply ruination for any woman and no satisfaction in it" (U, 18.89–98).

She also expresses her rejection of at least one of the sexual substitutes that Bloom not only offers but insists on. She remembers his extended pout "when I wouldnt let him lick me in Holles street"—sleeping on the floor "half the night naked the way the jews used when somebody dies belonged to them" and refusing to eat or speak (U, 18.1245–48). And though she recalls that she finally gave in "and let him," she indicates that the experience was far from satisfactory, as "he does it all wrong too thinking only of his own pleasure his tongue is too flat or I dont know what" (U, 18.1249–50). Molly's thought continues with a group of words that make no sense as they are printed in the 1984 and 1986 editions: "he forgets that wethen I dont" (U, 18.1250–51). The editors note that the nonsense word *wethen* is so written in the Rosenbach manuscript (U-G, 1706), though in both the 1934 and 1961 Random House editions it has been separated into two plain English words—*we* and *then*—which can easily be placed in two different elliptical clauses: "he forgets that we . . ." and "then I don't . . ." both of which can be completed to make sense, though possibly a slightly different sense for different readers. Elliptical as they are, however, they appear to reinforce Molly's negative response to this sexual evasion.

In the face of her rejection of Bloom's substitutes for intercourse, a reader can hardly see Molly as sexually satisfied. Her situation is thus analogous to that of the Ephesian widow, whose grief, Rank says, is "completely earnest and true, for in the final analysis [her] love for her husband, continuing beyond the grave, refers to the sexual satisfaction secured from him, which the widow sorely misses and wants to get back" (53). Molly's references to the sexual satisfaction she has secured from Leopold in the past are admittedly much less explicit than her recital of dissatisfactions with her present situation. Indeed, it is a puzzling fact of the text, for which I can offer no reason, that Molly details little or no sexual joy in her marriage, her joyful memories being restricted to her courtship. Nevertheless, her expression of gratitude after her afternoon with Boylan—"O thanks be to the great God I got somebody to give me what I badly wanted to put some heart up into me" (*U*, 18.732–33)—surely testifies to her deprivation, expressing the same sense of loss and the same yearning for restoration that Rank sees in the widow's grief.

Rank comes to his view of the widow as a faithful, grieving woman through his examination of the third essential element of the tale—the complex motif of the hanged man. Unlike the other elements of the tale, the details of the game of musical chairs that circles around the hanged man—the stolen corpse, the lover who is threatened with death by hanging as punishment, and the husband who is substituted for the stolen corpse—exhibit a range of variations, in which Rank discovers hidden clues to the original motivations of the story.

In all versions of the tale the lover is responsible for guarding the bodies of several hanged men, one of which is stolen while the lover dallies with the widow in the tomb. Also constant is the fact that the lover, faced with the punishment of death by hanging, seeks counsel from the widow, who saves him by suggesting the substitution of her husband's body for the missing corpse. The details of the events surrounding the switching of corpses, however, differ considerably. In Petronius's retelling of the tale, for example, the widow simply orders her husband's body to be transferred from the coffin to the cross and is not personally involved in carrying out the transfer, whereas in most other versions the widow is deeply involved. She not only suggests the substitution of her husband for the missing corpse, but is generally forced to hang him herself, the guard being unable to bring himself to do this because of his "tender conscience" (51–52). She often undertakes the substitution of her husband's body on the condition that the guard marry her, but after she saves his life, the guard refuses to do so *because* of the widow's desecration of her husband's body through hanging and her subsequent mutilation of the body, which is also a feature of most versions. At this point, according to Rank, "we come up against a crude unlikelihood in the tale" and should recognize in this a "rationalization attempt," behind which the "original meaning of the motif may lie hidden" (51).

He looks closely at the variations in the mutilation of the corpse of the husband, a mutilation that is generally necessary to provide a match with the corpse that has been stolen from the cross. The corpse may be missing a tooth or two teeth, a nose or a pair of ears, which the widow, Rank points out, with emphasis, must *"cut off* from [her husband]." This "threadbare motivation" for the mutilation rouses suspicion, Rank says, and the *kind* of mutilation makes it clear that these are "symbolic substitutes for *castration*," a single organ standing in for the phallus and a pair for the testicles (52; emphasis Rank's). Having established the "special significance of the mutilation" as symbolic castration,[22] Rank looks further to determine how this interpretation may contribute to an understanding of the original meaning of the tale. He suggests that the widow's plan to hang the husband, as well as the castration, may be perceived as "a touching passage of womanly faithfulness which stands in direct opposition to the manifest content and to the obtrusive tendency of the tale." The widow of the original tale, Rank says, grieves for the loss of her husband's phallus and wants to recover it after his death (53).

Though the emphasis on the phallus as a thing-in-itself is a notable feature of Molly Bloom's soliloquy, her husband, oddly enough, is all but exempt from her consideration of the subject. True, she remembers "touch[ing] his trousers outside"—again, a courtship memory—"dying to find out was he circumcised" (*U*, 18.312–15). She also notes that "Poldy has more spunk in him" than Boylan (*U*, 18.168), but, contrary to "Joe's" gibe in "Cyclops" about Bloom's sexual activity—"I wonder did he ever put it out of sight" (*U*, 12.1655)—Molly gives no evidence that her husband's penis was ever *in* her sight. This omission contrasts sharply with her reliving of the afternoon with Boylan, whose "tremendous big red brute of a thing . . . like iron or some kind of a thick crowbar" (*U*, 18.144–48) she admires both for its size (*U*, 18.150, 155, 1123) and for its erectile capability: "standing all the time he must have eaten oysters" (*U*, 18.148). Later, of course, she ridicules the same phenomenon as she complains about Boylan's unceremonious undressing, "standing out that vulgar way in the half of a shirt they wear to be admired like a priest or a butcher or those old hypocrites in the time of Julius Caesar" (*U*, 18.1373–75).

Her interest in the phallus as an object extends beyond her afternoon's experience into the past. Her curiosity about Poldy's circumcision is paralleled by her speculation about "a black mans," which she would like to try (*U*, 18.483–84) and even in her memory of Mulvey, "when I unbuttoned him and took his out and drew back the skin it had a kind of eye in it" (*U*, 18.815–16). The tenderness she expresses about the statue of Narcissus focuses on admiration for "his lovely young cock there so simple I wouldnt mind taking him in my mouth if nobody was looking as if it was asking you to suck it," and she contrasts him with "those pigs of men I suppose never dream of washing it from 1 years end to the other" (*U*, 18.1352–57).

She is, of course, anything but tender about the "pigs of men" who have exhibited themselves to her—fairly often, it seems—"some fellow or other trying to catch my eye as if it was 1 of the 7 wonders of the world," like the "wretch with the red head," for example, "pretending he was pissing standing out for me to see it with his babyclothes up to one side" (*U*, 18.551–52, 545–48). She is scornful in her description of "what a man looks like with his two bags full and his other thing hanging down out of him or sticking up at you like a hatrack no wonder they hide it with a cabbageleaf" (*U*, 18.542–44). But she has once tried to "draw a picture of it . . . like a sausage" (*U*, 18.557–58) and twice expresses a desire to be a man to "get up on a lovely woman" (*U*, 18.1146–47) and "to try with that thing they have swelling up on you so hard and at the same time so soft when you touch it" (*U*, 18.1382–83).

Molly's soliloquy thus echoes the phallic emphasis of Rank's interpretation of the widow's tale, though she displaces the focus from the husband to a variety of other men. Rank's further reconstruction of the widow's original motivation, however, finds contradictory echoes in Molly's assessment of her own case. Rank hypothesizes that hidden behind the "so thinly motivated mutilation of the husband" (56), found in most versions of the tale, is the original widow's desire, at a very primitive stage in the evolution of the tale, to possess her husband's phallus not only "as a loving memory, but also with the hidden fantasy of obtaining with it future sexual enjoyment and gratification" (53). Molly explicitly rejects the possibility of self-gratification as a solution very early in her musings when she considers "pay[ing] some nicelooking boy to do it since I cant do it myself" (*U*, 18.84–85), though she refers shortly afterwards to "finish[ing] it off myself" (*U*, 18.99) and much later to the effect of Bloom's "mad crazy letters" that "had me always at myself 4 and 5 times a day sometimes" (*U*, 18.1176–80). And she also remembers as a girl having "tried with the Banana but I was afraid it might break and get lost up in me somewhere" (*U*, 18.803–4). As her soliloquy draws to a close and she accuses Leopold of responsibility for her becoming "an adulteress," she angrily pictures ways she might "make his micky stand for him" and even supposes she might "put him into me" (*U*, 18.1509–10,

1514), a picture that is very close to the hidden fantasy that Rank attributes to the Widow of Ephesus.

Rank cites examples of customs and tales that reveal vestiges of the "fantasy of conserving the penis," including the legend of Isis and Osiris, in which, of course, Isis recovers and reanimates the pieces of her murdered brother/husband's body, except for the phallus, which she cannot find and for which she substitutes one made of wood (54). The substitution of a wooden phallus in turn has its counterpart in a sixteenth-century version of the tale of the Ephesian widow, except that the motif undergoes a further repression when a wooden figure of the whole body of the husband—"Johannes"—takes the place of the original embalmed penis (55–56). This substitution, however, is to a degree reversed in a later version that returns to something closer to the original. In this story the wooden figure becomes a wax form, which is then melted down to make candles for the wedding breakfast of the widow and her new lover. Since it is well known, Rank says, that candles are actually used as a "phallic substitute instrument," this account changes the "peculiar subterfuge of the 'wooden Johannes'" back to the import of the original story (55), which dealt, he concludes, "with the fantasy of an especially *faithful* widow, who after the death of her husband shunned every other sexual outlet, despite her desire, in order to give herself satisfaction with the cut off and embalmed genitals of her husband" (55–56; emphasis Rank's).

It is with this motivation on the part of the widow that Rank returns to the "*hanging* of the body," also weakly motivated in the reworked story, as a clue to hidden meaning. "It is a well known physiological fact," Rank writes, that "customarily a powerful erection appears in the hanged man" (56), connecting this fact with the purposes for which, in Rank's reconstruction of the original story, the widow castrates the corpse. The phallus is obviously no help to her unless it is rigid, a state that can be achieved by hanging.[23] Rank then retells an Honoré de Balzac story about an old maid and a hanged man, which depends for its "grim humor" on "the physiological fact of the erection of the hanged man."[24] In the final line of the story—"Oh, he feels better to me as hanged than *hanging*"—the old maid could be speaking for the Widow of Ephesus (56).

She could also be speaking for Molly Bloom, though the hanging motif, as Joyce uses it in *Ulysses*—with the same phallic associations as are emphasized by Rank—is separated from Molly and attached instead to Bloom,[25] even as the allusion to the faithless widow is introduced in connection with Bloom. The explicit mention of "another Ephesian matron" in "Oxen of the Sun" plus the two scenes—in "Cyclops" and in "Circe" —that focus on the erection of the hanged man so essential to Rank's interpretation, are all connected to Bloom, and more specifically to his sexual problems and peculiarities.

It is Bloom who sets up the allusion to the Ephesian matron in "Oxen of the Sun" after the birth of the Purefoy baby is announced. He comments to Mulligan, who is sitting next to him in the Maternity Hospital, on the pain Mrs. Purefoy has endured in childbirth "through no fault of her own," to which Mulligan responds that the fault is her husband's, "or at least it ought to be unless she were another Ephesian matron" (*U*, 14.884–86). On the surface, Mulligan's quip may well refer to the widow's traditional faithlessness, but it also may double in the text as a reference to Bloom's own lack of capability, echoed later by Molly's "was he not able to make [a son]" (*U*, 18.1445) and earlier by the harsh comments of the citizen in "Cyclops" about Bloom's manhood. "Do you call that a man? says the citizen" (*U*, 12.1654), and when he is reminded that the Blooms have produced two children, he responds, "And who does he suspect?" (*U*, 12.1657).

When Joyce highlights the hanging motif in "Cyclops" (*U*, 12.450–78), Bloom is also in center stage. The talk in Barney Kiernan's pub turns to capital punishment and "Bloom comes out with the why and the wherefore and all the codology of the business" (*U*, 12.450–52), the main point of which is, as Alf Bergan puts it, the effect on "the poor bugger's tool that's being hanged" (*U*, 12.457). Alf reports that in the case of a hanged Invincible, "it was standing up in their faces like a poker" when they cut him down (*U*, 12.459–62). Bloom then, as "Herr Professor Luitpold Blumenduft," in a long, Latinate contribution, reported in the inflated parody that follows Alf's report, describes the phenomenon as "a violent ganglionic stimulus of the nerve centres of the genital apparatus" (*U*, 12.472–73). The parody, which Garry Leonard calls "the funniest moment in the novel" (88), is followed immediately by the citizen's "gassing" about various Irish revolutionary groups and "all the fellows that were hanged, drawn and transported for the cause" (*U*, 12.480–83).

Thus, when Joyce again makes the point about the hanged man's erection in "Circe," the identity of the hanged man, who is The Croppy Boy, a generic symbol for Irish nationalism, establishes an association with the hanging motif in "Cyclops," where the motif is clearly associated both with nationalism and with Bloom. As The Croppy Boy "gives up the ghost, [a] violent erection of the hanged sends gouts of sperm spouting through his deathclothes on to the cobblestones," where three women— Mrs. Bellingham, Mrs. Yelverton Barry and the Honourable Mrs. Mervyn Talboys—"rush forward with their handkerchiefs to sop it up" (*U*, 15.4548–52).

These three women, labeled "the noble ladies" by Hugh Kenner in his summary of the principal fantasies of "Circe," provide a further link between the anomalous salutary effect of the hanging and Bloom's problematic sexuality, for they have earlier been witnesses against Bloom at the trial concerning his "deeper sexual guilt" (361). They accuse him variously of making "improper overtures" with a view to adultery, offering to supply them with pornographic reading material, writing them suggestive letters, showing them dirty pictures, begging them to satisfy his masochistic desires (*U*, 15.1013–119). These "noble ladies," in fact, provide the "evidence" that leads to the sentence on Bloom to "be hanged by the neck until he is dead" (*U*, 15.1170–71) or—in the special ambiguity of the hanging motif, suggested by Rank and exploited by Joyce— until he is sexually resurrected. The reappearance of "*H. Rumbold, master barber*" (*U*, 15.1177), whose letter offering his services as hangman touched off the discussion of this anomalous effect in "Cyclops" (*U*, 12.415–31), provides another link to the hanging motif in that episode. The chain of associations that links these three scenes to Bloom, in fact, may also be seen to link his situation to that of the dead husband in "The Woman of Ephesus," as Rank reconstructs it.

Rank finally posits an "original psychological identity" of the husband and lover, who embody the widow's contradictory attitudes toward her husband, the young lover thus representing for the widow "nothing other than a better new edition of the sexually incapacitated husband . . . the husband arisen to new life" (58). The figure of the lover is in fact another transformation of the original fantasy of conserving the penis. In this case, however, the widow rejects an "autoerotic substitute" in favor of an actual lover capable of performance, at the same time, however, seeing in the lover "only a substitute husband" (60).

The entry of the lover into the history of the tale thus represents a transformation in the hanging/castration motif: "the phenomenon of the erection and slackening of the male member, which underlies the fable, appears to be transferred to the whole body, which is considered, now 'dead,' like the slack penis [the husband], now 'arisen,' like the erect [the lover]." The real motivation for the widow's activity thus becomes, Rank says, "a matter . . . of helping the 'dead' man again to be capable of an erection" (58). And Rank refers to an example offered by Freud in his *Interpretation of Dreams* of the woman whose concern about her husband's impotence took mental form in a phrase that horrified her— "Go hang yourself!"—which Freud interpreted as "Get yourself an erection at any price!" (58 n. 2).[26]

Thus Rank identifies at the base of the story, not the fickleness of woman, but "the theme of potency" (59), a correction of perspective that applies also, I think, to Bloom's story in *Ulysses,* which is based at least as importantly on potency as on adultery. The problem of sexual impotence, which Rank presents as the Ephesian widow's problem and which Molly presents as a problem for herself in her monologue, is quite obviously Bloom's problem as well,[27] for which, as evidenced by his trial and sentence in "Circe," he feels a measure of guilt at some level. And the fact that the sentence of hanging, with its restorative implications, is never carried out suggests that his problem is never resolved in the novel.

The themes of adultery and impotence, of course, are hardly mutually exclusive, as Rank recognizes in his "final synthetic reconstruction of the fantasy construction" that underlies the tale of the widow of Ephesus. He acknowledges that some measure of hostility toward her husband because of his impotence must have been attached to the widow in the original tale and indeed helps to account for the focus on her infidelity in later versions. For the woman of the story is true, "not so much to her husband as to his penis and to this only so long as it is in a position to satisfy her" (59). Rank points to the "unambiguously vindictive significance of the castration" as evidence of a "fantasy of revengeful faithlessness." This fantasy, however, "with the conspicuous ambivalence which directly attaches to psycho-sexual impulses," coexists with the "tender fantasy of the love-starved widow, who is still faithful to the phallus of the dead husband" (59). In *Ulysses,* "Penelope" concludes with two contradictory fantasies that fit Rank's labels, as Molly's truly "revengeful" diatribe against Bloom (*U,* 18.1508–39) is followed almost immediately by a lyrical return to her original acceptance of him (*U,* 18.1571–609).

Apparently it is Molly's continuation of her earlier fantasy about Stephen as a possible new lover (*U,* 18.1300–67), embellished by a fantasied scene of bringing him his breakfast in bed (*U,* 18.1476–97), that trig-

gers her vengeful fantasy about Bloom. Beginning with a determination
equal to the widow's own to bring her "dead" husband's phallus back to
life, Molly visualizes exhibiting herself to Bloom in her "best shift and
drawers" (*U*, 18.1509)—since her husband is "mad on the subject of
drawers" (*U*, 18.289)—"to make his micky stand for him." She then sees
herself defiantly proclaiming her adultery: "Ill let him know if thats what
he wanted that his wife is fucked yes and damn well fucked too up to my
neck nearly and not by him 5 or 6 times handrunning" (*U*, 18.1510–12).
Her assertion that "its all his own fault if I am an adulteress" (*U*, 18.1516)
is followed shortly by her angry plan for some wifely prostitution, allow-
ing her husband to indulge in his sexual peculiarities in exchange for
money: "if he wants to kiss my bottom Ill drag open my drawers and
bulge it right out in his face as large as life he can stick his tongue 7 miles
up my hole as hes there . . . then Ill tell him I want £1 or perhaps 30/-" (*U*,
18.1520–23). Her fantasy includes a direct "revengeful" threat to Bloom:
"O wait now sonny my turn is coming" (*U*, 18.1533), but it ends with her
desire to "make him want me" (*U*, 18.1539).

With hardly a transition, Molly's thinking returns briefly to Stephen
as a reason to buy flowers for the house (*U*, 18.1549–54), apparently dismissing Boylan altogether. Her meditations become a kind of hymn to all
creation and to its Creator (*U*, 18.1557–71), which serves as a prelude to
the tender memory that counters her "revengeful diatribe." For she remembers the culmination of Bloom's courtship, "the day we were lying
among the rhododendrons on Howth head" and Bloom had told her she
"was a flower of the mountain . . . one true thing he said in his life and the
sun shines for you today yes that was why I liked him because I saw he
understood or felt what a woman is and I knew I could always get round
him and I gave him all the pleasure I could leading him on till he asked
me to say yes" (*U*, 18.1576–81). This often-quoted passage builds to the
final "Yes" of the novel, which, whatever its cosmic significance, is certainly a "yes" to Bloom, and the novel thus ends with a doubled return.
Bloom has returned to Molly, echoing the return of Odysseus to Penelope, and Molly has returned to Bloom, echoing perhaps the Odyssean
slaughter of the suitors. These are echoes which Joyce has publicly invited readers and critics to look for.

There are, however, other allusive possibilities that Joyce has signaled
only obliquely in the text itself (though no more obliquely than many of
the Homeric ones) among which Rank's 1913 psychoanalytic view of the

Widow of Ephesus may well be one. And with Molly's apparent replacement of Boylan by Stephen as the third corner of her fantasy-satisfying
triangle, the reader is returned to a triangular configuration that clearly
agrees with Rank's characterization of the husband and lover of the
widow's tale as "the self itself in two parts" (59) at the same time that it
conforms to a central motif in *Ulysses*. For Bloom and Stephen exactly fit
Rank's phrase. Their identity is insisted on in the text of *Ulysses* through
verbal and situational parallels, almost literally innumerable,[28] and it is
explicitly pictured in "Circe," where Stephen and Bloom together look in
a mirror and see the reflection of one face—a paralyzed Shakespeare,
wearing the horns of the cuckold (*U*, 15.3821–24).

But what about the explicit fictional triangle of Molly, Bloom, and
Blazes Boylan, the lover to whom Molly has succumbed on Bloomsday?
He, too, may be seen pairing with Bloom as "the self itself in two parts,"
though in a much more limited sense than Stephen. This view, however,
requires that we look beyond the fictional triangle to the unity behind
the fiction, to James Joyce himself. Indeed, as we follow Joyce through the
intricacies of the text of *Ulysses*, testing any hypothesis we may have, we
almost always reach a point that is like the "navel" Freud spoke about in
a dream—"the spot where it reaches down into the unknown" (*SE*,
5:525)—and in *Ulysses* the unknown often involves Joyce's experience
outside the text.

The place of autobiography in Joyce's fiction has been problematic in
Joyce criticism from its beginnings, and the persistent idea of Joyce as a
presence in his fiction has met with considerable resistance. But it continues to reappear, most recently in James McMichael's suggestion that
Joyce's presence in *Ulysses* is divided among a trinity of "Jamesy,"
Stephen, and James Joyce. McMichael also makes a case for D. B. Murphy
as another autobiographical character who, like the "cybernetic self-portrait" of Robert Scholes's analysis of Bloom, stands in for Joyce without
being "recognizable in his skin" (Scholes, 164–65). But this identification, McMichael points out, is possible only through "biographical information recoverable from writing other than *Ulysses*" (145–46).[29]

Similarly the notorious pornographic letters that Joyce wrote to Nora
in 1909 (*SL*, 181–93) provide incontrovertible evidence of an autobiographical source for the portrait of Bloom, as they reveal how many of
Bloom's sexual peculiarities duplicate Joyce's own.[30] A kind of aftershock
of Joyce's excruciatingly painful, indeed cataclysmic experience of jeal-

ousy, they establish, as nothing else could have, the autobiographical base for aspects of Bloom that were revealed to Joyce as a necessary part of his portrait of the artist. These letters, added to the testimony of contemporary witnesses to Joyce's experience of jealousy, have enabled Joyce's biographer to reconstruct the experience (*JJII*, 279–82), and this autobiographical context makes a difference in how we read Bloom.

It may also make a difference in how we read Blazes Boylan, for whom Richard Ellmann finds no clear model in the Dublin of 1904, and whom he labels Joyce's "villain" (*JJII*, 378). I suggest, on the contrary, that Blazes Boylan may instead be seen as heroic in a special sense and that he also arises from Joyce's experience of jealousy as the projection of a kind of ideal phallic self, a fantasy of unadulterated sexuality, prominent in the letters, that embodies Joyce's youthful libido as it relates to this highly charged period of his life. Like Bloom a "cybernetic" self-portrait, totally unrecognizable as "Joyce in his skin," Blazes Boylan memorializes a youthful self with whom the middle-aged self projected in Bloom is in a kind of psychic competition,[31] but a competition that is exclusively sexual. Thus he and Bloom may also take their places in a fictional triangle that is a specialized alternative to that of Stephen, Bloom, and Molly—the intensely libidinous younger self in one corner facing the notably nonlibidinous middle-aged self in the other, a view that is again strengthened by what we know of Joyce's life.

Budgen, for example, remembers his friend's bitter remarks about women when Joyce was about Bloom's age, as well as his own reminder to Joyce of an earlier time when Joyce had felt that "the woman's body was desirable, whatever else was objectionable about her." Joyce's reported response echoes proclivities he has assigned to Bloom in *Ulysses:* "Now I don't care a damn about their bodies. I am only interested in their clothes," which Budgen interpreted as "underclothes" ("Further Recollections, 535), since he was aware, as Molly is about Bloom, that his friend was "mad on the subject of drawers" (*U*, 18.289). Budgen is also the source for Ellmann's report of Nora Joyce's tearful confidence that "Jim wants me to go with other men so that he will have something to write about" (*JJII*, 445), testifying to an autobiographical base for Bloom's pervasive pandering. And Brenda Maddox, pointing to the fact that "the one ordinary human activity conspicuous by its absence in *Ulysses* is copulation," suggests that this textual fact is also grounded in autobiography, offering the "irresistible" speculation that "Joyce excluded it from his book because he had excluded it from his life" (164).

"Irresistible" or not, Maddox's suggestion remains a speculation only, one of those things we cannot know for sure, but it is an *informed* speculation, as is my own speculation that Joyce was aware of psychoanalytic reports of sexual perversities in real people that he has attributed to Bloom, as well as Rank's psychoanalytic interpretation of the tale of the Widow of Ephesus. I have here traced echoes of Rank's essay in Joyce's ambiguous treatment of the whole question of Molly's fidelity, even though we cannot know for certain whether or to what extent Joyce's reading of Rank's exposition of the hidden motivations behind the old tale may have offered him a universal dimension for a highly personal aspect of his own life that he then transfused into his fiction: we can only speculate. And the same may be said of textual echoes of psychoanalytic case studies that contribute to the portrait of Bloom.

But the echoes are there, and they make a difference in the texture of the novel. After all, Joyce appears to invite such speculation when, in a comment reported by Arthur Power, he affirms the basic psychoanalytic assumption of the reality of unconscious motivation: "Though people may read into *Ulysses* more than I ever intended, who is to say they are wrong: do any of us know what we are creating?" (74).

Oedipus and Ulysses

The Ongoing Dialogue

The "real world" and the "represented world," M. M. Bakhtin says, are "indissolubly tied up with each other and find themselves in continual mutual interaction." "The work and the world represented in it," he goes on, "enter the real world and enrich it, and the real world enters the work and its world as part of the process of its creation, as well as part of its subsequent life" (254). This complex proposition illuminates the interaction between Freud's twentieth-century translation of the legendary figure of Oedipus and Joyce's twentieth-century translation of the legendary figure of Odysseus/Ulysses. The centrality of the Oedipus complex—the "core complex" in Freud's structuring of the new psychology of the twentieth century, depended on Sophocles' tragic drama even as Joyce's *Ulysses*, a monument of twentieth-century literature, was structured around Homer's epic.

Each of these translations has at once resuscitated the traditional figure from which it was drawn and at the same time has to a degree preempted the place of that figure in the tradition. To say, that is, that in the twentieth century Oedipus has been important because of Freud, and Ulysses has been important because of Joyce may overstate the case, but only by a little. Thus both Freud's Oedipus and Joyce's Ulysses have, as Bakhtin puts it, "enter[ed] the real world and enriched it."

Indeed, recent end-of-the-century appraisals, however dubious these exercises may be, have dramatized the influence of both Freud and Joyce on the "real world" of the twentieth century. The Library of Congress exhibit titled "Sigmund Freud: Conflict and Culture," which opened in Washington, D.C., in October 1998, has aroused as much controversy as Freud's psychoanalytic theory did in its infancy. Harriet Barovick justly notes in a *Time* write-up that "the whole brouhaha shows how difficult it is for everyone to forget about Freud" (8), while Daphne Merkin, reporting on the exhibit in the *New Yorker*, observes that "what life was like before we came to believe that our difficulties in the present reside in a buried and traumatic past has become nearly impossible to imagine" (55). And *Time*, in its end-of-the-century listing of the "Great Minds" of the twentieth century, started the list with Freud.

As for Joyce, he has been proclaimed the "most influential writer" of the twentieth-century by *Time*, while his *Ulysses* tops a Modern Library panel's list of the hundred best novels of the century and has been included in many such lists, despite the limitations on its actual readership. And it is not insignificant that John Taylor has claimed in a Boston University alumni magazine that *Ulysses* "sells 100,000 copies a year, and three-quarters of a century after its publication has been dubbed 'the hottest literary property in the world'" (32). Granted the dubiety of this kind of summing up, it nonetheless reflects how insistently these notably elite figures have entered the consciousness of popular culture.

Even by the period of 1914 to 1922, when Joyce was writing *Ulysses*, Freud's work and that of his early disciples had already become a significant part of the "real world" of intellectual Europe, in particular the world of Trieste and Zurich, where Joyce lived during this period. And, as I have argued in the foregoing chapters, it is more probable than not that a range of this psychoanalytic literature entered the represented world of *Ulysses* "as part of the process of its creation." By the time Molly's final "Yes" concludes *Ulysses*, all three of the major figures in the novel have been touched, in different contexts and to different degrees, by the literature of psychoanalysis. Both Molly and Leopold include what have become well-worn Freudian clichés in their own discourse: Molly with her unuttered statement about the return to the womb—"theyre all mad to get in there where they came out of" (*U*, 18.806)—and Leopold with his Freudian slip on "the wife's admirers . . . advisers, I mean" (*U*, 12.767–69).[1] Like Stephen's reference to "the new Viennese school" (*U*, 9.780), these are superficial grace notes, but they are also reasonably straightforward signals that Freud's new psychology—new in large part because it insisted on the reality and the significance of the unconscious realm of the psyche—has found an anachronistic place in Joyce's record of Ulyssean wanderings on 16 June 1904.

Throughout this study I have followed traces of the inclusion of early psychoanalytic texts in the text of *Ulysses* and to a degree in *A Portrait*. To be sure, I can offer no solid evidence that Joyce in every instance had read the texts that appear to me to have left traces. But the traces, the echoes, the parallels, are there. And even though my selection of these texts does not claim to be comprehensive, the traces are considerable. Starting from around 1910 to 1913, the time of his acquisition in Trieste of Sigmund Freud's *Leonardo*, C. G. Jung's essay on "The Significance of the Father," and the German translation of Ernest Jones's original Hamlet and Oedipus essay, Joyce has selectively added fragments from these early psychoanalytic speculations to the autobiographical base for each of his main characters. I have developed my thesis throughout *as if* it were true without continually repeating an acknowledgment that this is an assumption every time—but a reasonable one.

To be sure, Joyce has also added fragments from innumerable other sources, and any attempt to describe the *way* Joyce integrates bits and pieces from other works into his own text must call on metaphors, none of which quite fits the case, but all of which are partially descriptive. Margot Norris has recently made excellent use of the metaphor of a web in her *Joyce's Web*, in which case the texts that contribute may be figured as woven threads, though a somewhat different kind of threads from the ones used in a tapestry, to which Joyce's work may also be compared. Joyce himself compared *Ulysses* to the "intricate illuminations" of the Book of Kells in which painting illuminates, but at the same time obscures, text (*JJII*, 545). And Valéry Larbaud saw Joyce's text as "a genuine example of the art of mosaic" (102), in which innumerable pieces of differing sizes and shapes are assembled to form a picture. Robert Motherwell, as I have earlier noted, identified Joyce's technique as analogous to the modernist painting technique of collage, with layer upon layer of *trouvés* or found objects, and I myself have sometimes thought of Joyce's text as layers of transparencies on an overhead projector that may produce shifting composites of differing outlines and densities.

Thus, Joyce's way with allusions, though similar to a number of techniques in various mediums, is uniquely his and perhaps uniquely complex as well as extraordinarily subtle. Motherwell, in his comments at the 1980 Provincetown Joyce Conference, delivered a remarkable cadenza testifying to this uniqueness, which I quote in part. "I doubt if ever again there will be a man who is a creative genius, who is in exile, who knows twelve languages, who has a thorough Jesuit education, . . . a mind like a razor, a sensuality like a Venetian *grand dame* . . . with a lyricism, with a quickness of pace, with a sense of the specific word, with a capacity for quadruple puns on one word, et cetera. . . . It's as though Joyce used art to such limits that the only person capable of grasping it as a totality is another Joyce, and that there will be another Joyce I very much doubt."[2]

The complexity of Joyce's way with words extends to the complicated effect of the imported psychoanalytic texts that are my subject. This is especially notable as these texts are combined with other texts, all of them, as Bakhtin says, "already populated with the social intentions of others," but "compel[led] to serve [Joyce's] own new intentions." And it is through this kind of focused textual agglutination that Joyce creates what Bakhtin calls "a unique artistic system orchestrating the intentional theme" with which he has begun (298–99). David Lodge was, I think, the first to point out how exactly Joyce's writing agrees with Bakhtin's descriptions even though Bakhtin does not mention Joyce.[3]

In a keynote address to a 1987 *Novel* conference on "Why the Novel Matters," Lodge posed the question whether books are "made out of the writer's observation and experience, or out of other books." And he presumed to speak for most writers when he answered "both" (131). Lodge's supposition is to a degree confirmed by Hugh Kenner's comment to the Frankfurt Symposium in 1984 that "a text by Joyce attracts other texts. Something outside the semantic system we have to bring before the text comes alive." The pervasive interrelationship of Joyce's texts with other texts is a critical fact that is a necessary part of any approach to his work, and even though the interrelationship between *Ulysses* and early psychoanalytic literature, with which I am here concerned, is only one aspect of the larger critical fact, it is significant—if for no other reason—because of the radical effect of Freud's theories on the social fabric of our time. Indeed, Paul Gray noted in a 1992 report the "remarkable degree" to which "Freud's ideas, conjectures, pronouncements have seeped well beyond the circle of his professional followers into the public mind and discourse," so that his "rich panoply of metaphors for the mental life has become, across wide swaths of the globe, something very close to common knowledge"[4]

But Freud's ideas were far from common knowledge when Joyce began his deliberate appropriation of psychoanalytic literature with his absorption of snatches from Freud's *Leonardo* into the prefiguring overture to *A Portrait*. Indeed, he has provided Stephen with a childhood memory that echoes Freud's reconstruction of meanings attached to a childhood memory recalled by Leonardo da Vinci. Joyce also works into *A Portrait* textual echoes of Freud's central assertion in his psychobiography of a causal connection between Leonardo's latent homosexuality and his relationship with his mother. This suggestion is carried over from *A Portrait* to *Ulysses*, where Mulligan replaces Cranly as a vaguely defined threat to Stephen's personhood that is at least colored by Freud's speculations about Leonardo. Bloom, too, who is already carrying the weight of Homer's Odysseus, is touched by Freud's *Leonardo*, as Joyce translates aspects of Freud's view of Leonardo's existential stance into his portrait of this twentieth-century Irish Jew. Beyond these echoes, the declared temperamental opposition of Stephen and Bloom as "artistic" and "scientific" also echoes a conflict in Freud's Leonardo. Both protagonists of the novel are thus weighted with ideas and facts that echo Freud's psychoanalytic re-creation of Leonardo da Vinci. In much the same way that he has appropriated fragments from Freud's *Leonardo* to piece out his characters and his story, Joyce has accumulated and used echoes from a range of other early psychoanalytic texts that were useful to him in deepening his own intentions for his work.

Though the basic frame of *Ulysses* is autobiographical,[5] this is a twentieth-century approach to autobiography, which takes into account both conscious and unconscious motivations, a perspective that obviously harmonizes with the aims and techniques of psychoanalysis. And Stephen, Bloom, and Molly are all implicated in the psychoanalytic intertext, which may well be even more extensive than the traces I have followed in this study. This psychoanalytic intertext in turn combines in various ways with other intertexts, including Christian doctrine and Shakespeare's *Hamlet*,[6] but, most significantly and certainly most publicly, with the Homeric intertext.

The Legendary Intertext

Most Joyceans are familiar with the fact that Joyce's identification with his epic hero went back to his schoolboy days, but perhaps not so familiar with the parallel fact that Freud was also exposed to his legendary intertext in his youth. Freud translated thirty-three verses of *Oedipus Rex* for his matriculation examination in Greek, receiving a mark of *good*—"the only one" in the class, he confided to his young friend Emil

Fluss in a letter of 16 June 1873 ("Some Early Unpublished Letters," 425). Indeed, David Willbern sees Freud's "eloquent Oedipal theory" as "a continuation of that translation," in which "Freud becomes the hero of his own translation; he interpenetrates the text of the myth" (107). Freud had just turned seventeen.

Joyce was a schoolboy at Belvedere and only twelve when he first met Ulysses in Charles Lamb's *Adventures of Ulysses* and chose him as the subject of an essay on "My Favorite Hero" (*JJII*, 46). Many years later Stanislaus Joyce, affirming his brother's contempt for epic heroes, "who, as it seemed to him, had developed their taurine bodies at the expense of their brains," remembered that "only Ulysses, astute and patient, did he find profoundly human" ("A Memoir," 497). These great originators had thus grown up with the legends that they eventually transposed into their own twentieth-century myths.

Freud's original text, Sophocles' *Oedipus Rex*, is a drama, in which the plot is central and the outcome is tragic. In fact, as Cynthia Chase observes—and it is an important observation—"the Oedipus complex draws its specificity from the *Sophoclean tragedy*, rather than just from the ostensible semantic content of the Oedipus legend" (54; emphasis Chase). Freud, in fact, saw the plot of *Oedipus Rex* as a model for the course of a psychoanalysis, in which a current crisis leads backward to its cause in the past, and the gradual unfolding of that past becomes the plot of the drama (*SE,* 16:330).

The Oedipus drama also connected intimately with Freud's self-analysis, which provided the backgrounds for his *Interpretation of Dreams* and later for his developed theory of the Oedipus complex, which, as Robert Steele points out, provides "a perfect demonstration of the fusion of art and science in [Freud's] work." For Freud uncovered evidence in his own dream life of feelings of murderous hostility toward his father and erotic desire for his mother, a pattern that he found confirmed in Sophocles' *Oedipus Rex* and in Shakespeare's *Hamlet*. The pattern was revealed through his "systematic observation" of his patients as well (114). He consequently assumed the universality of the construct that became the Oedipus complex and adopted the plot of the unfolding Oedipal drama as the master plot for his case histories and dream interpretations. Steele notes that "for a scientist, using literary works as evidence" represented a "bold tactic," but "the Oedipal insight," scientific or not, "connected Freud to all humanity" (94).

The original text for Joyce's *Ulysses*, on the other hand, is Homer's epic poem, the *Odyssey*, a connection that Joyce assiduously promoted both before and after the publication of his novel. When Valéry Larbaud introduced *Ulysses* to an audience in Sylvia Beach's book store in December of 1921, just before its publication the following February, he predicted that a reader who approached Joyce's novel "without the *Odyssey* clearly in mind will be thrown into dismay," for *Ulysses*, he asserted positively is "a book which has a key," and the key "is the title" (94, 97). Joyce's schema for the novel, a version of which he had lent to Larbaud before the introductory lecture, was first published in Stuart Gilbert's 1931 *Study*, with the now indispensable Homeric names for the episodes. But Joyce had sent the first known schema to Carlo Linati in 1920, then revised it for Larbaud's lecture, after which typed copies were circulated "under the most solemn injunctions of secrecy" (*JJII*, 521).[7]

The *Odyssey*, in contrast to the Sophoclean *Oedipus Rex*, featured a hero from a folktale tradition, in which the emphasis is on character rather than plot and the outcome is neither tragic nor conclusive. According to W. B. Stanford, "Homer alone [before Joyce] presented the whole man," and Homer's Odysseus was from the beginning endowed with a range of contrasting, even contradictory characteristics (*Ulysses Theme*, 211). Subsequent portraits in the tradition that sprang from Homer have varied widely as these contradictions were individually highlighted in different cultures by different artists with different personal responses to this multifaceted hero. Joyce's vision of his hero, stimulated first by Homer's "man of many devices" and at the same time surely colored by the accepted Christian analogy between Odysseus and Christ,[8] was inevitably influenced by these other portraits—the rebel/wanderer Ulysses of Dante's *Inferno* (canto 26), for example, as well as the "man of policies" of Shakespeare's *Troilus and Cressida*, to whom Stephen alludes in his Shakespeare lecture (Thornton, *Allusions*, 212; *Troilus and Cressida*, 3.3.115–23). But it was to Homer that Joyce regularly referred in comments about his hero.

As for plot, Aristotle, pointing out that the *Odyssey* "turns on character," summarizes its plot in three sentences:

A man is kept away from his home for many years; Poseidon is watching him with a jealous eye, and he is alone. The state of affairs at home is that his wealth is being squandered by his wife's suitors, and plots are being laid against his son's life. After being buffeted by many storms he returns home and reveals his identity; he falls upon his enemies and destroys them, but preserves his own life.

"There," Aristotle concludes, "you have the essential story of the *Odyssey;* the rest of the poem is made up of episodes" ("On the Art of Poetry," 67, 55–56). With some changes in the facts presented, this summary could be adapted to Joyce's *Ulysses,* which is, like the *Odyssey,* very nearly plotless in any classical sense.

Both *Oedipus Rex* and the *Odyssey* feature a basic triadic family situation of father-mother-son, in which the father is a king and the son is an only child. In both the tragic drama and the epic poem the son's relationship with the father is broken in early childhood so that—to different degrees—the father is unknown to the son. But here the similarities end. Laius, the father of Oedipus, threatened by the oracle with death by the hand of a son, has himself broken the paternal tie, condemning the baby son to death by exposure. Oedipus, to review briefly the well-known plot, is saved and brought up by other parents, but, discovering the prophecy that he will kill his father and marry his mother, he flees his adoptive parents. In the course of his flight he meets and quarrels with Laius at the famous crossroads and does indeed kill his father, who is a stranger to him. He enters Thebes, solves the riddle of the Sphinx, and marries his mother, also unknown to him. He becomes Oedipus the King.[9] And as Sophocles' tragedy opens, only the mother (wife) and son (husband) are in the nuclear family picture.

Homer's *Odyssey* also opens on a situation in which only mother and son represent the family triangle, with the free-loading suitors supplying the hostile element, indeed plotting against the son's life.[10] The father is absent, but here in Ithaca there is no hidden background of a father's murderous hostility, indeed, quite the opposite, as Joyce reminded Budgen. For Ulysses, Joyce pointed out, "tried to evade military service by simulating madness," but "the Greek recruiting sergeant was too clever for him and, while he was ploughing the sands [to demonstrate his madness] placed young Telemachus in front of his plough." And thus Ulysses went to war rather than endanger his son's life (*JJII,* 417). To be sure, Telemachus does not know his father any more than Oedipus does, but he does know from the beginning who his father is because his mother has told him, and he *knows* his mother, as Oedipus does not.

Only as the recapitulated drama of *Oedipus Rex* unfolds does Oedipus discover the identity of his father *and* his mother, who is also his wife. The meeting between both fathers and their sons is delayed until the sons reach adulthood. But when father and son in the *Odyssey* meet, after both return to Ithaca, their meeting leads to the cooperative project of slaughtering a common enemy, the usurping suitors. When Oedipus and his father meet, however, before the Sophoclean tragedy begins, Oedipus kills his father,

Freud, in his use of the Sophoclean Oedipus drama as a metaphor for the "nuclear complex" of neurosis, which he originally referred to as the "family complex," or even simply the child's relation with the "grown-ups,"[11] focused, as had Sophocles, on the son's role in the family triangle. The son's hostility toward the father on account of erotic feelings for the mother, basic to Freud's theoretical Oedipus complex and so decisively symbolized in the murder and incest that are central in *Oedipus Rex*, is in Freud's theory unconscious and therefore true to the drama, in which both patricide and incest are unknowing. The reigning point of view in the Oedipus story—legend, drama, or complex—is the son's, the Oedipal father being by and large ignored (see Rangell, 9–15). And through this story of the son, Freud simplified the family complex he was explaining psychoanalytically.[12]

For Joyce, however, both the family situation and the intertextual situation are considerably more complicated than in Freud's transposition of the Oedipus drama into his theory. In Homer's *Odyssey*, the hero is the father of Telemachus, but only incidentally.[13] An essential feature, in fact, of the hero's situation throughout his adventures is that, as Aristotle sums it up, "he is alone." And so is Telemachus. Isolated in Ithaca among his mother's suitors and threatened by plots on his life, he is not involved in any of his father's adventures as Odysseus struggles to return home from war. Furthermore, the fabled "search for the father," analogically embraced by early critics of *Ulysses* and still a significant part of the critical tradition, has a fairly skimpy textual base in Joyce's Homeric model (see Kimball, *Odyssey*, 3–4). True, Telemachus does leave Ithaca, on Athena/Mentor's advice, to inquire about his father in Pylos and Sparta, but this move is in large part a defensive response to danger for him in Ithaca. And once he gets to Sparta, he stays there, returning to Ithaca only when Athena/Mentor comes and gets him. At this point he finally meets his father and helps him in an auxiliary capacity in the slaughter of the suitors.

Complicating the Homeric heritage of Joyce's hero is the fact that, as Stanford reminded readers of *Ulysses* some years ago, Joyce was first introduced to Ulysses in Charles Lamb's *Adventures of Ulysses* (1808), a book that Joyce much later recommended to his Aunt Josephine as an aid to understanding *Ulysses:* "Buy at once the *Adventures of Ulysses* (which is Homer's story told in simple English much abbreviated) by Charles Lamb. . . . Then have a try at *Ulysses* again" (*Letters,* 1:193). In 1893 the Intermediate Examination Board determined on the first seven chapters of Lamb's *Adventures* as a text in the English course for Joyce's Preparatory Grade at Belvedere for the year 1893–1894, selecting John Cooke's edition, just published in Dublin. Cooke's edition included among its introductory materials Lamb's own "modest, one-page introduction," the first sentence of which points out that "this work is designed as a supplement to the adventures of Telemachus."[14]

Lamb is here referring to François Fénelon's *Les aventures de Télémaque,* which Joyce owned in a 1910 edition[15] and which, like Lamb's *Adventures,* is a children's book, described by Fénelon's biographer as "the first novel put into the hands of youth." A "prodigious success" when it was published in 1699, it was "translated into every language of Europe,"[16] and a perusal of the annotated table of contents for an 1859 English translation reveals the nature and extent of Telemachus's travels and adventures, some of which replicate those of his father. In book 1, for example, when Telemachus is washed up on Calypso's island shortly after his father's departure from Ogygia, the goddess "conceives a passion" for the son even as she had for his father and duplicates her offer of immortality as well.[17] Indeed, by the time Telemachus arrives in Ithaca in book 24 of Fénelon's story, he is world-famous in his own right, and Fénelon ends his account with the meeting of father and son at the dwelling of Eumaeus, a cutoff point that coincides with the closing of chapter 7 in Lamb, the end of the assigned reading for the schoolboy Joyce.

Since Lamb's *Adventures* is designed as a supplement to this fulsome account of Telemachus's exploits (over 350 pages in English), Lamb omits entirely the first four books of the *Odyssey*—the Telemachiad—limiting himself to passing references to Telemachus. His first chapter thus starts with the Cicones and the Lotus-eaters, chronologically the first of Ulysses' adventures after he left Troy, though delayed until book 9 of the *Odyssey* and until the fifth episode of Joyce's *Ulysses*. In addition, Joyce's initial reading of the *Odyssey*, which included only the first seven chapters of Lamb's book, ended with the hero's safe return home, indeed, with Ulysses "stooping down and kissing the soil" of his native land, an act that is famously figured in Bloom's goodnight kiss upon his return to Molly in "Ithaca." Thus the adventures of Ulysses disguised as a beggar as well as the slaughter of the suitors—the only adventures in which Telemachus is importantly involved—were not a part of Joyce's introduction to the *Odyssey*. Stanford points out that "the chief episodes in . . . *Ulysses* belong to those first seven chapters" ("Joyce's First Meeting," 105), and the "Ithaca" episode marks the conclusion of the narrative in Joyce's novel.

In the deterministic plot of Sophocles' drama, which Freud carried over to his theory, Oedipus as son is trapped in the original family triangle. This entrapment contrasts with a certain open-endedness in the Odyssean model, in which the ambiguity of the father-son relationship carries with it a freedom for both father and son that is realized in different degrees in Joyce's Odyssean sources and in his own novel. Father and son, whatever the ins and outs of their relationship may be, are separate individuals with separate stories in the *Odyssey* and even more in Lamb's *Adventures*, especially as that work subsumes Fénelon's *Adventures of Telemachus*.[18]

Such a separate delineation of these two members of the basic family triangle is also characteristic of Joyce's *Ulysses*, especially if we look at it as a sequel to his *Portrait of the Artist as a Young Man*, which is as purely the story of a son as is the Oedipus drama. Moreover, the first three episodes of *Ulysses* continue Stephen's story from *A Portrait* after a hiatus of a year, during which his mother has died, a feature dictated by autobiographical fact. And in a strangely offkey way Joyce's *Ulysses* also opens, like Sophocles' drama and Homer's poem, upon mother and son, for though Stephen's mother is dead, she is still very much with him, another presumably autobiographical fact that has produced a paralyzing crisis for Stephen, a crisis that haunts him through the day. And even as the first episodes of *Ulysses* focus exclusively on Stephen, the closing episode of the novel, paralleling the *Odyssey*'s return to Penelope and her problem with the suitors at its close, is entirely turned over to Molly.

This is a patterning that conforms superficially at least to the structure of Homer's *Odyssey,* in which the adventures of Odysseus form the center, with Telemachus in focus at the beginning and Odysseus's relationship with Penelope at the end. To be sure, the parallel is not exact; it seldom is with Joyce. In the "Wanderings" section at the center of *Ulysses,* Bloom is not "alone" in the same way that Homer's Odysseus or Lamb's Ulysses is. For in a number of the adventures Stephen joins Bloom—in "Aeolus" or "Oxen of the Sun" or "Circe," for example—and the two protagonists split the episode between them in differing proportions.

In addition, Homer's epic does not conclude with the reunion of Odysseus and Penelope. The final book of Homer's *Odyssey* covers the meeting between Odysseus and his father, as well as his confrontation with the angry Ithacans, whose sons Odysseus has so recently slaughtered. Athena/Mentor engineers a solution to the demand for retribution, and the way is cleared for Odysseus to return as king. But the central story is over, and this final book serves as an epilogue, tying up the loose ends.

Psychoanalysis and the "Subsequent Life" of *Ulysses*

This, then, is the "represented world" of Joyce's *Ulysses,* which is, according to the author's public declarations, a fictional world intentionally built on the fictional world of Homer's *Odyssey.* The analogy, however, is far from symmetrical, and whatever the structural similarities, there are clearly significant differences in the structuring of the two worlds. These differences are dictated by other intentions, not least the autobiographical intention that, in my view at least, motivates all of Joyce's work. The incorporation of fragments of texts other than Homer's has helped to realize Joyce's complicated intentions, and it has been the purpose of this study to trace echoes of psychoanalytic works that Joyce has included among the wealth of analogical intertexts that resonate with each other in *Ulysses.*

My assumption is that all these texts are congruent in one way or another with Joyce's own vision, though it is not always possible to identify how, and in a number of instances they are congruent also with each other. An assessment of the impact of any one of these intertexts perhaps has dubious reliability, since it is basically in combination that they produce their effects, but in combination psychoanalytic intertexts have had their separate effect on the way *Ulysses* has been read in the first century of its existence.

Joyce's incorporation into *Ulysses* of fragments from the literature of psychoanalysis has had an effect on the reading of the novel, I think, that may well have gone beyond Joyce's intention. There is good ground for assuming that Joyce's purchase of the texts by Freud, Jung, and Jones around 1910–1911 represented his first more than superficial acquaintance with psychoanalytic speculations, and this was very early in the history of the movement. It was a time when Freud had only recently coined the term "Oedipus complex"[19] and well before the concept had developed into a shibboleth of psychoanalytic theory and a catchword of pop-psychoanalysis. When Joyce began to introduce allusions from these texts into his work, psychoanalysis was new, and its remarkably expansive future could not have been predicted.

Even in 1918, when Joyce was writing "Scylla and Charybdis," the episode in which psychoanalysis enters *Ulysses*, as I have detailed in chapter 3, the development of the movement had been arrested because of World War I, so that neither Joyce nor anyone else could be expected to foresee that the language of psychoanalysis would enter the common speech of readers and critics to the extent it has and affect their response to his novel. And when Joyce worked the Oedipal triangle of Freud's theory—more or less as he found it in Jones's *Hamlet* essay—into the thematically suggestive discussion of fatherhood in "Scylla and Charybdis," he was dealing with an intertext whose enduring cultural weight was not yet established, in contrast to the authenticated values for the allusions to Shakespeare, Christian doctrine, and the church fathers with which it was combined. But historically, through Freud's insistent and powerfully persuasive extension of the application of the Oedipus legend—as he had originally found it in Sophocles—the Oedipus complex leaped beyond its therapeutic uses and gained wide acceptance as the master plot for the psychic life of every son, so that the erotic attraction to the mother, along with the hostility between son and father, came to seem almost a norm for the family triangle.

In "Scylla and Charybdis," Joyce incorporated this Oedipal triangle into one of the most examined passages in *Ulysses*, Stephen's disquisition on fatherhood, a passage that has provided quotable lines for generations of critics. And in this passage Freud's master plot is placed in the context of a competing biblical master plot—original sin—in an analogical relation to the sin of Adam and Eve in the Garden. Even as Freud assumes that every man has participated, through his now unconscious infantile desires, in the double sin of murder and incest committed—also unconsciously—by Oedipus, so also the Catechism assigns participation in original sin to all of Adam's descendants through inheritance. And this is the way Joyce translates his doubled biblical/psychoanalytic allusion into *Ulysses*: "*An* original sin and, *like* original sin, committed by another in whose sin he too has sinned" (*U*, 9.1008–9; emphasis mine).

The material on fatherhood provides a very showy set piece for Stephen, and early and late it has offered readers and critics a hold on some central meaning in *Ulysses* that hovers around the "paternity theme." But when Joyce added the Freudian context to the textual mix in Stephen's lecture, he set up a dialogue between competing views of the family triangle, especially the father-son relationship, which has at the least added to the ambiguity surrounding our interpretations of this relationship and may even have subverted Joyce's original intention.

For the Oedipal family triad is basically at odds with the Odyssean triangle of Joyce's advertised intention and also at odds, I think, with the autobiographical base that underlies and is reflected in the narrative of *Ulysses*. The son's hostility toward the father on account of his erotic feelings for the mother, basic to the Freudian Oedipus complex, appears to be absent in the Homeric family triangle,[20] as does the implication of the father's hostility toward the son that is expressed in King Laius's brutal exposure of the infant Oedipus.

Stephen's remarks in "Scylla and Charybdis" do not go beyond the Odyssean contrast between the unknown father and the surely known mother, and his internal references to his own father, which counterpoint his remarks on fatherhood, go no further than this "incertitude." Certainly they do not support the feelings of hostility or rejection with which critics have often invested his voiced comments here about a father as "a necessary evil" and paternity as "a legal fiction." There is, in fact, a note of near-tenderness in Stephen's memory of his meeting with Simon, "the widower," upon his return from Paris, an awareness in Stephen of "new warmth" in his father's voice and of "the eyes that wish me well," even though these responses are coupled with the recognition that the eyes "do not know me" (*U*, 9.824–27).[21]

The addition of the paternal factor to Stephen's crucial problem with his dead mother does not appear to be justified by Stephen's existential situation in the novel, even though the adumbrated outline of the Oedipus complex that is included in "Scylla and Charybdis" has encouraged readers and critics to read the Oedipal triangle into *Ulysses* as well. For Joyce, though, Bloom and Stephen remain stand-ins for Ulysses and Telemachus, whatever the complications of their connection to their Homeric heritage; they are "Ul and Tel" in Joyce's notes.

They are in addition "consubstantial," a peculiar fact that Joyce develops through various devices, among them the widely recognized interchange of thoughts that distinguishes their relationship in *Ulysses*. This somewhat mysterious consubstantiality is further indicated, though not defined, in Joyce's British Museum notesheets for "Circe," which contain the equation: "SD + LB = idem" (Adams, *Surface and Symbol*, 252 n. 1), which may be translated "the same" and, further, forms the stem for "identity." In the notesheets for "Eumaeus," Joyce notes that "Ul and Tel exchange unity," a note, A. Walton Litz points out, that is "crossed in blue pencil, a sign that Joyce found an adequate expression for this interchange" (22). This interchange, indeed, is realized textually midway through "Ithaca," when Stephen and Bloom part, Stephen becoming the "centrifugal departer," the Ulyssean wanderer, while Bloom reverts to the "centripetal remainer" (*U*, 17.1212). At this point the schematic Telemachus "exchanges unity" with the schematic Ulysses.

Of course, as Stanford has observed, Stephen throughout *Ulysses* (and even before) has represented one element in the Ulysses tradition, the "rebellious, destructive, home-abandoning" Ulysses of the line descending from Dante's view of the hero in the *Inferno*. And Stanford credits Joyce with "us[ing] Dedalus-Telemachus as a means of solving a radical antinomy in the tradition—the conceptions of Ulysses as a home-deserter and as a home-seeker" (*Ulysses Theme*, 215). In Joyce's treatment of the theme, in short, Telemachus and Ulysses, are both Ulysses. Like George Meredith's "Egoist," Joyce's Ulysses is "Son of Himself" and "likewise the Father."[22]

In the final analysis, Joyce remains faithful to the Odyssean patterns that he found in Lamb's version of the *Adventures of Ulysses* as this version built on parallel adventures for Telemachus in Fénelon's *Télémaque*. He splits the Homeric adventures between his designated Telemachus and his designated Ulysses in various ways, and the existential problems of Joyce's Stephen and Bloom duplicate those of their Homeric prototypes. At the same time these problems duplicate those of their creator at the separate stages of his life embodied in his two protagonists. For the son Stephen Dedalus, as for the son Telemachus, the problem of his life is to escape from enemies in his homeland, as it was for Joyce in 1904. For the father Leopold Bloom, as for the father Ulysses, the problem is to return to what he loves in his homeland, as it was, after all, for the self-exiled Joyce as the creator of the new and eternal Dublin.

Autobiography and myth thus merge in *Ulysses,* which is firmly bound to tradition through the Homeric parallels and also through Stephen, an identifiable artist-hero of the traditional *Künstlerroman* and a hero whose mind "is full . . . of borrowed words," also from the tradition, "half quotes" with which he sprinkles his discourse to himself and to others (*Letters,* 1:263). Stephen, as a reader sees him in *Ulysses* is almost all mind and all talk, but great talk. He is countered and completed by Bloom, the prophetic character in *Ulysses,* who embodies the "modern theme" as Joyce saw it and as it has proved to be—"the subterranean forces, those hidden tides which govern everything . . . the pathological and psychological body which our behaviour and thought depend on" (Power, 54, 56). Drawing undoubtedly on his own hidden life as well as the subterranean layer of the lives examined by the early psychoanalysts, Joyce has produced in Bloom one of the great figures of world literature. And Joyce, who denied Freudian influence, has perhaps done more, in his dual portrait of the artist, to transfuse Freud's new perspective into the mainstream of Western literature than many a declared disciple.

Notes

Chapter 1. Introduction

1. See Stanford, *Ulysses Theme*. See also Rahner, *Greek Myths*, especially his chapter on "Odysseus at the Mast," 328–86; and see Kimball, "Hypostasis," 422–25, for the specifically Christian connotations of Joyce's Odysseus/Ulysses figure.

2. See Ellmann, *Consciousness*, 97–134, for the listing of the library, and 54–56, for his comments on the effect of the psychoanalytic texts. See also Gillespie, *Inverted Volumes*, 11–23, for a comparison of Ellmann's listing and his own catalogue. And see Gillespie's *Catalogue* for the individual listings. Further reference in the text to these pamphlets will be to their English titles. See Anderson, "Leopold Bloom," 23–43, for an examination of echoes of Freud's *Psychopathology of Everyday Life* in *Ulysses*.

3. The journals, in the order of their founding, were *Jahrbuch für psychoanalytische und psychopathologische Forschungen* [Yearbook for psychoanalytic and psychopathological research] (1909), *Zentralblatt für Psychoanalyse* [Central bulletin for psychoanalysis] (1911), *Imago* (1912), and *Internationale Zeitschrift für arztliche Psychoanalyse* [International journal for medical psychoanalysis] (1913). I refer to these journals in the text by their shortened English titles.

4. On the "long and often speculative debate" about the relationship between Joyce's fiction and psychoanalysis, see Mierlo, 115.

5. The 1912 volume was extensively revised and published as *Symbols of Transformation: An Analysis of the Prelude to a Case of Schizophrenia*, volume 5 of Jung's *Collected Works*.

6. These pages refer to Joyce's second stay in Paris, though both periods had their miseries. The first stay lasted just three weeks, from 1 to 23 December 1902 (*JJII*, 111–16), after which he came back home, returning to Paris on 23 January 1903 (*JJII*, 120).

7. See Trilling, "Adventurous Mind of Dr. Freud," 1, and "James Joyce in His Letters," 56.

8. See also Thomas, 19, on Freud's *Interpretation of Dreams* as "vitally affiliated with the novel as a literary form."

9. See Hoffman's chapter on "Freudianism—American and English," 59–86.

10. See Jones, *Life and Work*, 2:8–10. See also Freud, *History, SE*, 14:25–26.

11. West does assume Freudian patterns, though not so specifically as Williams indicates, I think.

12. See Ellmann's index s.v. "psychoanalysis."

13. The pamphlets were not expensive (1 mark for Jung's essay, 1.50 for Jones's, and 2.50 for Freud's, as compared with 10 marks for Freud's *Traumdeutung*), but see Crivelli (186) on the Joyces as "always penniless (and in debt)." See also Crivelli's note on the "F. H. Schimpff" bookshop (178).

14. Although Jung had a powerful base in the Zurich School after his break with Freud, Rank's place in the history of psychoanalysis was for many years all but ignored, since, as Roazen has noted, a break from Freudian orthodoxy meant that the "heretic's work was no longer cited" (300). See Menaker and Lieberman, for re-evaluations of Rank.

15. See also Perkins, 11 and 35–36, on Joyce and his understanding of the "possibilities of the German language."

16. See *SE*, 4 and 5 for *The Interpretation of Dreams, SE*, 6 for *The Psychopathology of Everyday Life, SE*, 8 for *Jokes and Their Relation to the Unconscious*, and *SE*, 7 for "Fragment of an Analysis of a Case of Hysteria," 1–122, and *Three Essays on the Theory of Sexuality*, 123–245.

17. See Anzieu on the autobiographical nature of *The Interpretation of Dreams*.

18. The phrase is Rahner's (26). See also his note on Paul and the church fathers of the third and fourth centuries, who "took over words, images and gestures of the mystery religions . . . not as seekers after treasure but as possessors thereof" (11).

19. See Thornton, "Allusive Method," 235–49.

20. For a convenient summary of the implications of the wide variety of terms Bakhtin has used, see Dettmar, 26–37.

21. See also Dettmar's suggested explanation for Bakhtin's omission of any consideration of Joyce (27–28).

22. For the context provided by this allusion, see Kimball, "'Brainsick Words of Sophists,'" 399–400.

23. See "Former Student" in "Talk of the Town," *New Yorker*, 30 December 1991, 27. See also Hedberg, 441–42. And see *JJII*, 436, where Ellmann attributes this remembrance to Budgen, though in his note (24) he appears to identify it with Kraus.

24. The *Encyclopaedia Britannica* (1965) article on Trieste divides up a 229,510 population in 1910 as follows: 118,959 Italians; 59,319 Slovenes and Croats; 12,635 other Austrians, including Germans; and 38,597 foreigners. See also chap. 1 of Hartshorn's *James Joyce and Trieste*.

25. See also Staley, "Italo Svevo," 207, where he quotes Michel David on the "two cultures" in Trieste, one dominated by Vienna and the other by Florence. David's *La psicoanalis, nella culture italiana*, which is a source for both Bollettieri and Staley, has never been translated into English.

26. See Crivelli (164) on Joyce's students as "noblemen, businessmen, and intel-

lectuals." See also Pelaschiar (68) on the "social limbo" in which the Joyce brothers lived vis-à-vis their pupils in Trieste.

27. Bollettieri notes that Stanislaus claimed in a lecture given in Trieste that "Svevo tried vainly to convert James to psycho-analysis" (181).

28. See Kerr, *A Most Dangerous Method*, 9, on the status of the Zurich School at the time Freud and Jung formed their personal and professional association.

29. See Jones, *Life and Work*, 2:33, on the founding of the *Yearbook* and 2:44, on Jung's elevation to the presidency of the association.

30. "America Facing Its Most Tragic Moment—Dr. Carl Jung," sec. 5, 2. Jung's lecture at Fordham, according to Kerr, clarified a number of his differences with Freud ("Beyond the Pleasure Principle," 48–50).

31. See, for example, the continuing subject of "the incest problem," as well as Jung's conception of the libido theory, in the letters between Jung and Freud in the spring of 1912 (McGuire, 501–12).

32. See Jones, *Life and Work*, 2:137–51, for a summary of the drawn-out separation between Freud and Jung.

33. A check of accession records at the Zentralbibliothek Zurich reveals that besides these journals, the library had purchased, some time before Joyce left Zurich in 1919, a number of books by Freud, Jung, and Rank, including two copies of Freud's *Traumdeutung* [Interpretation of dreams] and copies of Rank's *Der Künstler* [The artist], *Der Mythus von der Geburt des Helden* [The myth of the birth of the hero], and *Das Inzest-Motiv in Dichtung und Sage* [The incest-motif in poetry and legend], the first two cited by Jones in his *Hamlet* essay.

34. This essay was cited by Freud in his study of Leonardo and also by Jones in his *Hamlet* essay.

35. Note that Faerber and Luchsinger also fail to mention the library. Compare Crivelli on the Trieste city library: "there is no formal evidence of Joyce entering this library . . . [but] the writer was definitely a frequent visitor" (195), as he surely was in Zurich.

36. Note that Gillespie, warning of the hazards of complete dependence on the Trieste collection in the investigation of Joyce's sources, has suggested the need for further work in the area of Joyce's library research (*Inverted Volumes*, 11, 21–23).

37. Several histories of the library exist, the most accessible of which is the summary by Cattani, "Milestones in Zurich's Library History," published in a special edition of the *Neue Zürcher Zeitung* for 1 November 1994 (B3), which celebrated the opening of the most recent reconstruction of the Zentralbibliothek in 1994.

38. See Wyss, esp. 16–41, on the *Stadtbibliothek* [City Library] and 54–58, on the *Kantonsbibliothek* [Canton Library]. See also Escher, 86–104.

39. See Faerber and Luchsinger (13–15) for Joyce's residences in Zurich and their location on a map, and note that Reinhardstrasse 7, Kreuzstrasse 19, and Seefeldstrasse 14 and 73 are all relatively close to the Limmatquai where the Wasserkirche and Helmhaus are located.

40. According to the accession records of the library, this volume was purchased in 1912.

41. See Owen, 87 and 89, for Joyce's translating jobs in Zurich, as well as a testimonial that his work was "faultless except for absentminded omissions of an occasional sentence or paragraph."

Chapter 2. Freud's *Leonardo*

1. On the relationship between the two novels, see Kimball, *Odyssey*, 41–56.

2. See Gabler, "Seven Lost Years," 35, on the probable late date of the completion of the opening section.

3. *SE*, 7:130–243. See also appendix 7, *SE*, 7:244–45, "List of Writings by Freud Dealing Predominantly or Largely with Sexuality."

4. Most comprehensively by Brivic in his "Joyce in Progress," 306–27, and his earlier "From Stephen to Bloom," 118–62. See the latter, 124 n. 14, for a representative list of discussions of Stephen's Oedipus complex. See also Shechner, "James Joyce and Psychoanalysis," 383–84. McKnight's "Unlocking the Word-Hoard" centers, as does Freud's analysis of Leonardo, on the ambiguity of the mother-son relationship. But her expanded conception of this relationship, as Shechner points out in the same issue, is really post-Freudian in perspective and "beyond Joyce's own myths," or indeed any "conceptual guides" he might have had ("Joyce and Psychoanalysis," 418).

5. An exception, in addition to my own "James Joyce and Otto Rank," 366–82, is Anderson's detailed evidence for Joyce's use of Freud's *Psychopathology of Everyday Life* in the "Lestrygonians" episode of *Ulysses*. See his "Leopold Bloom as Dr. Sigmund Freud." I have not included Anderson's analysis in this study.

6. Compare Shechner's note on Joyce's "deliberate mythmaking" as a response to his "need to tie his own emotional life to larger patterns of experience in order to universalize and aggrandize himself" ("Two Additional Perspectives," 417–18).

7. See the editor's discussion of Freud's mistranslation of the Italian *nibio* (*nibbio* in modern Italian) from Leonardo's notebooks. It is Italian for *kite*, whereas Freud translated it as *Geier* (vulture) (*L*, 60–62).

8. See "Baby Tuckoo," 141–42. Anderson's note that "tuckoo" is related to "tuck" as a word for food (142) seems to me reasonable and helpful, though I am not so ready to go along with his connection between the excretory birth theories of children and Simon's story, or indeed a number of features of his Freudian reading.

9. *SE*, 10:5–149. Other works by Freud that he cites in the Leonardo study are the following: "Fragment" (1905), *SE*, 7:7–122; "Character and Anal Erotism" (1908), *SE*, 9:169–75; "Sexual Theories of Children" (1908), *SE*, 9:109–26; *Three Essays* (1905), *SE*, 7:130–243.

10. Compare Stephen's recognition of the Jesuits as a separate species, outside male categories: "It was hard to think what [they would have become if they had not become jesuits] because you would have to think of them in a different way with . . . beards and moustaches" (*P*, 48).

11. There is no suggestion in Freud's Leonardo essay that this image is connected with castration anxiety (compare Brivic, "Stephen to Bloom," 127); the implication is that the problem is more nearly narcissistic (*L*, 95–99).

12. See *L*, 78–80. See also Hans's father's comment that "it is not clear to him in what way he belongs to me" (*SE*, 10:100), and see "On the Sexual Theories of Children" (*SE*, 9:211–14). See also *SE*, 10:133 n, on Freud's emendation to his first assumption that the primary riddle was that of birth.

13. See also Hans's dialogue with his father (*SE*, 10:61–63), in which his account of "looking-on" episodes with Berta runs into related episodes with his mother, and note Freud's observation that "the pleasure taken in looking on while someone one loves performs the natural functions" represents a "confluence of instincts" (*SE*, 10:127).

14. Note Freud's comment on "the great riddle of where babies come from . . . of which the riddle of the Theban Sphinx is probably no more than a distorted version" (*SE*, 10:133).

15. Freud's essay does not extend the literal self-punishment through the eyes to symbolic castration, which Brivic sees as a probable interpretation of the punishment in *A Portrait* ("Stephen to Bloom," 125).

16. See Freud's comment that if motherhood "represents one of the forms of attainable human happiness, that is in no little measure due to the possibility it offers of satisfying, without reproach, wishful impulses which have long been repressed and which must be called perverse" (*L*, 117). Note that this is followed by a reference to *Three Essays* (*SE*, 7:223), where he spells out the sexual nature of mother love. Note also that he introduces the idea of rivalry and antagonism between father and son (*L*, 117), which crops up in Stephen's discussion of fatherhood (*U*, 9.828–60).

17. *Joyce in Nighttown*, 27–28. Compare Brivic, "Stephen to Bloom," 129–30.

18. Compare Freud's elucidation (*SE*, 7:71–74) of the antithesis between fire and water as specifically related to bed-wetting and its sexual connotations in his analysis of one of "Dora's" dreams in "Fragment," to which he refers in the Leonardo study (*L*, 87), and note that there is also a reference in his analysis to the question of a kiss. Note also that Brivic sees this antithesis as related to the conflict in Stephen between "phallic threat" and "maternal haven" ("Stephen to Bloom," 126, and "Joyce in Progress," 308). He identifies as fetishistic not only the mother's slippers but also details of her farewell kiss ("Stephen to Bloom," 127).

19. This figure, used by the Ghost in *Hamlet*, apparently has a certain fascination for Stephen, who has misquoted it to himself in "Aeolus" (*U*, 7.750; Thornton, *Allusions*, 123). Here, he is applying the murder method to Shakespeare's "undoing," having just transferred it also to the poison of his own argument: "And in the porches of their ears I pour" (*U*, 9.465).

20. See Curtius, 311–12, on Joyce's "enchainment of associations" and note his axiom: "When two or more things have been once associated, one can be put for the other in the course of the stream of consciousness."

21. See *Odyssey,* book 12, where Circe tells Odysseus that he must sacrifice six of his men to Scylla to escape the whirlpool of Charybdis.

22. *As I Was Going,* 84. See also Lewis, 101, for a similar opinion, limited to Bloom as a Jew: "Usually the author . . . is alone performing before us."

23. "Structuralist Perspective," 164–65. See also Kimball, *Odyssey,* 65–71, on Stephen and Bloom as "I and Not-I."

24. See Kenner's defense of these figures, "Bloom's Chest," 505–8, and, for a reply, see Kimball, "The Measure of Bloom—Again," 201–4.

25. See Steinberg's "Reading Leopold Bloom," 397–416, for a comprehensive review, as of 1989, of the critical literature on the question of Bloom's Jewishness. See also Byrnes, "Bloom's Sexual Tropes," 303–23; and his "Weiningerian Sex Comedy, 267–81, for an intertextual view of the question. For Steinberg's most recent contribution to the question of Bloom's identity see "The Source(s) of Joyce's Anti-Semitism," 63–83.

26. See also *U,* 14.1062–63, where Bloom, surrounded by the young men at the hospital, reflects, "Now he is himself paternal and these about him might be his sons," paralleling the relationship that Freud sees for Leonardo with his young apprentices, whatever the emotional undertones. In Freud's interpretation of Leonardo, however, it was a *maternal* relationship (*L,* 102–4), an interpretation that agrees with a number of recent critical views of Bloom as maternal. See, for example Bormanis, 593, 599, and Henke, 121. See also Kimball, *Odyssey,* 120–21.

27. In *Ulysses* the birds of the scene in *A Portrait* appear to be paralleled by the bats that Bloom sleepily contemplates on the Strand (*U,* 13.1117–286), and Leonardo also compares the bird and the bat in connection with his efforts to build a flying machine. See McCurdy, 416.

28. Note that Freud links Leonardo's absent father with Leonardo's overdeveloped drive to investigate (*L,* 92) and with his freedom from any dogmatic religion (*L,* 124), both features that have found their way into the comic portrait of Bloom.

29. Compare *U,* 3.397–98, 7.522–25, and see also Anderson's interpretation of the "ugly fantasy—at once homosexual and incestuous" (136).

30. On Joyce's probable use of this work in *Finnegans Wake,* see Troy, 20–21, and Atherton, 197.

Chapter 3. Freud's *Hamlet* and Stephen's

1. For details on Stephen's sophistical tricks, see Kimball, "'Brainsick Words of Sophists,'" 400–401.

2. See also *JJII,* 155, 364, and note Ellmann's statement that "nothing has been admitted into the book which is not in some way attached and personal" (*JJII,* 364). See also Colum, 328, on this episode as indicating that "Joyce believes only in the autobiographical in art."

3. See Gogarty, *Mourning,* 41, for a description of Joyce when Gogarty first met him.

4. See *BK,* 232, 245, 254, on Joyce's change in outlook after his return from Paris

and his mother's death. See Stanislaus on his brother as "an artist first. He has too much talent to be anything else. If he was not an artist first, his talent would trouble him constantly like semen" (*CDD*, 52–53). Stanislaus's view of Gogarty as an instigator in Joyce's destructive lifestyle was apparently shared by Padraic Colum, who writes of "the comic *persona* with which Gogarty invested him" as a "Gogartian creation" (Colum and Colum, 76, 37–38). See also Curran, 66.

5. Colum and Colum, 29–30. Except for the following description by Byrne, descriptions of the librarians are those of Padraic Colum, 29–34.

6. "Das 'Schauspiel' im *Hamlet*," translated into English by Paul Lewinson as "The 'Play-Within-a-Play' in *Hamlet*." Citations in the text are to this translation ("Play").

7. See Schutte, 53, 63–64, and 174–75, for example, on the combination of fact and fiction in Stephen's information about the star that rose at Shakespeare's birth (*U*, 9.928–31). Budgen, *James Joyce*, 117–18, comments that "the evidence entirely contradicts Stephen's hypothesis" about Ann's adultery with the brothers, who were much younger than Shakespeare, while Ann was eight years older, and Schutte notes that Stephen could hardly have been "unaware of his distortion of the probabilities" in his charge (53).

8. Quillian has arranged and annotated these notes, now in three groups, in the James Joyce Collection at Cornell University, in three appendices to his *Hamlet and the New Poetic*, 79–145.

9. It is seldom acknowledged that Freud ends this footnote by pointing out that, like dreams, which "need to be ['over-interpreted'] in order to be fully understood, so all genuinely creative writings are the product of more than a single impulse in the poet's mind and are open to more than a single interpretation. In what I have written I have only attempted to interpret the deepest layer of impulses in the mind of the creative writer" (*SE*, 4:266).

10. See Jones's extended explanation (*H*, 94–97) of jealousy in children and its "close relation" to "the desire for removal of a rival by death," as well as the child's extremely limited understanding of death and his "non-adapted" sexual understanding as well.

11. Norris uses the web as a metaphor for Joyce's text in her *Joyce's Web*, describing her "critical procedure" as "a teasing apart and reknitting of writing intertexted with itself" (52). This procedure is equally necessary in the process of analyzing the effect of outside intertexts, and throughout this study I have often "teased apart" for analysis strands that have a unified effect in the text.

12. Rank's *Der Mythus von der Geburt des Helden*, acquired by the Zurich library in 1911, was translated into English in 1914 by F. Robbins and Smith Ely Jelliffe. References in the text are found in Philip Freund's *The Myth of the Birth of the Hero and Other Writings*, cited as *MBH*.

13. Any quotations I use from Freud's essay are from James Strachey's translation, "Family Romances," *SE*, 9:236–41 (abbreviated *FR* in the text).

14. Compare Freud, "Creative Writers" (*SE*, 9:150), on "His Majesty the Ego, the hero alike of every day-dream and of every story."

15. For Rank's summaries, see *MBH*, 65 and 72. Note also traces of the hero myth in Stephen's perception of his relation to his family in *A Portrait* (presumably too early for any suggestion of influence), as "the mystical kinship of fosterage, fosterchild and fosterbrother" (*P*, 98).

16. For an extended Freudian interpretation of paternity in *Ulysses*, see Brivic, *Joyce Between Freud and Jung*, 123–216. See also Epstein's discussion of the "theory of symbolic fatherhood" in *Ulysses, Ordeal*, 5–11.

17. In the following discussion, details on allusions not otherwise documented will be found in order in Thornton, *Allusions*, 199–204.

18. See *Jerusalem*, chap. 2, pl. 46 [41], ll. 25–26, in *Complete Writings*, 676. See also pl. 27, ll. 81–82, "A man's worst enemies are those / Of his own house & family," 652, and note that Thornton lists neither of these allusions.

19. Note that Jones quotes the central section of Hamlet's soliloquy, including the Hecuba question, as evidence of Hamlet's certainty about his mission—and also his despairing recognition of his vacillation in carrying it out (*H*, 88; *Hamlet* 2.2.582–613). I assume that in the German translation it was quoted in English, even as Jones mixes untranslated German into the original English version. Rank also quotes Hamlet's question in English in the 1907 edition of *Der Künstler* (41) in a discussion of artistic sublimation and the persistence of the original affect of what has been repressed, even with the transformation of the material.

20. Compare Joyce's letter of 7 August 1909 to Nora, in which his first anguish at Nora's supposed unfaithfulness found expression in the question: "Is Georgie my son? . . . Perhaps they laugh when they see me parading 'my' son in the streets" (*Letters*, 2:232–33).

21. Compare Rank, on "the psychological evidence that this glorification of a friend is, fundamentally, self-glorification. . . . In this sense, not only are the sonnets in fact self-dedicated—as is creative work of every description—but they reveal that peculiar attitude of the creative instinct towards the creative ego which seeks to glorify it by artistic idealization" (*Art and Artist*, 56).

22. Compare Stephen on Cissy Caffrey: "Addressed her in vocative feminine. Probably neuter. Ungenitive" (*U*, 15.4376).

23. This passage parallels the earlier question-and-answer section about mother and daughter (*U*, 9.423–31), containing the controversial "love passage," restored in the Gabler edition. I discuss this restoration and its psychoanalytic context in a later chapter.

24. See Schutte, 117–19, on the lapwing's "addiction for concealment and pretense," and compare Graves, 36–37, on the lapwing as one of a trio of mythic symbols whose common significance is some form of "Disguise the Secret."

25. *The Incest Theme in Literature and Legend*, 175. Gregory Richter has translated the 1912 edition. Translations in the text, also based on the 1912 edition, which was the one available to Joyce, are my own, but I give page numbers in the English

translation, which is more readily available than the original German edition. Some of my citations come from footnotes, which Richter sometimes does not translate at all, or, alternatively, works into the text of the translation. For these I give approximate pages in the English translation and/or the page number in the original *Inzestmotiv*, accompanied by the abbreviation *IM*.

26. Stephen's relationship with his "old father," the "hawklike man" Daedalus, is undoubtedly also a part of this bird/father context.

27. Stephen's point that Shakespeare identifies with the Ghost is often stated as an identification with King Hamlet *instead of* his son. See, for example, Kellogg, 151, and Sultan, 156. But Stephen never claims that Shakespeare does not identify with Prince Hamlet, only that he *does* identify with the Ghost as well, echoing Rank's point about a double identification. Thus Stephen's agreement with Eglinton's "all in all" statement (*U*, 9.1018–19) is not a retraction but a reiteration.

28. Rank points out (*Incest Theme*, 181) that Shakespeare originated the identity of names in *Hamlet*. See Rank's *Die Lohengrinsage* (99) on the combination of motives for this fantasy.

29. Compare Rank, *Art and Artist*, 27–28, on the self- appointment of the artist, whose "creativity begins with the individual himself—that is, with the self-making of the personality into the artist."

30. See Freud (*SE*, 147, and *FR*, 238), and compare Rank (*MBH*, 85) on the subordination of the conflicting attitudes toward the parents to "the motivation of vindication of the individual through the hero."

31. See Kimball, *Odyssey* 102–4, on these identifications.

Chapter 4. Psychoanalytic Contexts for "The Mother"

1. See chapter 2 on the "homosexual threat," 35–40.

2. Both *Marius the Epicure* and *The Renaissance* were in Joyce's Trieste Library. See Gillespie, *Catalogue*, s.v. "Pater." In *Ulysses* see esp. *U*, 9.376–78, for the "weaving and unweaving" of bodies and the artist's image, an allusion to Pater's *Renaissance*. See Thornton's *Allusions* index for other allusions.

3. *Wandlungen und Symbole der Libido*, part 1, *Jahrbuch*, vol. 3 (1911): 120–227; part 2, vol. 4 (1912): 162–464. References in the text to this work are taken from the English translation, *Psychology of the Unconscious*, accompanied by the abbreviation *PU*. According to the accession records of the Zentralbibliothek, the 1912 volume was acquired "*nach 1919.*"

4. See, for example, Homans, 27, where he notes that Jung himself repeatedly said that the contents of the 1912 work were "the source of his break with Freud."

5. For more complex examples of traces that do carry thematic significance, see Kimball, *Odyssey*, 83–85.

6. Herring, *Joyce's Notes and Early Drafts for "Ulysses,"* 194. See 211–49, for the first draft, 244–46, for the encounter with the mother.

7. In the foreword to the second edition of the essay on "The Significance of the Father," Jung so identified his *Wandlungen und Symbole der Libido*, in which "it

became clear to me . . . why not only the father, but the mother as well, is such an important factor in the child's fate" (*CW*, 4:301).

8. See also Freud, in *Psychopathology*, which Joyce purchased in Zurich: "The strange fact that the [Oedipus] legend finds nothing objectionable in Queen Jocasta's age seemed to me to fit in well with the conclusion that in being in love with one's own mother one is never concerned with her as she is in the present but with her youthful mnemic image carried over from one's childhood" (*SE*, 6:178).

9. Note the English translations listed for these two adjectives: *frightful, terrible, awful, dreadful, horrible, hideous.*

10. For an extended examination of the mother's textual association with love and death, see Kimball, "Love and Death in *Ulysses*," 152–55.

11. Page references in the following paragraphs are to "The Psychology of the Unconscious Processes."

12. Note that Stephen's accompanying cry of "The intellectual imagination!" echoes his identification in "Proteus" of Lucifer as "proud lightening of the intellect." Note also that there is the same mix of Christ and Satan in both passages, with Stephen's Christ-derived "Come, I thirst" opposed to Lucifer in "Proteus" (*U*, 3.485–86) and The Mother's identification with Christ in "Circe"—"Inexpressible was my anguish when expiring with love, grief and agony on Mount Calvary" (*U*, 15.4239–40)—opposed to Stephen's identification with Satan.

13. Compare Bakhtin, 128, on "the seamier side of sexual love, love alienated from reproduction, from a progression of generations, from the structures of the family and the clan."

14. Note the echo of "All or not at all" in Stephen's destruction of The Mother in "Circe" (*U*, 15.4227–28).

Chapter 5. The "Viennese View" Beyond Oedipus

1. See Jones, *Life and Work*, 2:6–8, on the probable date of the founding of this informal group.

2. "Introductory Essay," *Incest Theme*, xx–xxi. See these pages for Rudnytsky's discussion of Rank's *Incest Motif* in its historical context and also in the context of present day critical approaches.

3. See Holland, 89–90, for a summary of Rank's special view of *Hamlet*.

4. The 1926 edition, following Rank's break with Freud, was revised to reflect his defection from Freudian orthodoxy.

5. See Rank's introduction, *Incest Theme*, 3–18, esp. 13–15, and his conclusion, 569–73.

6. Rank makes no connection between this sister-complex and Shakespeare's life, and though Stephen mentions a sister, she plays no part in his theory either. When Stephen sees his sister Dilly in "Wandering Rocks," however, his final vision of her comes close to the drowned Ophelia (*U*, 10.875–80).

7. See Hoffman, 21 n. 46, 123, and 148–49, on the incest motif in *Finnegans Wake*.

8. See Rank's comments on this melding of the psychology of father and son in Sophocles' Oedipus trilogy, especially in *Oedipus at Colonus* (*Incest Theme*, 145, 323, and 487).

9. See Adams, 249–53. See also Brivic, "Stephen to Bloom," esp. 122–23 on "union through separation," and Kimball, "Hypostasis," esp. 424–25.

10. As Ellmann suggests (*JJII*, 268–69), Nora's miscarriage may well have been the autobiographical base for Rudy.

11. Compare Stanislaus's diary entry: "My voice tires my throat and bores me" (*CDD*, 21), and note that Stephen in "Telemachus" is "depressed by his own voice" (*U*, 1.188).

12. See Schutte, 53–54, on the dubious validity of Stephen's presentation.

13. The significance of sibling relationships has been highlighted in recent years by a number of researchers. See, for example, Bank and Kahn, *The Sibling Bond* and Lamb and Sutton-Smith, *Sibling Relationships*. And see Kimball, "'*Lui, c'est moi,*'" 234, on the relationship between James and Stanislaus as one identified by Bank and Kahn as "intense sibling loyalty," which nevertheless coexists with "rivalry, conflict, and competition."

14. See Nunberg and Federn, 1:6–29, for discussions of Rank's preliminary manuscript for *Das Inzest-motiv*, which remained the topic of discussion during the first three meetings for which minutes exist—10, 17, and 24 October 1906.

15. Note that Rank, like Stanislaus Joyce, was a younger brother, whose older brother, Paul, was much favored. See Lieberman, 2–3, on the situation of these brothers, which in many ways was similar to that of the Joyce brothers.

16. Compare Stanislaus's diary entry: "He has used me, I fancy, as a butcher uses his steel to sharpen his knife" (*CDD*, 20).

17. See Edel's characterization of Stanislaus as "one of the martyred siblings of literary history," 485, and Cixous on Stanislaus as a "victim" of his brother's "cannibalism," *Exile*, 120. Compare Kimball's view of the relationship between the brothers as one of "psychic reciprocity" akin to the *participation mystique* of brothers in primitive tribes, "James and Stanislaus Joyce," 75–76.

18. Beebe, *Ivory Towers*, 264–65. See also Rank, *Art and Artist*, 199–202, on the "building sacrifice" and the connections between fratricide and artistic creation, esp. 202: "The mortal 'double' must be sacrificed if the immortal ego is to live on in the work."

19. See Kimball, "*Lui, c'est moi*," 229–30, on further Stanislaus/Bloom parallels.

20. See also the chapter "A House of Joyces," 109–32.

21. See Susan Sutliff Brown, 8–28, for an ingenious discussion of an autobiographical base for the Shakespeare brothers, based on the feminized names of Joyce's brothers.

22. From the unsent letter to his father, which Ellmann dates 1910, in the Ellmann Collection at the MacFarlin Library, Tulsa.

23. See my further discussion of the reverberations of Joyce's 1909 experience of jealousy in chapter 6.

24. Compare Brivic, "Stephen to Bloom," 149.

25. Compare chapter 2, 35–40, on the homosexual threat in *Ulysses* as an echo of Freud's *Leonardo*.

26. "The Theme of *Ulysses*," 132, 145. See also Joyce's notes for act 2 of *Exiles* where he considers the possibility of Richard and Robert's being "united . . . carnally through the person and body of Bertha as they cannot, without dissatisfaction and degradation, be united man to man" (*E*, 123).

27. Beaumont and Fletcher are already linked with *Hamlet* through Stephen's reference to Shakespeare as "the ghost, the king, a king and no king" (*U*, 9.164–65). *A King and No King* is a 1611 play by Beaumont and Fletcher, featuring the question of brother-sister incest, a recurring theme in their plays according to Rank (*Incest Theme*, 441).

28. *BK*, 232, 245–54. Note that here and in his diary Stanislaus sees a villain in Gogarty, who is "treacherous in his friendship," as well as "jealous of Jim and wishes to put himself before him by every means he can," but still "has friendship for Jim" (*CDD*, 25–26). Shechner, noting that Stanislaus is not always accurate, makes a case for the liberating effect of his mother's death on Joyce (*Joyce in Nighttown*, 233 n and 237–40). Since *Ulysses* in some way dramatizes the transition from dislocation to creativity, both interpretations may be right.

29. Herring, *Joyce's "Ulysses" Notesheets*, 24. Ford has made a case for Bloom's incestuous thoughts about his daughter as evidence of actual incest in "Why Is Milly in Mullingar?" 436–49, and also in her *Patriarchy and Incest*, 125–37. Like much in the text of *Ulysses*, the evidence is ambiguous at best, and I do not read it the same way Ford does.

30. "*Der Sinn der Griselda Fabel*" [The meaning of the Griselda tale], 34–48. See also *Incest Theme*, 308 and 311–12.

31. See Perkins, 1–15, on the history of the manuscript of Joyce's translation of *Vor Sonnenaufgang*. See also Joyce's comment in a 1905 letter to Stanislaus about Hauptmann as "a very beautiful type of civilisation. . . . I wish I had leisure enough to interpret him" (*Letters*, 2:85), as well as his request of Ezra Pound more than twenty-five years later to obtain Hauptmann's autograph for *Michael Kramer*, "a play which I still admire greatly" (*Letters*, 1:398).

32. See *Griselda*, scene 10, 6:278–80. See also the discussion of the motivations in this play by the Vienna Psychoanalytic Society, Nunberg and Federn, 2:185–94.

33. This is the unfortunately tagged "love passage," probably the most publicized and controversial of the changes in Gabler's edition, which itself became the subject of considerable controversy. For an overview of the larger controversy, see *James Joyce Literary Supplement* 3 (Fall 1989), devoted to discussion of Gabler's *Critical and Synoptic Edition;* also *Studies in the Novel* 22/2 (Summer 1990), "A Special Issue on Editing *Ulysses*," esp. Rossman's bibliography, 257–69. On the "love passage," see "The Love Passage," *James Joyce Literary Supplement* 3 (Fall 1989): 17–18; also Kimball, "Love and Death" and "Love in the Kidd Era."

34. "The Love Word," *James Joyce Literary Supplement* 3 (Fall 1989), 18.

35. Alternatively the granddaughter, "his daughter's child." It is possible to read father-daughter incest into "his daughter's child," who might, in Stephen's ambiguous rhetoric, be also Shakespeare's child. I myself think that Joyce intends the hint to be present, even though the whole connection remains ambiguous.

36. The contribution of these images to coherence in Stephen's musings on the artist's relation to his work is in reality considerably more complicated than this, but a complete development would take me too far afield from the present argument. See my "Love in the Kidd Era," 370–73.

Chapter 6. Ghost Stories in *Ulysses*: The Psychic Origins of Bloom

1. Later published in their entirety in Joyce's *Selected Letters* (*SL*, 181–93).

2. Compare Solomon (114) on the "inescapable impression that one single 'true subject' underlies both characterizations," so that the end result is "an overview which transcends all divergent points of view."

3. *Projection* has become a part of our pop-psych vocabulary, but see LaPlanche and Pontalis, *Language of Psycho-Analysis*, 349–55, s.v. "projection."

4. See C. G. Jung's personification of the conscious and unconscious personalities as Ego and Shadow, *CW*, 9/2:3–10, esp. 8–9 on "the *emotional* nature" of the repressed contents that constitute the Shadow. See also Kimball, *Odyssey*, esp. 59–80.

5. Compare Hogenson's discussion of the works of Freud and Jung as "so mythic and self-reflexive, for all their claim to scientific objectivity, that they can only be seen as expressions of what I am terming 'metabiography'" (22–27). And see Von Phul on Joyce's "highly subjective autobiography" as the "formal determinant of the tetralogy" of *A Portrait, Ulysses, Exiles,* and *Finnegans Wake* (241).

6. See Rader, "Logic of *Ulysses*" (568); and his "Exodus and Return" (154). Caraher also argues for the epic nature of *Ulysses* from the base of Stephen's definition (191–93). And see Schwarz, "'Tell Us in Plain Words'" on *Ulysses* as a "modern epic novel" (27–29).

7. See also Lewis's discussion of *Ulysses* as "an immense nature-morte" (91–93).

8. Rose, 129. See also Stanford, *Ulysses Theme*, 214, on the two time-levels in *Ulysses*.

9. Ellmann's generally accepted speculation that 16 June marks the day that Joyce "began to fall in love" with Nora (*JJII*, 155–56) is questioned by Owen (*Beginnings*, 9–11), who feels the date was chosen because it offered the closest correspondence to the first day back in Ithaca for Homer's Odysseus. I myself feel that 16 June could well have been chosen because it was a Thursday, as was 2 February 1882, Joyce's birthdate, and thus connects with Joyce's rebirth, "as a man," through Nora.

10. On Joyce's disorientation following his mother's death, see Kimball, "James and Stanislaus" (101–3); see also Kimball, *Odyssey* (97–111), on Stephen's psychic shift between his mother and Molly.

11. Scholes and Kain, 103. See Rader's assertion that Joyce called his book *Ulysses* because "its most basic informing and constitutive act is Joyce's imaginative return home" ("Logic of *Ulysses*," 570).

12. Rank, "Homer" (133–69), and "Folk Epic" (372–93). Parenthetical page numbers in the text, not otherwise identified, refer to the original essay, and translations of material from the German are my own, an endeavor supported by a summer stipend from the National Endowment for the Humanities.

13. See Rank, "Folk Epic," 392, for the extended reference to Schlegel, as well as the analogy between the fusing of times in the epic and the technical achievement of perspective in painting; and see 159–60 for his commentary on anachronisms and the "mixed culture" characteristic of the epic. See also Scholes and Corcoran, 692–93, for their discussion of the German background for Stephen's whole theory of aesthetic forms.

14. This footnote (*IM*, 483 n. 1) is not included in the English translation (*Incest Theme*, 397–98). Rank refers to an article by von Winterstein on the psychoanalysis of travel (344–45), which in turn refers back to Rank's *Incest Motif* and repeats Rank's list of poets (496 n).

15. Quoted in Lewis, "Analysis," 369. See also 89 on *Ulysses* as a "time-book" of the "great time-school" of "Bergson-Einstein, Stein-Proust."

16. The same thing happens in the nightdream, except that, as Rank points out, everything in the nightdream "will *regularly* be represented and felt as present" (374). Freud's original essay concerns conscious fantasizing and thus does not touch on the nightdream.

17. Freud's realization that his patients' memories of childhood seductions were more fiction than fact appeared initially to destroy his theory of the neuroses, throwing him into a state of "helpless bewilderment." See Jones, *Life and Work*, 1:263–67, for a useful summary of this "dividing line" in Freud's discovery of psychoanalysis.

18. "Childhood Memories and Screen Memories," *SE*, 6:48, 147–48. See also *Leonardo* (*L*, 83–84) on the analogy between childhood memories and the epic; and see "Screen Memories," *SE*, 3:318, on the measure of validity in childhood memories.

19. See the picture of the demolition of 7 Eccles Street on the cover of the *James Joyce Literary Supplement* 11/2 (Fall 1997).

20. This indignity is recorded in the unfinished letter that Stanislaus wrote to his father in 1910, which outlines the "heartless and thankless sweating of me that has been Jim and his wife's chief profit" since Stanislaus's arrival in Trieste. It was particularly galling because the original plan called for Stanislaus to take Giorgio back to Dublin. Ellmann's typed copy of this draft is in the Ellmann papers at the McFarlin Library at Tulsa.

21. See, for example, Frank, "The Shadow That Had Lost Its Man," in Willard Potts's *Portraits*. Note also Gillet's description of Joyce as "not of this world. He was a stranger, a phantom whose shadow only was among us ("Farewell to Joyce," in Potts, 168).

22. Joyce's notes for *Exiles* give evidence of his fascination with the experience of jealousy, as he implicitly compares his own treatment of the theme in *Exiles*—"its baffled lust converted into an erotic stimulus"—with Shakespeare's in *Othello* (*E*,

114). See Empson, 144–46, on the "contorted attitude to sexual jealousy" in this "disgusting play," as well as his characterization of these notes as "the public sweat of monks."

23. See Empson, 134, on "the Bloom Offer."

24. See Adams, 35–43; Sultan, 431–44; and Hayman, who "lays the ghost of [Molly's] checkered past," 113–14.

25. See Ellmann's attempts to identify models (*JJII*, 378) and Adams (68–69) for a similar, inconclusive attempt.

26. See Bruce Williams, 545–46, on the "longitudinal phallacy" in Molly's soliloquy and Molly as "the perennial masculine fantasy."

27. Compare the passage quoted by Weir, from a Victorian pornographic publication (*The Pearl: A Journal of Facetiae and Voluptuous Reading*), detailing a similar uncovering and showing of the "glories" of "delicious buttocks," 127 n. 31.

28. Sadger's development of the connections to flagellantism have particular relevance for the Circean development of Bloom's sexual peculiarities, especially in the episode with "the noble ladies." See Kenner, "Circe," 361; *U*, 15.1013–121).

29. Ellmann, *Ulysses on the Liffey*, 163. See also his comparison of the Linati and Gorman-Gilbert schemas, following 187.

30. See Grinstein, 1720–23, for Sadger's writings, and note that Nunberg and Federn label Sadger's contributions to the understanding of the perversions "outstanding" (*Minutes*, 1:xxxvi).

31. This was not always the case, as witness Dr. Joseph Collins's characterization of Bloom as a "moral monster, a pervert and an invert" in his review of *Ulysses*, excerpted in Deming, 1:122–26. For an extended examination of the shifting attitudes toward Bloom in the years since 1922, see Kimball, *Odyssey*, 119–22 and 143–45.

32. Horace Gregory, in his review of the first American edition of *Ulysses*, quoted in Deming, 1:240.

33. West, *Strange Necessity*, 31; McLuhan, *Understanding Media*, 296.

34. Power, 54. See also Nabokov on Bloom as "a good clinical example of extreme sexual preoccupation and perversity with all kinds of curious complications" (296).

35. Compare Freud on Goethe as "not only a great self-revealer, but also, in spite of the abundance of autobiographical records, a careful concealer" ("Address Delivered in the Goethe House at Frankfurt" [*SE*, 21:212]). See also Anzieu's comment on Freud's own "hide-and-seek ploy," during his lifetime and with posterity (x–xi). And see Freud's own admission that "in scarcely any instance have I brought forward the *complete* interpretation of one of my own dreams, as it is known to me. I have probably been wise in not putting too much faith in my readers' discretion" (*SE* 4:105 n).

Chapter 7. Freudian Contexts Chez Bloom

1. See chapter 2, 40–45. On Molly's contradictions, see, for example, Card (17–26), and compare Adams's dictum that "in the context of real life, Bloom's attitudes

are quite impossible; in the context of the fiction, they are merely wooden and improbable" (105).

2. From Nat Halper's impromptu interview with Motherwell at the first Provincetown Joyce Conference, 15 June 1980. See also Kenner, "Cubist *Portrait*," 172–73, where he explains his statement that "Joyce's *Portrait* may be the first piece of cubism in literary history."

3. See Joyce's review of Allen's *Mettle of the Pasture*, from which he apparently appropriated the idea of "two roaring worlds" in "Wandering Rocks" (*U*, 10.824), *Critical Writings*, 118 n. 2.

4. McGuire, 177F, 291; 77F, 130.

5. Translations for all essays are my own.

6. I have not attempted to use gender-neutral pronouns in paraphrasing these studies, since the subjects are almost universally presumed to be masculine.

7. That Sadger's observation was not far-fetched is suggested by a recent series of letters to an advice columnist from wives whose husbands insist on urinating in the yard.

8. Gifford gives no gloss for the paragraph (479), and as a woman, I have no direct experience of this. See Cheng, "'Godinpotty'" (91 n. 6), for relevant quotations from Lindsey Tucker and William York Tindall.

9. See the discussion of Sadger's paper in *Minutes* (Nunberg and Federn, 2:577–82), especially the reservations expressed about the connection between urination and love. Note also Eduard Hitschmann's comment: "That Sadger's patients are invariably such swine is probably due to the fact that, under a close going-over, every neurotic simply looks like that" (2:578).

10. Compare Bloom's testimony to the "overpower[ing]" effect of "sit[ting] where a woman has sat" (*U*, 15.3424–27), though it is unclear what event this may refer to.

11. Note the striking similarity between Abraham's patient, whose interest in women was directed "not to the naked body, but to its covering" (560) and the Joyce of the 1930s, who remarked to Budgen: "But now I don't care a damn about their bodies. I am only interested in their clothes" ("Further Recollections," 535). And see Brenda Maddox (164) on the absence of copulation in *Ulysses*.

12. See, for example, Devlin (383–96) and Parkes (283–301).

13. "Weiningerian Sex Comedy" (274). See also Byrnes's "Bloom's Sexual Tropes."

14. Oppenheim points out the sadomasochistic nature of this situation, and observes that "in *no* case of morbid jealousy is the sadistic component absent" (74; emphasis Oppenheim's). Bloom's masochistic tendencies are a critical commonplace. Dervin, who comments that Bloom's "polymorphous perverse trends balance well . . . with his vacillating affirmations of genital primacy," nevertheless terms masochism Bloom's "perversion of choice" and finds the evidence of this "so overwhelming" that "it renders the many-sided wanderer all too onesided" (250).

15. Compare Molly's echo of Bloom's attitude in "Penelope": "showing him my photo . . . I wonder he didnt make him a present of it altogether and me too after all why not" (*U*, 18.1302–5). Or her comment on jealousy: "why cant we all remain friends over it instead of quarrelling" (1392–93).

16. Knapp, *Fernand Crommelynck* (48). I have depended on her chapter, "The Magnificent Cuckold: A Phallic Ritual (1920)" (48–69), for details of the nature and plot of the play.

17. See also Joyce's notes for *Exiles* (*E*, 114) on Richard's jealousy, which is "separated from hatred . . . its baffled lust converted into an erotic stimulus." Richard "is jealous, wills and knows his own dishonour and the dishonour of her."

18. Contemporary versions of the tale are found in Fry's *A Phoenix Too Frequent* and in scenes 18–23 of Federico Fellini's *Satyricon* (159–65). See also Bakhtin's discussion of the "folkloric base" of the tale (221–24).

19. Parenthetical page references in this section not otherwise identified are to this work, and translations are my own, a part of a project supported by a 1985 Summer Stipend from the National Endowment for the Humanities. On Rank's place in the early movement, see Freud, *SE*, 14:24–25.

20. Chapters 111 and 112 of Petronius's *Satyricon* (122–25).

21. Compare Dervin (254), on the effect of Rudy's death.

22. Compare Dervin on Bloom's sexual abstinence as conforming to "the classical oedipal tradition of self-castration" (256).

23. For a recent examination of the widespread knowledge of this phenomenon, see Meyers (345–48). It is true that in Petronius's tale, which is probably the one with which Joyce was familiar, the husband is crucified, not hanged, but Rank makes no such distinction, and what I am tracing here are the echoes of Rank's interpretation.

24. See Balzac, *Droll Stories* (116–20), for the old maid's story, the final jest in the chapter titled "The Merry Jests of King Louis the Eleventh."

25. Molly does consider hanging in connection with an actual case of a woman involved in a triangle, recalling Rank's comment that the widow in many versions of the tale finally hangs herself out of guilt for her faithlessness (51). Molly, however, concludes that "theyre not brutes enough to go and hang a woman surely are they" (*U*, 18.244–45).

26. See *SE* 5:291 for Freud's recounting of the case.

27. There continues to be a reluctance to label Bloom's problem as impotence, and his achievement of an ejaculation in "Nausicaa" is sometimes cited as evidence that he is not impotent. Masters and Johnson, however, define *impotence* as "a disturbance of sexual function in the male that precludes satisfactory sexual coitus" (341), a definition that agrees with dictionary definitions in its emphasis on satisfactory or successful sexual intercourse and one that fits Bloom's case in *Ulysses*.

28. See Kimball, "Hypostasis," 429–31, for the textual parallels, and compare Brivic's listing of "synchronicities" in his *Joyce the Creator*, 145–53. See also

Kimball, *Odyssey*, chapter 5, on Stephen and Bloom as the Jungian Ego and Shadow, contradictory aspects of one personality, in confrontation.

29. On the case for D. B. Murphy, see McMichael, 144–54.

30. They also establish Joyce's experiential context for the psychoanalytic literature on perversity that he has used (in my view) in constructing Bloom's character, though it would be a mistake, I think, to assume that these perversions were of the same quality or weight in Joyce's life as they are in Bloom's characterization.

31. Compare Joyce's notes for *Exiles*, where this kind of partitioned self is suggested in the relationship between Bertha and Richard: "the part of Richard which neither love nor life can do away with; the part for which she loves him: the part she must try to kill, never be able to kill and rejoice at her impotence" (*E*, 118).

Chapter 8. Oedipus and Ulysses: The Ongoing Dialogue

1. See also Anderson's "Analytical List of Bloom's Parapraxes and Other Freudian Clues in 'Lestrygonians,'" in his "Leopold Bloom as Dr. Sigmund Freud" (26–32).

2. Kelly, in his recent study, asks the question "Who benefits from [Joyce's 'image' as a genius]?" (223) and appears to answer that the scholarly critics have benefited in some not quite legitimate way. It seems to me, however, that Joyce's genius—and he is an authentic genius, whatever his lack in common sense or compassion—benefits anyone who reads *Ulysses* with attention and love, including scholarly critics. Compare Ezra Pound's comment, quoted by Ellmann, *JJII*, 480 n: "I never had any respect for his common sense or for his intelligence, apart from his gifts as a writer."

3. See Lodge's review of Bakhtin's *Dialogic Imagination* in the *James Joyce Broadsheet* (1).

4. Gray, 47. See also Lear's defense against the "Freud bashers" in his recent *Open Minded*, especially his chapter "On Killing Freud (Again)" (16–32).

5. But see McBride's caution against the autobiographical assumption (29–37).

6. See Toynbee, on *Hamlet* as "the secondary mythological framework" of *Ulysses* (257).

7. See Gilbert (30) for the schema. See also Ellmann's introductory note to his comparison of the Linati schema with that published by Gilbert (*Ulysses on the Liffey*, 186–87.)

8. See, for example, Rahner's chapter on "Odysseus at the Mast" (328–86, esp. 378 and 375) on Christ as "the heavenly Odysseus" and the cross as "our mast and our sail-bearing yard-arm."

9. See Jonathan Lear's annotated retelling of the plot of the Oedipus drama, which concludes that "Oedipus' acts are so ridiculous that, were his fate not horrific, this would be the stuff of hilarious comedy" (47).

10. A true Freudian could doubtless consider the suitors—or at least Antinuous—as a stand-in for the hostile father in the classic Oedipus triangle, but this is not my perspective.

11. Forrester (90). See 84–96, for his "History of the Oedipus Complex, 1897–1910," outlining the steps in the development of Freud's use of the term.

12. See Forrester on "the introduction of the Oedipus complex as the central *explanatory* concept of psychoanalysis" and on the "simplification—perhaps even the reductionism—that the story of mama and papa attains" (148–49; emphasis Forrester's).

13. See Stanford's comment that "in Homer's *Odyssey* the relationship between father and son was never more than conventional" (*Ulysses Theme*, 215).

14. Stanford, "Joyce's First Meeting with Ulysses" (99). See also McCleery, "One Lost Lamb" and "The Gathered Lambs" on McCleery's search for a copy of Cooke's edition of Lamb's *Adventures*. Having been found, the volume has now been "reset in its entirety and published by the Split Pea Press, Edinburgh" ("Gathered Lambs," 562).

15. See Gillespie, *Catalogue*, s.v. "Fénelon," and note that Fénelon is included in Stanislaus's list of the authors Joyce read in preparation for writing *Ulysses* (Stanford, *Ulysses Theme*, 214 n. 6).

16. Janet (155). The biographer also notes that on its publication *Télémaque* was seen as a political satire and only later became "the reading book of children."

17. See the table of contents, complete with summaries of the action (xvii–xxii). In his discussion of *Télémaque* (155–71), Janet points out that to begin with it was "an imitation of Homer's *Odyssey*," but in addition Fénelon borrowed from Virgil, Sophocles, Plato, Horace, and others so that Fénelon's *Télémaque* "is not a work of creation and invention, but a series of imitations and literary reminiscences" (Janet, 156, 168), all of which may sound familiar to readers of *Ulysses*.

18. Even in Homer, Penelope, in her dealings with the problem of the suitors, as well as her testing of her husband after his return, has a separate development of sorts, as does Telemachus—again, to a degree. In Joyce's *Ulysses*, this separation in the situations of the main characters is more evident, and it is even more striking in Gerhart Hauptmann's *The Bow of Ulysses*, also identified by Stanislaus as part of his brother's reading for *Ulysses* (Stanford, *Ulysses Theme*, 214 n. 6).

19. See Forrester, 91–92, on the first use of the term.

20. There is a lost epic, the *Telegony*, in which Telegonus, the son of Odysseus by Circe, like Oedipus, kills his father unknowingly. This also concludes with semi-incestuous marriages between Penelope and Telegonus and Circe and Telemachus. Homer, however, omits this aspect.

21. Joyce's attitude toward his father is not without its ambivalences, but in a letter to Harriet Shaw Weaver after John Stanislaus Joyce's death, he acknowledged his father's "extraordinary affection" for him, as well as the fact that "I was very fond of him always, being a sinner myself" (*Letters*, 1:312). Stanislaus, whose relationship with his father was strikingly different from his brother's, identified Joyce's "attachment to his father" as "one of the dominant motives of his character" (*BK,*

57). See also Kimball, "James and Stanislaus" (93–98), on the brothers' contrasting attitudes toward their father.

22. See chapter 39 of George Meredith, *The Egoist*. And see Stanislaus's opinion that "*The Egoist* has to be written again," and "the man who will write it must be able to write without a 'plot,' directly from his characters," a statement that may serve as a prophecy of his brother's *Ulysses* (*CDD*, 121).

Bibliography

Abraham, Karl. *"Bemerkungen zur Psychoanalyse eines Falles von Fuss- und Korsettfetischismus* [Remarks on the psychoanalysis of a case of foot- and corset-fetishism]." *Jahrbuch* 3 (1912): 557–67.

Adams, Robert M. *Surface and Symbol: The Consistency of James Joyce's "Ulysses."* New York: Oxford University Press, 1962.

"America Facing Its Most Tragic Moment—Dr. Carl Jung." *New York Times Magazine,* 29 September 1912, sec. 5, 2.

Anderson, Chester. "Baby Tuckoo: Joyce's 'Features of Infancy.'" In *Approaches to "Ulysses": Ten Essays,* ed. Thomas F. Staley and Bernard Benstock, 135–71. Pittsburgh: University of Pittsburgh Press, 1976.

———. "Leopold Bloom as Dr. Sigmund Freud." *Mosaic* 6 (Fall 1972): 23–43.

Anzieu, Didier. *Freud's Self-Analysis.* Trans. Peter Graham. Madison, Conn.: International Universities Press, 1986.

Aristotle. *Generation of Animals.* Trans. A. L. Peck. Loeb Classical Library 366. Cambridge: Harvard University Press, 1963.

———. *Nichomachean Ethics.* Trans. David Ross. Rev. by J. O. Jonson. New York: Oxford University Press, 1980.

———. "On the Art of Poetry." In *Classical Literary Criticism,* ed. and trans. T. S. Dorsch, 29–75. London: Penguin, 1975.

———. "On Sophistical Refutations." In *On Sophistical Refutations [and] On Coming-to-Be and Passing Away,* trans. E. S. Forster, and *On the Cosmos,* trans. D. J. Furley, 11–155. Loeb Classical Library. Cambridge: Harvard University Press, 1955.

Atherton, James S. *The Books at the Wake: A Study of Literary Allusions in James Joyce's "Finnegans Wake."* New York: Viking, 1960.

Bakhtin, M. M. *The Dialogic Imagination: Four Essays.* Ed. Michael Holquist. Trans. Caryl Emerson and Michael Holquist. Austin: University of Texas Press, 1981.

Balzac, Honoré de. *Droll Stories.* New York: Liveright, 1928.

Bank, Michael Steven, and Michael Kahn. *The Sibling Bond.* New York: Basic Books, 1982.

Barovick, Harriet. "A Man and His Couch." *Time,* 12 October 1998, 8.

Beebe, Maurice. *Ivory Towers and Sacred Founts: The Artist as Hero in Fiction from Goethe to Joyce*. New York: New York University Press, 1964.

———. "Joyce and Stephen Dedalus: The Problem of Autobiography." In *A James Joyce Miscellany, Second Series*, ed. Marvin Magalaner. Carbondale: Southern Illinois University Press, 1959.

Benstock, Bernard. "Text, Sub-Text, Non-Text: Literary and Narrational In/Validities." *James Joyce Quarterly* 11 (Summer 1979): 355–65.

Bertschinger, H. "*Illustrierte Halluzinationen*" [Illustrated hallucinations]. *Jahrbuch* 3 (1911): 69–100.

Blackmur, Richard. "The Jew in Search of a Son." *Virginia Quarterly Review* 2 (1948): 96–116.

Blake, William. *The Complete Writings of William Blake with All Variant Readings*. Ed. Geoffrey Keynes. New York: Nonesuch Press, 1957.

Bollettieri [Bosinelli], Rosa Maria. "The Importance of Trieste in Joyce's Work, with Reference to His Knowledge of Psycho-Analysis." *James Joyce Quarterly* 7 (Spring 1970): 177–85.

Boone, Joseph A. "Representing Interiority: Spaces of Sexuality in *Ulysses*." In *Languages of Joyce: Selected Papers from the Eleventh James Joyce Symposium*, ed. Rosa M. Bollettieri Bosinelli et al., 70–84. Philadelphia and Amsterdam: John Benjamins Publishing Co., 1992.

Bormanis, John. "'in the first bloom of her new motherhood': The Appropriation of the Maternal and the Representation of Mothering in *Ulysses*." *James Joyce Quarterly* 29 (Spring 1992): 593–606.

Brandell, Gunnar. *Freud, A Man of His Century*. Trans. Iain White. Atlantic Highlands, N.J.: Humanities Press, 1979.

Brivic, Sheldon. "James Joyce: From Stephen to Bloom." In *Psychoanalysis and the Literary Process*, ed. Frederick Crews, 118–62. Cambridge, Mass.: Winthrop Publishers, 1970.

———. *Joyce Between Freud and Jung*. Port Washington, N.Y.: Kennikat Press, 1980.

———. *Joyce the Creator*. Madison: University of Wisconsin Press, 1985.

———. "Joyce in Progress: A Freudian View." *James Joyce Quarterly* 13 (Spring 1976): 306–27.

Brown, Richard. *James Joyce and Sexuality*. Cambridge: Cambridge University Press, 1985.

Brown, Susan Sutliff. "The Joyce Brothers in Drag: Fraternal Incest in *Ulysses*. In *Gender in Joyce*, ed. Jolanta W. Wawrzycka and Marlene G. Corcoran, 8–28. Florida James Joyce Series. Gainesville: University Press of Florida, 1997.

Budge, E. A. Wallis. *The Gods of the Egyptians or Studies in Egyptian Mythology*. 2 vols. 1904. Reprint, New York: Dover Publications, 1969.

Budgen, Frank. "Further Recollections of James Joyce." *Partisan Review* 23 (Fall 1956): 530–44.

———. *James Joyce and the Making of "Ulysses."* New York: H. Smith and R. Haas, 1934.

———. "Joyce's Chapters of Going Forth By Day." In *James Joyce: Two Decades of Criticism,* ed. Seon Givens, 343–67. 2d ed. New York: Vanguard Press, 1963.

———. *Myselves When Young.* New York: Oxford University Press, 1970.

Byrne, John Francis. *Silent Years: An Autobiography with Memoirs of James Joyce and Our Ireland.* New York: Farrar, Straus, and Young, 1953.

Byrnes, Robert. "Bloom's Sexual Tropes: Stigmata of the 'Degenerate' Jew." *James Joyce Quarterly* 27 (Winter 1990): 303–23.

———. "Weiningerian Sex Comedy: Jewish Sexual Types Behind Molly and Leopold Bloom." *James Joyce Quarterly* 34 (Spring 1997): 267–81.

Callow, Heather Cook. "'Marion of the Bountiful Bosoms': Molly Bloom and the Nightmare of History." *Twentieth-Century Literature* 36 (Winter 1990): 464–76.

Caraher, Brian. "A Question of Genre: Generic Experimentation, Self-Composition, and the Problem of Egoism in *Ulysses.*" *ELH* 54 (Spring 1987): 183–214.

Card, James Van Dyck. "'Contradicting': The Word for Joyce's 'Penelope.'" *James Joyce Quarterly* 11 (Fall 1973): 17–26.

Cattani, Alfred. "Milestones in Zurich's Library History." *Neue Zürcher Zeitung,* 1 November 1994, B3.

Chase, Cynthia. "Oedipal Textuality: Reading Freud's Reading of Oedipus." *Diacritics* 9 (March 1979): 54–68.

Cheng, Vincent. "'Godinpotty': James Joyce and the Language of Excrement." In *Languages of Joyce: Selected Papers from the Eleventh James Joyce Symposium,* ed. Rosa M. Bollettieri Bosinelli et al., 85–99. Philadelphia: John Benjamins Publishing Co., 1992.

Cixous, Hélène. *The Exile of James Joyce.* Trans. S.A.J. Purcell. New York: David Lewis, 1972.

Collins, Joseph. "James Joyce's Amazing Chronicle." *New York Times Book Review,* 28 May 1922: 6, 17.

Colum, Mary. "The Confessions of James Joyce." In *The Freeman Book, 1920–1924,* 327–55. New York: B. W. Huebsch, 1924.

Colum, Mary, and Padraic Colum. *Our Friend James Joyce.* Garden City, N.Y.: Doubleday, 1958.

Crivelli, Renzo S. *James Joyce: Triestine Itineraries.* Trieste, Italy: MGS Press, 1996.

Curran, Constantine. *James Joyce Remembered.* New York: Oxford University Press, 1968.

Curtius, Ernst Robert. "Technique and Thematic Development of James Joyce." *transition* 15–17 (June 1929): 310–25.

David, Michel. *La psicoanalis, nella culture italiana.* Turin, Italy: Boringhieri, 1966.

Deming, Robert H., ed. *James Joyce: The Critical Heritage.* 2 vols. New York: Barnes and Noble, 1970.

Dervin, Daniel. "Bloom Again? Questions of Aggression and Psychoanalytic Reconstruction." *American Imago* 47 (Fall–Winter 1990): 249–69.

Dettmar, Kevin. *The Illicit Joyce of Postmodernism: Reading Against the Grain*. Madison: University of Wisconsin Press, 1996.

Devlin, Kimberly. "The Romance Heroine Exposed: 'Nausicaa' and *The Lamplighter*." *James Joyce Quarterly* 22 (Summer 1985): 383–96.

Edel, Leon. "The Genius and the Injustice Collector." *American Scholar* 49 (1980): 467–87.

Eliot, T. S. "*Ulysses*, Order and Myth." In *James Joyce: Two Decades of Criticism*, ed. Seon Givens. 2nd ed. New York: Vanguard Press, 1963.

Ellenberger, Henri. *The Discovery of the Unconscious: The History and Evolution of Dynamic Psychiatry*. New York: Basic Books, 1970.

Ellmann, Richard. *The Consciousness of Joyce*. New York: Oxford University Press, 1977.

———. *Ulysses on the Liffey*. New York: Oxford University Press, 1972.

———. *Yeats: The Man and the Masks*. New York: Macmillan, 1948.

Empson, William. "The Theme of *Ulysses*." In *A James Joyce Miscellany, Third Series*, 127–54. Carbondale: Southern Illinois University Press, 1962.

Epstein, Edmund. *The Ordeal of Stephen Dedalus: The Conflict of the Generations in James Joyce's "A Portrait of the Artist as a Young Man."* Carbondale: Southern Illinois University Press, 1971.

Escher, H. "*Die Errichtung der Zentralbibliothek in Zürich*." [The building of the central library in Zurich]. *Zentralblatt für Bibliothekswesen* 32 (1915): 86–104.

Esman, Aaron H. "The Study of Lives: Discussion of Tashjian and Shaw." *Adolescent Psychiatry* 10 (1982): 99–105.

Faerber, Thomas, and Mark Luchsinger. *Joyce und Zürich*. Zurich: Schweizerische Bankgesellschaft, 1982.

Fellini, Federico. *Fellini's Satyricon*. Ed. Dario Zanelli. Trans. Eugene Walter and John Matthews. New York: Ballantine, 1970.

Fénelon, François de Salignbac de la Mothe. *Adventures of Telemachus*. Trans. John Hawkesworth. New York: D. Appleton and Co., 1859.

Ford, Jane. *Patriarchy and Incest from Shakespeare to Joyce*. Gainesville: University Press of Florida, 1998.

———. "Why Is Milly in Mullingar?" *James Joyce Quarterly* 14 (Summer 1977): 436–49.

Forrester, John. *Language and the Origins of Psychoanalysis*. New York: Columbia University Press, 1979.

Frank, Nino. "The Shadow That Had Lost Its Man." Trans. Jane Carson. In *Portraits of the Artist in Exile: Recollections of James Joyce by Europeans*, ed. Willard Potts, 74–105. Seattle: University of Washington Press, 1979.

Freud, Sigmund. "Analysis of a Phobia in a Five-Year-Old Boy." *SE*, 10:1–147.

———. *Leonardo da Vinci and a Memory of His Childhood*. *SE*, 11:59–137.

———. *On the History of the Psycho-Analytic Movement*. *SE*, 14:1–66.

————. "The Psycho-Analytic View of Psychogenic Disturbance of Vision." *SE*, 11:209–18.

————. "Some Early Unpublished Letters of Freud." *International Journal of Psycho-Analysis* 50 (1969): 419–27.

————. *The Standard Edition of the Complete Psychological Works of Sigmund Freud*. Trans. and ed. James Strachey with Anna Freud et al. 23 vols. London: Hogarth Press and the Institute of Psycho-Analysis, 1953–1974.

Fry, Christopher. *A Phoenix Too Frequent*. London: Oxford University Press, 1959.

Gabler, Hans Walter. "The Seven Lost Years of *A Portrait of the Artist As a Young Man*." In *Approaches to Joyce's "Portrait": Ten Essays*, ed. Thomas Staley and Bernard Benstock, 25–60. Pittsburgh: University of Pittsburgh Press, 1976.

Gay, Peter. "Sigmund Freud." *Time*, 29 March 1999, 66–69.

Gifford, Don, with Robert J. Seidman. *Notes for Joyce: "Dubliners" and "A Portrait of the Artist as a Young Man*." New York: E. P. Dutton, 1967.

Gilbert, Stuart. *James Joyce's "Ulysses": A Study*. New York: Vintage Books, 1955.

Gillespie, Michael Patrick. *Inverted Volumes Improperly Arranged: James Joyce and His Trieste Library*. Ann Arbor: UMI Research Press, 1983.

Gillespie, Michael Patrick, with Erik Bradford Stocker. *James Joyce's Trieste Library: A Catalogue of Materials at the Harry Ransom Humanities Research Center, The University of Texas at Austin*. Austin: Harry Ransom Humanities Research Center, 1986.

Gillet, Louis. "Farewell to Joyce." Trans. Georges Markow-Totevy. In *Portraits of the Artist in Exile: Recollections of James Joyce by Europeans*, ed. Willard Potts, 163–69. Seattle: University of Washington Press, 1970.

Godwin, Murray. "Three Wrong Turns in *Ulysses*." *Western Review* 15 (Spring 1951): 221–25.

Gogarty, Oliver St. John. *As I Was Going Down Sackville Street: A Phantasy in Fact*. New York: Reynal and Hitchcock, 1937.

————. *Mourning Became Mrs. Spendlove and Other Portraits Grave and Gay*. New York: Creative Age, 1948.

Graves, Robert. *The White Goddess: A Historical Grammar of Poetic Myth*. New York: Creative Age Press, 1948.

Gray, Paul. "The Assault on Freud." *Time*, 29 November 1993, 47–51.

Grinstein, Alexander. *Index of Psychoanalytic Writings*. New York: International Universities Press, 1956–.

Hart, Clive. "The Sexual Perversions of Leopold Bloom." In *"Ulysses": Cinquante Ans Après*, ed. Louis Bonnerot et al., 131–36. Paris: Didier, 1992.

Hart, Clive, and Leo Knuth. *A Topographical Guide to James Joyce's "Ulysses*." Colchester, U.K.: A Wake Newslitter, 1976.

Hartshorn, Peter. *James Joyce and Trieste*. Contributions to the Study of World Literature. Westport, Conn.: Greenwood Press, 1997.

Hauptmann, Gerhart. *Griselda*. Trans. Ludwig Lewisohn. In *The Dramatic Works of*

Gerhart Hauptmann, ed. Ludwig Lewisohn, 6:159–280. 8 vols. New York: B. W. Huebsch, 1915.

Hayman, David. "The Empirical Molly Bloom." In *Approaches to "Ulysses": Ten Essays,* ed. Thomas Staley and Bernard Benstock, 103–35. Pittsburgh: University of Pittsburgh Press, 1970.

Hedberg, Johannes. "Hans Kraus, Jan Parandowski, and James Joyce." *James Joyce Quarterly* 33 (Spring 1996): 441–42.

Henke, Suzette. *James Joyce and the Politics of Desire.* New York: Routledge, 1990.

Herring, Phillip. *Joyce's Notes and Early Drafts for "Ulysses": Selections from the Buffalo Collection.* Charlottesville: University Press of Virginia, 1976.

———. *Joyce's "Ulysses" Notesheets in the British Museum.* Charlottesville: University Press of Virginia, 1972.

Hoffman, Frederick J. *Freudianism and the Literary Mind.* 2d ed. Baton Rouge: Louisiana State University Press, 1957.

Hoffmeister, Adolf. "Portrait of Joyce." Trans. Norma Rudinsky. In *Portraits of the Artist in Exile: Recollections of James Joyce by Europeans,* ed. Willard Potts, 127–36. Seattle: University of Washington Press, 1970.

Hogenson, George. *Jung's Struggle with Freud.* Notre Dame: University of Notre Dame Press, 1983.

Holland, Norman. *Psychoanalysis and Shakespeare.* New York: McGraw-Hill, 1964.

Homans, Peter. *Jung in Context: Modernity and the Making of a Psychology.* Chicago: University of Chicago Press, 1979.

Hutchins, Patricia. *James Joyce's Dublin.* New York and London: Grey Walls Press, 1950.

Janet, Paul. *Fénelon: His Life and Works.* Ed. and trans. Victor Leuliette. 1914. Reprint, Port Washington, N.Y.: Kennikat Press, 1970.

Jones, Ernest. *The Life and Work of Sigmund Freud.* Vol. 1, *The Formative Years and the Great Discoveries, 1856–1900.* New York: Basic Books, 1955.

———. *The Life and Work of Sigmund Freud.* Vol. 2, *Years of Maturity: 1901–1919.* New York: Basic Books, 1955.

———. "The Oedipus-Complex as an Explanation of Hamlet's Mystery: A Study in Motive." *American Journal of Psychology* 21 (January 1910): 72–113.

Joyce, James. *The Critical Writings of James Joyce.* Ed. Ellsworth Mason and Richard Ellmann. New York: Viking Press, 1959.

———. *Dubliners.* New York: Viking, Compass, 1968.

———. *Exiles: A Play in Three Acts.* New York: Viking, Compass, 1961.

———. *Finnegans Wake.* New York: Viking, 1958.

———. *The Letters of James Joyce.* 3 vols. Vol. 1, ed. Stuart Gilbert. Vols. 2 and 3, ed. Richard Ellmann. New York: Viking, 1966.

———. "A Portrait of the Artist" (1904). In *The Workshop of Daedalus: James Joyce and the Raw Materials for "A Portrait of the Artist as a Young Man,"* ed. Robert

E. Scholes and Richard M. Kain, 56–74. Evanston: Northwestern University Press, 1965.

———. *A Portrait of the Artist as a Young Man.* New York: Viking, Compass, 1964.

———. *Selected Letters of James Joyce.* Ed. Richard Ellmann. New York: Viking, 1975.

———. *Stephen Hero.* Ed. John J. Slocum and Herbert Cahoon. New York: New Directions, 1944, 1963.

———. *Ulysses: The Corrected Text.* Ed. Hans Walter Gabler with Wolfhard Steppe and Claus Melchior. New York and London: Garland Publishing, 1984, 1986.

Joyce, Stanislaus. *The Complete Dublin Diary of Stanislaus Joyce.* Ed. George H. Healey. Ithaca: Cornell University Press, 1971.

———. "James Joyce: A Memoir." *Hudson Review* 2 (1949): 487–514.

———. *My Brother's Keeper: James Joyce's Early Years.* Ed. Richard Ellmann. New York: Viking, 1958.

Jung, C. G. *Analytical Psychology: Notes of the Seminar Given in 1925 by C. G. Jung.* Ed. William McGuire. Bollingen Series, 99. Princeton: Princeton University Press, 1989.

———. *The Collected Works of C. G. Jung.* Ed. H. Read et al. Trans. R. F. C. Hull. 18 vols. New York/Princeton: Bollingen Foundation and Princeton University Press, 1953–1978.

———. *Memories, Dreams, Reflections.* Rev. ed. Recorded and ed. Aniela Jaffe. Trans. R. F. C. Hull. New York: Bollingen Foundation and Princeton University Press, 1989.

———. *Psychology of the Unconscious: A Study of the Transformations and Symbolism of the Libido.* Trans. Beatrice M. Hinkle. New York: Moffat, Yard, 1916.

———. "The Psychology of the Unconscious Processes." Trans. Dora Hecht. In *Collected Papers on Analytical Psychology,* ed. Constance E. Long, 352–444. New York: Moffat, Yard, 1917.

———. *Wandlungen und Symbole der Libido: Beiträge zur Entwicklungsgeschichte des Denkens* [Transformations and symbols of the libido: Contributions to the developmental history of thought]. Leipzig and Vienna: Franz Deuticke, 1912.

Kain, Richard. "An Interview with Carola Giedion-Welcker and Maria Jolas." *James Joyce Quarterly* 11 (Winter 1974): 94–122.

Kellogg, Robert. "Scylla and Charybdis." In *James Joyce's "Ulysses,"* ed. Clive Hart and David Hayman, 147–79. Berkeley and Los Angeles: University of California Press, 1974.

Kelly, Joseph. *Our Joyce: From Outcast to Icon.* Austin: University of Texas Press, 1998.

Kenner, Hugh. "Bloom's Chest." *James Joyce Quarterly* 16 (Summer 1979): 505–8.

———. "Circe." In *James Joyce's "Ulysses,"* ed. Clive Hart and David Hayman, 341–62. Berkeley and Los Angeles: University of California Press, 1974.

———. "The Cubist *Portrait.*" In *Approaches to Joyce's "Portrait": Ten Essays,* ed.

Thomas F. Staley and Bernard Benstock, 171–84. Pittsburgh: University of Pittsburgh Press, 1976.

———. *Joyce's Voices*. Berkeley and Los Angeles: University of California Press, 1978.

———. "The *Portrait* in Perspective." In *James Joyce: Two Decades of Criticism*, ed. Seon Givens, 132–74. 2nd ed. New York: Vanguard, 1948.

Kerr, John. "Beyond the Pleasure Principle and Back Again: Freud, Jung, and Sabina Spielrein." In *Freud: Appraisals and Reappraisals*, ed. Paul E. Stepansky, 3–79. Vol. 3 of *Contributions to Freud Studies*. Hillsdale, N.J.: Analytic, 1988.

———. *A Most Dangerous Method: The Story of Freud, Jung, and Sabina Spielrein*. New York: Knopf, 1993.

Kidd, John. "Joyce and Freud: 'Only Namesakes,'" *James Joyce Quarterly* 22 (Fall 1984): 81–83.

Kimball, Jean. "An Ambiguous Faithlessness: Molly Bloom and the Widow of Ephesus." *James Joyce Quarterly* 31 (Summer 1994): 455–72.

———. "Autobiography as Epic: Freud's Three-Time Scheme in Joyce's *Ulysses*." *Texas Studies in Literature and Language* 31 (Winter 1989): 475–96.

———. "'Brainsick Words of Sophists': Socrates, Antisthenes, and Stephen Dedalus," *James Joyce Quarterly* 16 (Summer 1979): 399–405.

———. "Family Romance and Hero Myth: A Psychoanalytic Context for the Paternity Theme in *Ulysses*." *James Joyce Quarterly* 20 (Winter 1983): 161–73.

———. "Freud, Leonardo, and Joyce: The Dimensions of a Childhood Memory." *James Joyce Quarterly* 17 (Winter 1980): 165–82.

———. "Growing Up Together: Joyce and Psychoanalysis, 1900–1922." In *Joyce through the Ages: A Nonlinear View*, ed. Michael Patrick Gillespie, 25–45. Gainesville: University Press of Florida, 1999.

———. "The Hypostasis in *Ulysses*." *James Joyce Quarterly* (Summer 1973): 422–38.

———. "James and Stanislaus Joyce: A Jungian Speculation." In *Blood Brothers: Siblings as Writers*, ed. Norman Kiell, 73–113. New York: International Universities Press, 1983.

———. "James Joyce and Otto Rank: The Incest Motif in *Ulysses*." *James Joyce Quarterly* 13 (Spring 1976): 366–82.

———. "Jung's 'Dual Mother' in *Ulysses*: An Illustrated Psychoanalytic Intertext." *Journal of Modern Literature* 17 (Spring 1991): 477–90.

———. "Love and Death in *Ulysses*: 'word known to all men.'" *James Joyce Quarterly* 24 (Winter 1987): 143–60.

———. "Love in the Kidd Era: An Afterword." *James Joyce Quarterly* 29 (Winter 1992): 369–77.

———. "'*Lui, c'est moi*': The Brother Relationship in *Ulysses*." *James Joyce Quarterly* 25 (Winter 1988): 227–35.

———. "The Measure of Bloom—Again." *James Joyce Quarterly* 18 (Winter 1981): 201–4.

———. *Odyssey of the Psyche: Jungian Patterns in Joyce's "Ulysses."* Carbondale: Southern Illinois University Press, 1997.

Knapp, Bettina. *Fernand Crommelynck.* Twayne's World Authors Series. Boston: Twayne Publishers, 1978.

Kristeva, Julia. "Word, Dialogue, Novel." In *Desire in Language: A Semiotic Approach to Literature and Art.* Ed. Leon S. Roudiez. Trans. Thomas Gora, Alice Jardine, and Leon S. Roudiez. New York: Columbia University Press, 1980.

Lamb, Charles. "Adventures of Ulysses." In *The Works of Charles and Mary Lamb,* ed. E. V. Lucas. Vol. 3, *Books for Children.* London: Methuen and Company, 1903.

Lamb, Michael E., and Brian Sutton-Smith. *Sibling Relationships: Their Nature and Significance Across the Life-span.* Hillsdale, N.J.: Lawrence Erbaum Associates, 1982.

LaPlanche, Jean, and J.-B. Pontalis. *The Language of Psycho- Analysis.* Trans. Donald Nicholson Smith. New York: Norton, 1974.

Larbaud, Valéry. "The 'Ulysses' of James Joyce." *Criterion* 1 (October 1922): 94–103.

Lawrence, Karen. *The Odyssey of Style in "Ulysses."* Princeton: Princeton University Press, 1981.

Lear, Jonathan. *Open Minded: Working Out the Logic of the Soul.* Cambridge, Mass.: Harvard University Press, 1998.

Leonard, Garry. "Cultural Contexts and Poststructuralism: The Truth about Joyce's Fiction." *Novel* 24 (Fall 1990): 86–92.

Lewis, Wyndham. "An Analysis of the Mind of James Joyce." In *Time and Western Man,* 75–113. New York: Harcourt, 1928.

Lieberman, E. James. *Acts of Will: The Life and Work of Otto Rank.* New York: Free Press, 1985.

Litz, A. Walton. *The Art of James Joyce: Method and Design in "Ulysses" and "Finnegans Wake."* London: Oxford University Press, 1961.

Lodge, David. "Double Discourses: Joyce and Bakhtin." *James Joyce Broadsheet* 11 (June 1983): 1–2.

———. "The Novel Now: Theories and Practices." *Novel* 21 (Winter/Spring 1988): 125–37.

Lowes, John Livingston. *The Road to Xanadu: A Study in the Ways of the Imagination.* Boston: Houghton Mifflin, 1927.

Maddox, Brenda. *Nora: The Real Life of Molly Bloom.* Boston: Houghton Mifflin Company, 1988.

Maddox, James. *Joyce's "Ulysses" and the Assault upon Character.* New Brunswick: Rutgers University Press, 1978.

Masters, William H., and Virginia E. Johnson. *Human Sexual Response.* Boston: Little, Brown, 1966.

McBride, Margaret. *"Ulysses" and the Metamorphosis of Stephen Dedalus.* Lewisburg, Pa.: Bucknell University Press, 2001.

McCarthy, Jack, with Danis Rose. *Joyce's Dublin: A Walking Guide to "Ulysses."* New York: St. Martin's Press, 1986, 1988.

McCleery, Alistair. "The Gathered Lambs." *James Joyce Quarterly* 31 (Summer 1994): 557–63.

———. "One Lost Lamb." *James Joyce Quarterly* 27 (Spring 1990): 635–39.

McCurdy, Edward, ed. *The Notebooks of Leonardo da Vinci.* New York: Braziller, 1958.

McGuire, William, ed. *The Freud-Jung Letters: The Correspondence Between Sigmund Freud and C. G. Jung.* Trans. Ralph Manheim and R.F.C. Hull. Bollingen Series, 94. Princeton: Princeton University Press, 1974.

McKnight, Jeanne. "Unlocking the Word-Hoard: Madness, Identity and Creativity in James Joyce." *James Joyce Quarterly* 14 (Summer 1977): 420–33.

McLuhan, Marshall. *Understanding Media: The Extensions of Man.* New York: McGraw-Hill, 1964.

McMichael, James. *"Ulysses" and Justice.* Princeton: Princeton University Press, 1991.

Menaker, Esther. *Otto Rank: A Rediscovered Legacy.* New York: Columbia University Press, 1982.

Meredith, George. *The Egoist: A Comedy in Narrative.* New York: Scribner's, 1910, c. 1897.

Merkin, Daphne. "Freud Rising." *New Yorker,* 9 November 1998, 50–55.

Meyers, Jeffrey. "Erotic Hangings in 'Cyclops.'" *James Joyce Quarterly* 34 (Spring 1997): 345–48.

Mierlo, Wim van. "The Freudful Couchmare Revisited: Contextualizing Joyce and the New Psychology." *Joyce Studies Annual* 8 (Summer 1997): 115–53.

Nabokov, Vladimir. *Lectures on Literature.* New York: Harcourt, 1980.

Noon, William. "James Joyce: Unfacts, Fiction, and Facts." *PMLA* 76 (June 1961): 254–76.

Norris, Margot. *Joyce's Web: The Unraveling of Modernism.* Austin: University of Texas Press, 1992.

Nunberg, Herman, and Ernst Federn, eds. *Minutes of the Vienna Psychoanalytic Society.* Trans. M. Nunberg. Vol. 1, 1906–1908, Vol. 2, 1908–1910. New York: International Universities Press, 1962, 1967.

Oppenheim, Hans. *"Zur Frage der Genese des Eifersuchtswahnes." Zentralblatt für Psychoanalyse* 2 (1912): 67–78. English abstract, "Discussion of the Genesis of the Delusion of Jealousy." *Psychoanalytic Review* 1 (1913): 114–15.

Owen, Rodney Wilson. *James Joyce and the Beginnings of "Ulysses."* Ann Arbor: UMI Research Press, 1983.

Parkes, Adam. "'Literature and instruments for abortion': 'Nausicaa' and the *Little Review* Trial." *James Joyce Quarterly* 34 (Spring 1997): 283–301.

Pelaschiar, Laura. "Stanislaus Joyce's 'Book of Days': The Triestine Diary," *James Joyce Quarterly* 36 (Winter 1999): 61–71.

Perkins, Jill. *Joyce and Hauptmann: Before Sunrise.* San Marino, Calif.: Huntington Library, 1978.

Petronius. *The Satyricon of Petronius.* Trans. William Arrowsmith. Ann Arbor: University of Michigan Press, 1959.

Plato. *The Republic.* Trans. Benjamin Jowett. New York: Heritage Press, 1944.

Power, Arthur. *Conversations with James Joyce.* Ed. Clive Hart. New York: Barnes and Noble, 1974.

Quillian, William H. *Hamlet and the New Poetic: James Joyce and T. S. Eliot.* Ann Arbor: UMI Research Press, 1975, 1983.

Rader, Ralph. "Exodus and Return: Joyce's *Ulysses* and the Fiction of the Actual." *University of Toronto Quarterly* 48 (Winter 1978): 149–71.

———. "The Logic of *Ulysses;* or Why Molly Had to Live in Gibralter." *Critical Inquiry* 10 (June 1984): 567–78.

Rahner, Hugo. *Greek Myths and Christian Mystery.* Trans. Brian Battershaw. New York: Harper and Row, 1963.

Rangell, Leo. "The Role of the Parent in the Oedipus Complex." *Bulletin of the Menninger Clinic* 19 (1955): 9–15.

Rank, Otto. *Art and Artist: Creative Urge and Personality Development.* Trans. Charles Atkinson. New York: Knopf, 1932.

———. "Der Doppelganger" [The double]. *Imago* 3 (1914): 150–64.

———. *The Double: A Psychoanalytic Study.* Trans. and ed. Harry Tucker, Jr. Chapel Hill: University of North Carolina Press, 1971.

———. "Homer: Psychologische Beiträge zur Entstehungsgeschichte des Volksepos" [Homer: Psychological contributions to the origins of the folk epic]. *Imago* 5 (1917): 133–669.

———. *Das Inzest-Motiv in Dichtung und Sage: Grundzüge einer Psychologie des dichterischen Schaffens.* Leipzig: Deuticke, 1912.

———. *The Incest Theme in Literature and Legend: Fundamentals of a Psychology of Literary Creation.* Trans. Gregory C. Richter. Baltimore: Johns Hopkins University Press, 1992.

———. *Die Lohengrinsage.* Vienna: Deuticke, 1911.

———. "Die Matrone von Ephesus; ein Deutungsversuch der Fabel von der treulosen Witwe" [The woman of Ephesus: An attempt at interpretation of the story of the faithless widow]. *International Zeitschrift für Psychoanalyse* 1 (1913): 50–60.

———. *The Myth of the Birth of the Hero and Other Writings.* Ed. Philip Freund. Trans. F. Robbins and Smith Ely Jelliffe. 1915. Reprint, New York: Vintage Books, 1964.

———. "The 'Play-Within-a-Play' in *Hamlet:* A Contribution to the Analysis and Dynamic Understanding of the Play." Trans. Paul Lewinson. *The Otto Rank Association Journal* 6 (1971): 5–21.

———. "Das 'Schauspiel' im *Hamlet*: Ein Beitrag zur Analyse und zum dynamischen Verstandnis der Dichtung." *Imago* 4 (1915): 41–51.

———. "Der Sinn der Griselda Fabel" [The meaning of the Griselda story]. *Imago* 1 (1912), 34–48.

————. "Das Volksepos: Die dichterische Phantasiebildung" [The folk epic: The poetic fantasy-construction]." *Imago* 5 (1917): 372–93.

Roazen, Paul. *Freud and His Followers.* New York: Knopf, 1975.

Rogers, H. E. "Irish Myth and the Plot of *Ulysses.*" *ELH* 15 (1948): 306–27.

Rose, Danis. "The Source of Mr. Bloom's Wealth." *James Joyce Quarterly* 25 (Fall 1987): 128–32.

Rosenzweig, Saul. *Freud, Jung, and Hall the King-Maker: The Historic Expedition to America (1909), with G. Stanley Hall as Host and William James as Guest.* St. Louis: Rana House, 1992.

Rossman, Charles, ed. "A Special Issue on Editing *Ulysses.*" *Studies in the Novel* 22 (Summer 1990).

Rudnytsky, Peter. Introductory essay to *Incest Theme in Literature and Legend: Fundamentals of a Psychology of Literary Creation.* Trans. Gregory C. Richter. Baltimore: Johns Hopkins University Press, 1992, xi–xxxv.

Rycroft, Charles. *A Critical Dictionary of Psychoanalysis.* 2d ed. London: Penguin Books, 1995.

Sadger, (J.) Isidore. "Über Gesässerotik." *International Zeitschrift für artzliche Psychoanalyse* 1 (1913): 351–58. English abstract, "Eroticism of Posteriors." *Psychoanalytic Review* 1 (1913–14): 466–69.

————. "Über Urethralerotik." *Jahrbuch* 2 (1910): 409–50. English abstract, "Concerning Urethral Eroticism." *Psychoanalytic Review* 5 (1918): 114–20, 228–29.

Scholes, Robert E. "*Ulysses:* A Structuralist Perspective." *James Joyce Quarterly* 10 (Fall 1972): 161–71.

Scholes, Robert E., and Marlena Corcoran. "The Aesthetic Theory and the Critical Writings." In *A Companion to Joyce Studies,* ed. Zack Bowen and James F. Carens, 689–705. Westport, Conn.: Greenwood, 1984.

Scholes, Robert E., and Richard M. Kain. "The First Version of 'A Portrait.'" *The Workshop of Daedalus: James Joyce and the Raw Materials for "A Portrait of the Artist as a Young Man."* Evanston, Ill.: Northwestern University Press, 1965.

Schutte, William. *Joyce and Shakespeare: A Study in the Meaning of "Ulysses."* New Haven: Yale University Press, 1957.

Schwaber, Paul. *The Cast of Characters: A Reading of "Ulysses."* New Haven: Yale University Press, 1999.

Schwarz, Daniel. "'Tell Us in Plain Words': An Introduction to Reading Joyce's *Ulysses.*" *Journal of Narrative Techinque* 17 (Winter 1987): 25–38.

Seldes, Gilbert. Review of *Ulysses.* In *James Joyce: The Critical Heritage,* ed. Robert Deming, 1:235–39. 2 vols. New York: Barnes and Noble, 1970.

Shechner, Mark. "James Joyce and Psychoanalysis: A Selected Checklist." *James Joyce Quarterly* 13 (Spring 1976): 383–84.

————. "Joyce and Psychoanalysis: Two Additional Perspectives." *James Joyce Quarterly* 14 (Summer 1976): 416–19.

————. *Joyce in Nighttown: A Psychoanalytic Inquiry into "Ulysses."* Berkeley and Los Angeles: University of California Press, 1974.

Solomon, Margaret C. "Character as Linguistic Mode: A New Look at Streams-of-Consciousness in *Ulysses*." In *"Ulysses": Cinquante Ans Après*, ed. Louis Bonnerot et al. Paris: Didier, 1974.

Staley, Thomas. "Italo Svevo and the Ambience of Trieste." In *Atti del Third International James Joyce Symposium*, 204–10. Trieste, Italy: Universita degli Studi, 1974.

Stanford, W. B. "Joyce's First Meeting with Ulysses." *The Listener*, 19 July 1951, 99, 105.

———. *The Ulysses Theme: A Study in the Adaptability of a Traditional Hero*. 2d ed. Ann Arbor: University of Michigan Press, Ann Arbor Paperbacks, 1968.

Steele, Robert, with consulting editor Susan V. Swinney. *Freud and Jung: Conflicts of Interpretation*. London: Routledge and Kegan Paul, 1982.

Steinberg, Erwin. "Reading Leopold Bloom/1904 in 1989." *James Joyce Quarterly* 26 (Spring 1989): 397–416.

———. "The Source(s) of Joyce's Anti-Semitism in *Ulysses*." *Joyce Studies Annual* (1999): 63–83.

Stoppard, Thomas. *Travesties*. New York: Grove Press, 1975.

Sultan, Stanley. *The Argument of "Ulysses."* Columbus: Ohio State University Press, 1965.

———. "Joycesday." In *Joyce Studies Annual* (2000): 27–48.

Taylor, Robert. "The Triumph of John Kidd—Copy Righter." *Bostonia* (Winter 1997–1998): 31–33.

Thomas, Ronald R. *Dreams of Authority: Freud and the Fictions of the Unconscious*. Ithaca: Cornell University Press, 1990.

Thomas Aquinas, Saint. *Charity*. Trans. R. J. Batten. Vol. 34 (1975). In *Summa Theologica*. 60 vols. New York: McGraw, 1964–76.

Thornton, Weldon. *Allusions in "Ulysses": A Line-by-Line Reference to Joyce's Complex Symbolism*. New York: Simon and Schuster, Touchstone, 1973.

———. "The Allusive Method in Ulysses." In *Approaches to "Ulysses": Ten Essays*, ed. Thomas F. Staley and Bernard Benstock, 235–49. Pittsburgh: University of Pittsburgh Press, 1970.

Tindall, William York. *A Reader's Guide to James Joyce*. New York: Farrar, Strauss, 1959.

Toynbee, Philip. "A Study of James Joyce's *Ulysses*." In *James Joyce: Two Decades of Criticism*, ed. Seon Givens, 243–84. 2d ed. New York: Vanguard Press, 1963.

Trilling, Lionel. "The Adventurous Mind of Dr. Freud." *New York Times Book Review*, 11 October 1953, 1.

———. "James Joyce in His Letters." *Commentary* 45 (February 1968): 53–64.

Troy, Mark L. *Mummeries of Resurrection: The Cycle of Osiris in "Finnegans Wake."* Uppsala, Sweden: Almquist and Wiksell, 1976.

Von Phul, Ruth. "Joyce and the Strabismal Apologia." In *A James Joyce Miscellany*, ed. Marvin Magalaner, 119–32. Second Series. Carbondale: Southern Illinois University Press, 1959.

Weir, David. *James Joyce and the Art of Mediation.* Ann Arbor: University of Michigan Press, 1996.

West, Rebecca. *The Strange Necessity.* Garden City, N.Y.: Doubleday, 1928.

Willbern, David. "Freud and the Inter-penetration of Dreams." *Diacritics* 9 (March 1979): 98–110.

Williams, Bruce. "Molly Bloom: Archetype or Stereotype." *Journal of Marriage and the Family* 33 (August 1971): 545–46.

Williams, William Carlos. "A Point for American Criticism." *transition* 15–17 (Winter 1929): 157–66.

Wilson, Edmund. *Axel's Castle.* New York: Charles Scribner's Sons, 1931.

Winterstein, F. von. "Zur Psychoanalyse des Reisens." *Imago* 1 (1912): 489–506. English abstract, "The Psychology of Travel." *Psychoanalytic Review* 2 (1914): 344–45.

Wyss, Wilhelm von. *Zürichs Bibliotheken.* Zurich: Schulthess and Co., 1911.

Index

—Relationships other than maternal: with
Dilly (his sister), 200n.6; with father,
tender tone of memory of meeting, 66
(denial of homosexual component in
father-son relationship, 70); with Mulligan, Bloom as alternative to, 69 (homosexual echoes in, 67–68; telegram to, 74;
as threat to family continuity, 95)
—Shakespeare lecture: and "adulterous"
brother, 108; fatherhood material in, as
guide to overall meaning, 187; on father-
son relationship in *Hamlet*, 99, 102; focus
on psychology of creative artist in, 99;
on Hamlet as "dispossessed son," 108;
and *Hamlet* theory, 98; on *Hamlet*, 100;
on influence of Shakespeare's life on art
re father-daughter incest, 113; and interchange of fathers and daughters in
Pericles and *A Winter's Tale*, 115–16; and
interplay of images, 116–18; layering of
allusions in, 65–66; on Shakespeare (and
Ann Hathaway, 36; in role of Ghost, 101;
identification with Hamlet, father and
son, 101); and Shakespeare's on sundering and reconciliation in Shakespeare's
work, 111; and women in Shakespeare's
life, 108–9
Dervin, Daniel: on Bloom's perversions,
206n.14; on Bloom's sexual abstinence,
207n.22
Dettmar, Keith: on Bakhtin's failure to mention Joyce, 17; on critical terms used by
Bakhtin, 192n.20

Edel, Leon: on Stanislaus Joyce, 201n.17
Eliot, T. S.: on Joyce's "mythical method,"
16; "*Ulysses*, Order and Myth" and
Freudian influence on *U*, 9
Ellenberger, Henri: on affinity between
dynamic psychology and spirit of late
nineteenth century literature, 8
Ellmann, Richard: *Consciousness*, listing
of "Trieste library" in, 2, 10, 191n.1; on
dating of Bloomsday, 203n.9; on Joyce's
identification with great figures, 28; on
Joyce's response to psychoanalysis, 10;

Joyce's use of Stanislaus's "Trieste diary"
in facts of Bloom's household, 107; on
lemniscate (lying-down 8) as symbol for
time in "Penelope," 141; on notion of binary self, 8; on "A Portrait of the Artist,"
27; on Rudy Bloom and Nora's miscarriage, 201n.10; and story of Joyce's experience of jealousy, 132; translation of
newspaper reports on Joyce's Trieste
Hamlet lectures by, 60–61
Empson, William: and "Bloom offer,"
110–11
Epstein, Edmund: on Stephen's quest, 74

Faerber, Thomas, and Mark Luchsinger:
Joyce's residences in Zurich, 193n.39
Fénelon, François: *Adventures of
Télemachus*, and Lamb's *Adventures*, 1–2,
183–84
Ford, Jane: on incest between Bloom and
Milly, 202n.29
Forrester, John: on development of concept
of Oedipus complex, 209n.11
Freud, Sigmund: on artist as precursor of
psychoanalysis, 2–3; controversy surrounding opening of 1998 exhibition,
174; on death of father, 101; and discovery that remembered "seductions" were
fiction, 204n.18; effect of theories on
social fabric of twentieth century, 177;
evaluation of Rank's *Incest-Motif*, 98;
as founder of psychoanalysis, 8–9; on
Goethe as "self revealer" and "careful
concealer," 205n.35; Oedipus complex,
pattern of, confirmed in patients and in
self-analysis, 179 (as master plot for case
studies, 179; as translation of Sophocles'
Oedipus Rex into twentieth century, 174;
in Paris, compared to Joyce, 7; on plot of
Oedipus Rex as model for psychoanalytic
treatment, 179; on Sadger, 147; youthful
translation of *Oedipus Rex*, 178–79. *See
also* Freudian concepts; Freud-Jung relationship
—Works
"Analysis of a Phobia" ("Little Hans"): in

Jean Kimball is an adjunct associate professor of English at the University of Northern Iowa, Cedar Falls. She is the author of *Odyssey of the Psyche: Jungian Patterns in Joyce's "Ulysses"* (Southern Illinois University Press, 1997).

The Florida James Joyce Series
Edited by Zack Bowen

The Autobiographical Novel of Co-Consciousness: Goncharov, Woolf, and Joyce,
by Galya Diment (1994)
Bloom's Old Sweet Song: Essays on Joyce and Music, by Zack Bowen (1995)
Joyce's Iritis and the Irritated Text: The Dis-lexic Ulysses, by Roy Gottfried (1995)
Joyce, Milton, and the Theory of Influence, by Patrick Colm Hogan (1995)
Reauthorizing Joyce, by Vicki Mahaffey (paperback edition, 1995)
Shaw and Joyce: "The Last Word in Stolentelling," by Martha Fodaski Black
(1995)
Bely, Joyce, Döblin: Peripatetics in the City Novel, by Peter I. Barta (1996)
Jocoserious Joyce: The Fate of Folly in Ulysses, by Robert H. Bell (paperback edi-
tion, 1996)
Joyce and Popular Culture, edited by R. B. Kershner (1996)
Joyce and the Jews: Culture and Texts, by Ira B. Nadel (paperback edition, 1996)
Narrative Design in Finnegans Wake: *The Wake Lock Picked,* by Harry Burrell
(1996)
Gender in Joyce, edited by Jolanta W. Wawrzycka and Marlena G. Corcoran (1997)
Latin and Roman Culture in Joyce, by R. J. Schork (1997)
Reading Joyce Politically, by Trevor L. Williams (1997)
Advertising and Commodity Culture in Joyce, by Garry Leonard (1998)
Greek and Hellenic Culture in Joyce, by R. J. Schork (1998)
Joyce, Joyceans, and the Rhetoric of Citation, by Eloise Knowlton (1998)
Joyce's Music and Noise: Theme and Variation in His Writings, by Jack W.
Weaver (1998)
Reading Derrida Reading Joyce, by Alan Roughley (1999)
Joyce through the Ages: A Nonlinear View, edited by Michael Patrick Gillespie
(1999)
Chaos Theory and James Joyce's Everyman, by Peter Francis Mackey (1999)
Joyce's Comic Portrait, by Roy Gottfried (2000)
Joyce and Hagiography: Saints Above!, by R. J. Schork (2000)
Voices and Values in Joyce's Ulysses, by Weldon Thornton (2000)
The Dublin Helix: The Life of Language in Joyce's Ulysses, by Sebastian D. G.
Knowles (2001)
Joyce Beyond Marx: History and Desire in Ulysses *and* Finnegans Wake, by
Patrick McGee (2001)
Joyce's Metamorphosis, by Stanley Sultan (2001)
Joycean Temporalities: Debts, Promises, and Countersignatures, by Tony Thwaites
(2001)
Joyce and the Victorians, by Tracey Teets Schwarze (2002)
Joyce's Ulysses *as National Epic: Epic Mimesis and the Political History of the
Nation State,* by Andras Ungar (2002)